Outline Studies in Christian Doctrine

by

George P. Pardington

CHRISTIAN PUBLICATIONS

Camp Hill, Pennsylvania

Christian Publications
3825 Hartzdale Drive, Camp Hill, PA, 17011

The mark of ✝ *vibrant faith*

ISBN: 0-87509-116-4
© by Christian Publications
Printed in the United States of America

CONTENTS

CHAPTER III. ANGELOLOGY.

CHAPTER IV. ANTHROPOLOGY.

CHAPTER V. HAMARTIOLOGY.

CHAPTER VI. CHRISTOLOGY.

CHAPTER VII. PNEUMATOLOGY

CHAPTER VIII. ECCLESIOLOGY

CHAPTER IX. ESCHATOLOGY.

INTRODUCTION.

It is at once a pleasing and painful service to place on record a word of appreciation for this volume, which bears the name of our beloved and lamented brother, George P. Pardington.

The writer had the privilege of knowing him from his very boyhood, and having some part in the training of his mind and the shaping of his ministry. Beginning with the great advantage of a liberal and careful education, the power and usefulness of his ministry were further heightened by the intense earnestness and devotion of his heart and life. To him theology was not a cold science gathered from books and lectures, but sprang as a molten stream from his own living experience of the truths he believed and his Spirit-baptized study of the Scriptures for himself. He accepted no truths second-hand, but believed his beliefs and proved his convictions in a victorious and deeply tested life.

Victorious suffering was perhaps the prominent feature of his earthly life, and it gave a touch of reality to all he believed and taught.

His system of Christian doctrine, which is reproduced in this volume, grew out of his professional labors as a teacher of Bible students, ministers, and missionaries. Repeated from year to year and melted down in the furnace fire of practical class work and considerable criticism, these lectures came to represent at length the deep and settled convictions of a highly trained mind and a deeply consecrated spirit.

Perhaps the best credential of the author was the love, admiration, and appreciation of his large and ever-changing classes and the glorious fruition that came back to him in their consecrated lives as they went forth from the heavenly atmosphere of his class room and his "Quiet Hour" to live the gospel he taught and to be witnesses for Christ and His fulness in every part of this land and to the uttermost part of the earth.

We thank God for the precious and abiding heritage our beloved brother has left us in this volume in which the Holy Spirit has enabled him to crystallize "the faith once for all delivered unto the saints."

A. B. SIMPSON.

PRELUDE.

I. DEFINITION OF THEOLOGY.

"**Theology** is the science of God and of the relations between God and the universe" (Strong).

Theology is the "science of things divine" (Hooker).

1. Derivation.

Theology comes from two Greek words, namely, *theos,* God, and *logos,* speech or reason. Etymologically, theology means a reasoned discourse or treatise about God.

2. Use.

As a term, theology has both a narrow and a broad use:

a. In its narrow use, theology means the doctrine of God, His being and works.

b. In its broad use, theology means the sum of Christian doctrines.

NOTE: By the Church Fathers St. John is called "the theologian," because he treats of the inner relations of the Trinity. Gregory Nazianzen was so called because he defended the deity of Christ against the Arians (A. D. 325-390), and since his time it has been the prevailing usage to employ the term theology in the broad sense.

3. Possibility.

According to Dr. Strong's definition, theology has a threefold ground, viz:

a. "In the existence of a God who has relations to the universe."

b. "In the capacity of the human mind for knowing God and certain of these relations."

c. "In the provision of means by which God is brought into actual contact with the mind, or, in other words, in the provision of revelation."

4. Necessity.

The science of theology finds its necessity in these grounds:

a. In the instinct of the mind for system.

"Theology is a rational necessity. If all existing theological systems were destroyed today, new systems would arise tomorrow. So inevitable is the operation of this law that those who most decry theology show, nevertheless, that they have made a theology for themselves, and often one sufficiently meager and blundering. Hostility to theology, where it does not originate in mistaken fears for the corruption of God's truth or in a naturally illogical structure of mind, often proceeds from a license of speculation which cannot brook the restraints of a complete Scriptural system" (Strong).

b. In the importance of systematic truth to the development of Christian character.

Theology should be dignified, not disparaged. Its study has sometimes been decried as deadening the religious affections. This is a mistake, since it deals with those truths which are best adapted to nourish the religious affections. Genuine piety is not weakened but strengthened by the systematic study of religious truth. Other things being equal, he is the strongest Christian who has the firmest grasp on the great fundamental truths of Christianity. It has been well said that "Christian morality is a fruit that grows only from the tree of doctrine and that Christian character rests upon Christian truth as its foundation" (Farr). "Some knowledge is necessary to conversion—at least, knowledge of sin and knowledge of a Saviour; and the putting together of these two great truths is the beginning of theology" (Strong). See Col. 1.10; II Peter 3.18. Texts representing truth as food, Jer. 15.16; Matt. 4.4; I Cor. 3.1, 2; Heb. 5.14; Job 23.12.

c. In the importance to the believer of definite and just views of divine truth.

Especially true is this of the preacher: Eph. 6.17; II Tim. 2.2, 25. "To mutilate it or misrepresent it (the teaching of the Scripture) is not only sin against the Revealer of it—it may prove the ruin of men's souls. The best safeguard against such mutilation or misrepresentation is the diligent study of the several doctrines of the faith in their relations to one another, and especially to the central theme of theology, the person and work of Jesus Christ" (Strong).

d. In the close relation between correct doctrine and the safety and aggressive power of the church: I Tim. 3.15; II Tim. 1.13.

"Defective understanding of the truth results sooner or later in defects of organization, of operation, and of life. Thorough comprehension of Christian truth as an organized system furnishes, on the one hand, not only an invaluable defense against heresy and immorality, but also an indispensable stimulus and instrument in aggressive labor for the world's conversion" (Strong). "A creed is like a backbone. A man does not need to wear his backbone in front of him; but he must have a backbone and a straight one, or he will be a flexible if not a humpbacked Christian" (H. Osgood).

e. In the injunctions of Scripture, both direct and indirect: Jno. 5.39; I Cor. 2.13; Col. 1.27, 28; Eph. 4.11, 12; I Tim. 3.2; II Tim. 2.15; Titus 1.9.

II. DEFINITION OF RELIGION.

"**Religion** in its essential idea is a life in God, a life lived in recognition of God, in communion with God, and under control of the indwelling Spirit of God" (Strong). "The life of God in the soul of man."

1. Derivation.

This is uncertain. Two views are held:

a. By some it is taken from the Latin verb *religare,* signifying "to bind back," that is, man to God.

b. Others, with perhaps greater accuracy, take it from the Latin verb *religere,* signifying "to go over again," "to ponder carefully," that is, a reverent observance of one's duties to God.

2. Relation to Theology.

Theology is a science; religion is a life. "One may be a theologian and not a religious man. One may know some things about God and not know God Himself" (Farr).

NOTE: Some would make religion a kind of knowing, while others would make it exclusively a matter of feeling; but as Dr. Strong says, "Since it is a life, it cannot be described as consisting solely in the exercise of any one of the powers of intellect, affection, or will. As physical life involves the unity and cooperation of all the organs of the body, so spiritual life involves the united working of all the powers of the soul. To feeling, however, we must assign the logical priority, since holy affection toward God, imparted in regeneration, is the condition of truly knowing God and of truly serving Him."

3. Relation to Morality.

Morality is a law; religion is a life. "**Morality** is conformity to an abstract law of right, while religion is essentially a relation to a person, from whom the soul receives blessing and to whom it surrenders itself in love and obedience" (Strong). From the Latin *mos,* plural *mores,* comes the word moral. The original word means a way of acting and the English word signifies a right way of acting. "Ethical" comes from the Greek and has the same force. "Hence the law which tells men how they should act with reference to right and wrong is called **moral law,** and man is said to have a moral nature because he is capable of acting right" (Farr). See Titus 2.1-15.

4. Relation to Worship.

Worship is an art: religion is a life. "**Worship** is the outward expression of religion. In it God speaks to man and man to God. It therefore properly includes the reading of Scripture and preaching on the side of God, and prayer and song on the side of the people" (Strong). Worship, of course, may be both private and public.

NOTE: "We judge a man's theology by his creed. We judge of a man's religion by his life. Theology is of the head, religion is of the heart. God judges us not by what is in our heads, but by what is in our hearts. Religion, not theology, is the final test by which we stand or fall. Many a one who did not subscribe to the Westminster Catechism may be in heaven after all, while another, well grounded in the Five Points of Calvinism and with the Thirty-nine Articles at his tongue's end, may find himself in hell, damned in spite of his theology" (Farr).

III. SOURCES OF THEOLOGY.

The sources of theology are twofold, viz: Nature

and the Scriptures. See Rom. 1.20; Psa. 8.3; 19.1; II John 9.

1. Nature.

"The universe is a source of theology. The Scriptures assert that God has revealed Himself in nature. There is not only an outward witness to His existence and character in the constitution and government of the universe, but an inward witness to His character in the heart of every man. The systematic exhibition of these facts, whether derived from observation, history, or science, constitutes natural theology" (Strong). Outward witness: Rom. 1.18-20, 32; 2.15.

2. The Scriptures.

"The Christian revelation is the chief source of theology. The Scriptures plainly declare that the revelation of God in nature does not supply all the knowledge which a sinner needs: Acts 17.23; Eph. 3.9, 10. This revelation is therefore supplemented by another in which divine attributes and merciful provisions only dimly shadowed forth in nature are made known to men. This latter revelation consists of a series of supernatural events and communications, the record of which is presented in the Scriptures" (Strong).

NOTE: There are four mistaken sources of theology, namely: traditionalism, rationalism, confessionalism, and mysticism.

1. TRADITIONALISM.

Rome elevates her interpretations of the Scriptures to a plane of equality with the Scriptures themselves.

2. RATIONALISM.

Rationalists subject the teaching of the Scriptures to the criterion of human reason, rejecting what is contrary thereto.

3. CONFESSIONALISM.

The symbol and creed of the church interpret and explicate the Scriptures, but can add nothing thereto in the way of new knowledge.

4. MYSTICISM.

Christian experience is a witness to the truth of Scripture, but is not an independent source of knowledge of divine things.

IV. LIMITATIONS OF THEOLOGY.

These are found:—

1. In the finiteness of the human mind: Job 11.7; Rom. 11.33.

2. In the imperfect state of science.

The so-called conflict between science and revelation grows out of either an imperfect knowledge of science or an imperfect knowledge of revelation. They cannot conflict when rightly understood, for both are from the same mind and hand: Psa. 19.

3. In the inadequacy of human language: I Cor. 2 13; II Cor. 3.5, 6; 12.4.

It is impossible perfectly to express divine truth in human words. Even the Greek language, the most perfect medium of human communication known, is not subtle enough to catch shades of divine truth. The New Testament writers had to give new meanings to old words, thus: *logos, hamartia, mysterion, katallasso,* etc.

4. In the incompleteness of our knowledge of the Scriptures: Psa. 119.18; Luke 24.32, 45.

5. In the silence of the written revelation: Deut. 29.29; Luke 13.23, 24; John 13.7; I Cor. 2.9.

Observe the silence of Scripture: On the life and death of the virgin Mary, the personal appearance of Jesus, the origin of evil, the method of the atonement, the state after death. Little is said about social and political questions, such as slavery, the liquor traffic, governmental corruption, capital and labor, etc. Of course principles of right action are laid down, but specific injunctions about many things are lacking.

6. In the lack of spiritual discernment caused by sin. "The spiritual ages make the most progress in theology. Witness the half-century succeeding the Reformation and the half-century succeeding the great revival in New England in the time of Jonathan Edwards" (Strong).

2

V. QUALIFICATIONS FOR THE STUDY OF THEOLOGY.

In order to study theology to the best advantage one should have:

1.   A well-disciplined mind.

2.   An intuitional habit of mind.

The student should trust his intuitive **convictions** as well as his logical reasoning. "The theologian must have insight as well as understanding. He must accustom himself to ponder spiritual facts as well as those which are sensible and material; to see things in their inner relations as well as in their outward forms; to cherish confidence in the reality and unity of truth" (Strong).

3.   Some acquaintance with science: Physical, mental, and moral.

4.   Some knowledge of the original languages of the Bible: At least of their genius and idiomatic structure. This of course is not indispensable, but yet a great help.

5.   A holy affection toward God: Psa. 25.14; I Cor. 2.14.

"Only the renewed heart can properly feel its need of divine revelation, or understand that revelation when given" (Strong). "It is the heart that makes the theologian."

6. The illumination of the Holy Spirit: Psa. 119.18; Luke 24.32, 45; I Cor. 2.10-12.

Dr. G. R. Crooks of Drew Theological Seminary used to say: "One needs but three things to understand the Scriptures; a knowledge of the original languages, the illumination of the Holy Spirit, and common sense."

VI. DIVISIONS OF THEOLOGY.

Theological science is generally divided into exegetical, historical, systematic, and practical theology.

1. Exegetical Theology.

This is the study of the original languages of the Bible, the Hebrew and Aramaic of the Old Testament and the Greek of the New Testament.

2. Historical Theology.

This is the study of the facts of Christianity. "As giving account of the shaping of the Christian faith into doctrinal statements, Historical Theology is called the History of Doctrine. As describing the resulting and accompanying changes in the life of the church, outward and inward, Historical Theology is called Church History" (Strong).

3. Systematic Theology.

Besides Systematic Theology, which is theology proper, two other terms are used, namely: Biblical Theology and Dogmatic Theology. These three need to be carefully distinguished.

a. Biblical Theology. This "aims to arrange and classify the facts of revelation, confining itself to the Scriptures for its material, and treating of doctrine only so far as it was developed at the close of the Apostolic Age" (Strong).

Biblical Theology traces the development of revelation in successive books of the Bible and compares the same revealed truth as treated by various writers, as Paul, Peter, James, etc.

b. Dogmatic Theology. This is the study of the theology of the creeds and confessions of faith of the Christian Church. It often lays more stress upon these symbols than upon the revelation of Scripture.

c. Systematic Theology. This "takes the material furnished by Biblical and by Historical Theology and with this material seeks to build up into an organic and consistent whole all our knowledge of God and of the relations between God and the universe, whether this knowledge be originally derived from nature or from the Scriptures" (Strong).

d. There is yet another term to be preferred either to Biblical or to Systematic Theology. It is Christian Doctrine. The word doctrine comes from the Latin *doctrina*, signifying teaching or instruction. It is a New Testament word; see Matt. 7.28; John 7.16, 17; Acts 2.42; 5.28; 13.12; 17.19; Rom. 6.17; I

Cor. 14.6; II Tim. 4.2; Titus 1.9; Heb. 6.2; 13.9; II John 9, etc. Christian Doctrine partakes in part of the character of Biblical Theology and in part of the character of Systematic Theology. That is, while not ignoring the material of Natural Theology (the universe) it yet lays chief emphasis upon the contents of revelation. **Christian Doctrine** may be defined as the cardinal doctrines or truths of the Bible arranged in systematic form. This is the term which has been chosen for this course; and the expression *Outline Studies* has been adopted because the lectures are not exhaustive of the subject.

"The Scriptures are rich in doctrinal material, but in elementary form; and it is only through a scientific mode of treatment that these elements can be brought into a theology in any proper sense of the term" (Miley).

4. Practical Theology.

This is "the system of truth considered as a means of renewing and sanctifying men, or, in other words, theology in its publication and enforcement" (Strong).

VII. VALUE OF THE STUDY OF THEOLOGY.

A good working knowledge of theology is of very great value:

1. It forms the basis of Christian experience: Titus **2**; II John 9.

2. It is the touchstone of error: Matt. 22.29; Gal. 1.6-9; II Tim. 4.2-4.

3. It is the foundation of teaching: I Tim. 4.13.

VIII. METHODS OF THEOLOGY.

Various have been the methods of treating the material of theology. Thus, the Analytical method begins with blessedness, which is the end of all things, and then treats of the means by which it is secured. The Trinitarian method regards Christian Doctrine as a manifestation successively of the Father, the Son, and the Spirit. The Federal method treats theology under the old and the new covenants. The Anthropological method begins with man's disease, sin, and ends with redemption, the remedy for this disease. The Christological method treats of God, man, and sin as presuppositions of the person and work of Christ. The Historical method discusses, chronologically, the history of redemption. The Allegorical method describes "man as a wanderer, God as the end, life as a road, the Holy Spirit as a light, and heaven as a home." This is done in Bunyan's "Holy War." Opposed to all these is the Synthetic method, so called, which "starts from the highest principle, God, and proceeds to man, Christ, redemption, and finally to the end of all things" (Hagenback, Hist. Doctrine, 2:152).

We adopt the Synthetic method with some modifications from the usual treatment. The following are the cardinal doctrines of the Bible. Around them may be grouped all the teachings of revelation: God, angels (including Satan), man, sin, Christ (His person and work), the Holy Spirit (His person and work), the church, and the future. The doctrines of Christ and the Holy Spirit are usually classed together under another doctrine called Soteriology, the doctrine of salvation. But preliminary to the study of all these doctrines is the study of the Bible itself as the source and support of divine truth. Accordingly, we begin with the Holy Scriptures. We may now exhibit the doctrines, which will comprise our course of lectures in this subject:

1. **Bibliology:** Doctrine of the Bible.

2. **Theology:** Doctrine of God.

3. **Angelology:** Doctrine of Angels (including Satan).

4. **Anthropology:** Doctrine of Man.

5. **Hamartialogy:** Doctrine of Sin.

6. **Christology:** Doctrine of Christ, His Person and Work.

7. **Pneumatology:** Doctrine of the Holy Spirit, His Person and Work.

8. **Ecclesiology:** Doctrine of the Church.

9. **Eschatology:** Doctrine of the Future.

DOCTRINE ONE: BIBLIOLOGY.

Topics.

I. Revelation.

II. Canonicity.

III. Genuineness.

IV. Authenticity.

V. Divine Authority.

VI. Inspiration.

VII. Ultimate Authority.

CHAPTER I.

BIBLIOLOGY.

TOPIC ONE: REVELATION.

I. DEFINITION.

Revelation may be defined as a supernatural communication from God to man, either oral or written. The term is usually understood of a written communication. "Revelation is a discovery by God to man of Himself, or of His will over and above what He has made known by the light of nature or reason" (Horne).

II. METHOD.

A twofold method of revelation is possible:

1. An immediate revelation to each person.

But to this there are serious objections:—

a. It would interfere with the freedom of the will. Some persons might not be willing to receive a revelation from God direct, but according to the theory it would have to be forced upon them.

b. It would have to be repeated to each one. Even on the part of God this would be, so to speak, a waste of time and effort.

c. It would open the way for contradiction and imposture. Human nature being what it is, people would not agree as to the revelation they had received. Moreover, some would not only delude themselves as to what they had received, but would claim to have received what they knew they never had received.

2. A written revelation once given and thoroughly accredited.

This method has marked advantages:

a. It is more fair and open than oral tradition.
b. It is more certain than oral tradition.
c. It is more permanent than oral tradition.
d. It is required by the importance of the subject.
e. It is more satisfactory, when properly accredited.

The credentials of a written revelation are attested miracle and fulfilled prophecy.

NOTE: Some of God's ways of making known His will to man are: signs (as Moses' rod), symbols (as the pillar of cloud and fire), dreams (such as Joseph, Pharaoh, etc. had), face-to-face communications (as Moses had), the urim and thummin (probably by the changing of the color of the stones), the lot, visions, miracles, prophecy, the incarnation, answered prayer, providential events, the voice of the Lord in the heart, etc., etc.

III. SOME REASONS FOR BELIEVING IN A SPECIAL DIVINE REVELATION.

1. It is possible.

Granted the omnipotence of God, He is able to make His mind known to man.

2. It is probable.

Granted the wisdom and goodness of God, these would prompt Him to communicate with man. Philosophers of all ages have thought a divine revelation probable, and have expected it.

3. It is credible.

Granted that a special divine revelation is both possible and probable, it is natural and easy to believe that one has been given. Human nature is more credulous than incredulous. Thus, in all ages mankind has been prone to believe in alleged supernatural revelations. Witness the sacred books of the East, The Koran, Book of Mormons, Records of Spiritism, Mrs. Eddy's "Science and Health, Key to the Scriptures," etc.

4. It is necessary.

a. The imperfect light of nature calls for the perfect light of revelation. Nature throws no light on the Trinity, the atonement, pardon, method of worship, personal existence after death, etc. "Even the truth to which we arrive by our natural powers needs divine confirmation and authority when it addresses minds and wills perverted by sin. To break this power of sin and to furnish encouragement to moral effort, we need a special divine revelation of the merciful and helpful aspect of the divine nature. . . . While conscience gives proof that God is a God of holiness, we have not, from the light of nature, equal evidence that God is a God of love. Reason teaches man that, as a sinner, he merits condemnation; but he cannot from reason alone know that God will have mercy upon him and provide salvation. His doubts can be removed only by God's own voice, assuring him of 'redemption . . . the forgiveness of . . . trespasses,' Eph. 1.7, and revealing to him the way in which that forgiveness has been rendered possible" (Strong).

b. The healing power of nature and her delay in meting out justice to the transgressor of her laws is a parable of the divine way of salvation for the sinner: II Pet. 3.9.

c. The dense ignorance, low morality, and abject helplessness of man in his natural state demand the illumination, righteousness, and power which the Scriptures reveal and provide. The Babylonians worshiped nature; the Egyptians, animals; the Greeks and Romans, the deified passions of humanity, etc.

d. Man's spiritual longings require satisfaction:
Job 31.35.

e. Man needs a final authority for creed and conduct.

IV. CERTAINTY OF A SPECIAL DIVINE REVELATION.

The above grounds afford strong presumption for
the reasonableness of believing in a revelation from
God; that is, the Holy Scriptures. But we are not
left without absolute certainty that the Bible is such
a revelation. By the twofold proof of attested miracle
and fulfilled prophecy God has certified His Book.

NOTE: "For two reasons God has given us a written revelation: Because He is absent; and 'Lest we forget': Josh. 1.13;
Mal. 4.4; Jude 17" (Chapell).

TOPIC TWO: CANONICITY.

I. DEFINITION OF CANON.

Canon (from the Greek *kanon*—reed or measuring rod) is a rule of life or doctrine. Thus, there are
canons of music, art, criticism, etc., which are the
fundamental principles of these subjects.

II. CANON OF SCRIPTURE.

The canon of Scripture comprises the sixty-six

books of the Old and New Testaments, which being inspired of God constitute the infallible *rule* of faith and practice of the Christian Church and the individual believer.

III. DEFINITION OF CANONICITY.

The **canonicity** of any book of the Bible means its right to a place in the sacred canon. Canonicity is used of a single book; canon, of the whole volume.

IV.   LAW OF CANONICITY FOR THE OLD TESTAMENT.

To have a place in the Old Testament, a book must have been written, edited, or endorsed by a prophet.

Christ, the "Great Prophet," Deut. 18.15, endorsed the Old Testament Scriptures, and thus forever established the right of all the books to a place therein: Luke 24.27, 44; Jno. 5.39. The three recognized divisions of the Old Testament were: the Law, the Prophets, and the Psalms.

Note: In the New Testament are 263 direct quotations and about 350 indirect allusions to the Old Testament. All but seven Old Testament books are referred to, viz: Obadiah, Nahum, Ecclesiastes, Song of Solomon, Esther, Ezra, and Nehemiah. However, as Dr. Schaff says: "The absence of quotation in the New Testament of any Old Testament book argues nothing against its canonicity." The Apocrypha—hidden, covered—consists of 14 books not found in the Hebrew Old Testament.

but in the Septuagint (Greek LXX), and also in the Vulgate (Latin), Versions. It is accepted by the Roman Catholic Church. The Lutheran and the Episcopalian Churches appoint it to be read for "example of life and instruction in manner, but not the establishing of doctrine."

V. LAW OF CANONICITY FOR THE NEW TESTAMENT.

To have a place in the New Testament, a book must have been written or endorsed by an Apostle, or received as divine authority in the Apostolic Age. Thus, Mark was endorsed by Peter; Hebrews, by Paul.

NOTE 1. Luther's law of canonicity was the power of a book to teach Christ. James, he called "A right straw-y epistle," because he believed James contradicted Paul on the subject of Faith and Works: Rom. 4 and Jas. 2. Jude, Luther called "An unnecessary epistle." He also rejected Hebrews and Revelation.

NOTE 2. There is a well-founded tradition that the Old Testament canon was formed by Ezra. The New Testament canon was not, as many suppose, formed arbitrarily by decree of Church Council. It is true that the Council of Laodicea, A. D. 363, (which was not an Ecumenical Council), did ratify the canon, but only as already accepted by the churches. But the canon of the New Testament was formed gradually under the providence of God, the Holy Spirit in the churches, we believe, giving the needed discernment to accept the genuine and reject the spurious. The fact that certain books were for some time held in doubt, but later were accepted simply shows what care was exercised. These books are seven in number

3

and are called "Antilegomena," that is, spoken against. They are: Hebrews, James, II Peter, II and III John, Jude, and Revelation. The New Testament books were read in the churches, I Thess. 5.27; were circulated among the churches, Col. 4.16; II Peter 3.15, 16; and the churches were warned against forgeries, II Thess. 2.2.

TOPIC THREE: GENUINENESS.

I. DEFINITION.

The **Genuineness of the Scriptures** involves two questions, *authorship* and *date*. Were the various books of the Bible written by the men to whom they are ascribed? And, were they written at the time, approximately, to which they are assigned?

NOTE: Genuineness is opposed to spuriousness. A corrupt text is an altered text.

II. GENUINENESS OF THE OLD TESTAMENT.

This, like its canonicity, or rather the canonicity of the books, was settled by Christ: Luke 24.27, 44. Christ's witness to the Old Testament, as a whole or any part thereof, is a sufficient answer to Higher Criticism. For example, take Jonah. See Matt. 12.39, 40; Luke 11.29. Also, the "Deutero-Isaiah": Matt. 8.17; Luke 4.17, 18, etc.

III. GENUINENESS OF THE NEW TESTAMENT.

If we had Christ's witness to the New Testament, as we have His witness to the Old Testament, this would be sufficient; but in its absence we resort to what is known as external and internal evidence.

1. External proof.

There is satisfactory evidence that the New Testament, as we now have it, was accepted as genuine before A. D. 200. This would necessitate a long-continued previous existence, since the transcription of manuscripts and their circulation were very slow.

NOTE 1. Irenæus (A. D. 120-200) refers to the four Gospels. Polycarp (A. D. 80-166) was his teacher and friend. And Polycarp's teacher and friend was John, the Beloved Apostle. See John Urquhart's "Structure of the Bible."

NOTE 2. A chain of four links binds the 20th to the 1st century:

A. The printed Bible. From the American Standard Version to the Bibles of Coverdale, Tyndale, and Wyclif of the 15th century.

B. The Greek Manuscripts of the 4th century. Of these, the greatest are three: *The Vatican Manuscript,* at Rome, under charge of the Roman Catholic Church; *The Sinaitic,* at London, in the British Museum (purchased from Russia, 1933), and *The Alexandrian,* at London, under the charge of the Protestant Church. Including fragments, there are fully 2,000 manuscripts of the Old Testament and 3,000 of the New Testament. Of the Old Testament Manuscripts, there are none older than the sixth or seventh century. At this time, the

Massorites, a school of Jewish Rabbis at Lake Tiberias, having invented a system of vowel points to pronounce the Hebrew text, destroyed all the manuscripts they could find. (Of the classic authors, there are sometimes not more than 20 manuscripts, none being older than the 10th century.)

C. Quotations found in the writings of the Church and Apostolic Fathers. These are of the 2nd and 3rd centuries, and are sufficient in variety and number to reproduce the entire New Testament.

D. Early Versions, dating, perhaps, as early as A. D. 150. Of these, the most valuable are: *The Syriac,* of the Eastern Church, and *The Vulgate,* or Old Latin, of the Western Church.

The original autographs have been lost. It is improbable, though not impossible, that they will ever be found.

2. Internal proof.

Internal evidence of the genuineness of the Scriptures proceeds upon questions of language, style, history, etc., which cannot properly be discussed here, as they belong to Biblical Introduction.

TOPIC FOUR: AUTHENTICITY.

I. DEFINITION.

The **Authenticity of the Scriptures** means their credibility or truthfulness.

II. AUTHENTICITY OF THE OLD TESTAMENT.

This was established by Christ: Luke 24.27, 44.

III.   AUTHENTICITY OF THE NEW TESTAMENT.

This is established by proving from the books themselves that the writers were competent, upright, and trustworthy.

1.   Competency is proved:

a.   From the common sense and good judgment of the writers "They do not write like enthusiasts or fanatics."

b.   From the more-than-average intelligence of the writers.   In this respect, they were superior to men of their time.

c.   From the consideration that the facts they record could be tested by the senses: I John 1.1.   In order to record accurately simple matters of every-day occurrence, a liberal education and a special training are not required.

2.   Uprightness is proved:

a.   From the seriousness of tone of the writings. A moral earnestness pervades the writings of the New Testament.

b.   From the spirituality of the teaching.

c.   From the absence of sufficient motive for fraud.

3.   Trustworthiness.

This is proved from competency and uprightness. As

competent, they were able to tell the truth; as upright, they were in duty bound to do so.

TOPIC FIVE: DIVINE AUTHORITY.

I. DEFINITION.

The **Divine Authority of the Scriptures** constitutes them the final court of appeal in all matters of Christian faith and practice.

II. SOURCE.

The divine authority of the Old Testament rests upon the testimony of Christ: Luke 24.27, 44. But so also does that of the New Testament, as the following facts prove:

1. Christ stated plainly that He would leave unfinished the revelation of truth: John 16.12.

2. He promised that the revelation should be completed after His departure: John 16.12.

3. He chose certain persons to receive such additional revelations and to be His witnesses, preachers, and teachers after His departure: John 15.27; 16.13; Acts 1.8; Matt. 28.19, 20; Acts 9.15-17.

4. Knowing beforehand what they would write, He gave to their words precisely the same authority as His own: Matt. 10.14-15; Luke 10.16; John 13.20; 17.20.

TOPIC SIX: INSPIRATION.

I. DEFINITIONS

There are three terms which need to be distinguished, viz: Revelation, Inspiration, and Illumination.

1. Revelation.

Revelation may be defined as that act of God by which He communicates to the mind of man truth not known before and incapable of being discovered by the mind of man unaided. Revelation is also used of the truth thus communicated.

2. Inspiration.

Inspiration may be defined as the divine influence which renders a speaker or writer infallible in the communication of truth, whether previously known or not.

"By the **Inspiration of the Scriptures** we mean that special divine influence upon the minds of the Scripture writers in virtue of which their productions, apart from errors of transcription and when rightly interpreted, together constitute an infallible rule of faith and practice" (Strong).

3. Illumination.

Illumination may be defined as the divine quickening of the human mind in virtue of which it is enabled to understand truth already revealed. By "truth already revealed" is meant the teachings of the Holy Scriptures.

NOTE: Illumination reveals no new truth, but gives an understanding of old truth: Luke 24.32, 45.

What light is to the eye, illumination is to the mind: Matt. 16.17; I Cor. 2.10, 14. Revelation concerns the discovery of truth; Inspiration, the communication of truth; and Illumination, the understanding of truth. Or,

Revelation—Discovery.

Inspiration—Communication.

Illumination—Understanding.

It may help our understanding of terms above employed, if we adduce instances of:

1. Inspiration, without Revelation, as in Luke or Acts: Luke 1.4.

2. Inspiration, including Revelation, as in the Apocalypse: Rev. 1.1-11.

3. Inspiration, without Illumination, as in the Prophets: I Pet. 1.11.

4. Inspiration, including Illumination, as in the case of Paul: I Cor. 2.12.

II. THE NATURE OF INSPIRATION.

The nature of inspiration is brought out in two striking New Testament passages, viz: II Tim. 3.16 and II Peter 1.21.

In the first passage, the Greek word rendered "inspired of God," or "given by inspiration of God," signifies, literally, "God-breathed" (*Theopneustos*). The Authorized Version is more faithful to the Greek than the Revised Version. Says Dr. Wm. Evans:

"If Paul had said, 'All Scripture that is divinely inspired is also profitable, etc.,' he would virtually have said, 'There is some part of the Scripture, some part of the Bible, that is not profitable, etc., and, therefore, not inspired.' This is what the spirit of rationalism wants, namely, to make human reason the test and judge and measure of what is inspired and what is not. One man says such and such a verse is not profitable to him; another says such and such a verse is not to him. The result is that no Bible is left. Is it possible that anyone need be told the flat and sapless tautology that all divinely inspired Scripture is also profitable? Paul dealt in no such meaningless phrases. The word translated *also* does not mean also here. It means *and*. Its position in the sentence shows this. Again, the Revised rendering is shown to be openly false because the revisers refused to render the same Greek construction in the same way, which convicts them of error. In Heb. 4.13 we have: 'All things are naked and laid open before the eyes of him with whom we have to do.' The form and construction are identical with those of II Tim. 3.16. Were we, however, to translate this passage as the revisers translated the passage in Timothy, it would read: 'All naked things are also open to the eyes of him with whom we have to do.' All uncovered things are also exposed things! All naked things are also open things! Again, I Tim. 4.4, 'Every creature of God is good and nothing is to be rejected.' According to the principles the revisers adopted in rendering II Tim. 3.16, this passage would read, 'Every good creature of God is also nothing to be rejected.' The Greek language has no such meaningless syntax. The place of the verb *is,* which must be supplied, is directly before the word *inspired,* and not after it. The great rationalistic scholar, DeWette, confessed candidly that the rendering the revisers adopted here cannot be defended. In his German version ·of the text, he gave the sense thus: 'Every sacred writing, i. e., of the canonical Scriptures, is inspired of God and is useful for doctrine,' etc. Bishops Moberly and Wordsworth, Archbishop Trench and others of the Revision Committee disclaimed any responsibility for the rendering. Dean Burgon pronounced it, 'The most astonishing as well as calamitous literary blunder of the age.' It was condemned by Dr. Tregelles."

In the other passage, II Peter 1.21, the Greek verb rendered "moved" (Revised Version, "being moved") signifies, literally, to be moved upon, or to be borne along, i. e., as by a strong current or mighty influence. The verb-form is the passive participle, and may be rendered "when moved upon or borne along by," etc. This distinctly teaches that the Scripture was not written by mere men, or at their suggestion, but by men moved upon, prompted, yea indeed, driven by the promptings of the Holy Spirit. Dr. Evans continues:

"The statements of the Scripture (viz: in II Tim. and II Peter) may be summed up as follows: Holy men of God, qualified by the infusion of the breath of God, wrote in obedience to the divine command, and were kept from all error, whether they revealed truths previously unknown or recorded truths already familiar."

NOTE: Inspiration comes from two Latin words, *in* and *spiro*, signifying "to breathe in." So aspire (*ad*) means "to breathe to"; transpire, "to breathe across"; expire, "to breathe out," etc.

III. THE EXTENT OF INSPIRATION.

What is the extent of inspiration? Is it confined to the essential ideas, the "concept," so called, or does it include the language of Scripture? Shall we say, the Bible *contains* the Word of God, or, the Bible *is* the Word of God? If we are to have accuracy and authority, there can be no such thing as inspired thoughts apart from inspired words; for language is the expression of thought—its embodiment and vehicle. The Bible is the Word of God.

The very words of Scripture are inspired. This is called plenary (i. e., full), verbal inspiration.

A. Testimony of the Old Testament Writers.

1. Balaam: Num. 22.38; 23.12.
2. Moses: Ex. 4.10-17; Num. 17.2-3; Deut. 4.2; 6.1; 29.1.
3. Joshua: Josh. 1.1-8.
4. David: II Sam. 23.2.
5. Solomon: Prov. 30.5-6.
6. Isaiah: Isa. 5.24; 8.1.
7. Jeremiah: Jer. 1.7-9; 7.27; 13.12; 30.1-2; 36.1, 2, 4, 11, 27-32.
8. Ezekiel: Ezek. 2.7; 3.10, 11; 24.2.
9. Daniel: Dan. 12.8, 9.
10. Micah: Micah 3.8.
11. Habakkuk: Hab. 2.2.
12. Zechariah: Zech. 7.8-12.

B. Testimony of the New Testament Writers.

1. Paul: I Cor. 2.13; 14.37; I Thess. 2.13.
2. Peter: I Pet. 1.10-11; II Pet. 1.20-21; 3.1-2.
3. See also Matt. 10.20; Mark 13.11; Luke 12.12; 21.14-15; Acts 2.4; 4.31; Jude 17; Rev. 2.7.

IV. THEORIES OF INSPIRATION.

Nowhere in Scripture is the nature of inspiration fully explained — the *modus operandi*, so to speak. In every work of the Holy Spirit, there is a profoundly mysterious element, else it would not be a work of the Spirit. However, Bible students have not been content to accept the fact of inspiration and such hints of its nature as we have found recorded in II Tim. 3.16 and II Pet. 1.21. They have insisted on formulating theories of inspiration. Of such, the principal ones are the following:

1. Intuitional Theory.

This consists in a so-called "exaltation of intuitional consciousness." It may be called natural inspiration. The view admits little more than a preeminent degree of genius, such as Shakespeare, Milton, etc., possessed. This theory is held by Unitarians, at least by many of them.

2. Illuminational Theory.

This consists in a preeminent degree of spiritual illumination, such as may be possessed by all believers. "If this be the true view, there seems to be no plausible reason why a new Bible should not be possible today. And yet no individual, however extreme his claims to inspiration may be, has ever ventured such a task" (Evans).

3. Mechanical Theory.

This view holds that the writers of the Bible were mere tools, passive instruments, automatons, or unconscious penmen of the divine Spirit. It is the Dictation Theory, ignoring the human element, and giving the writers no scope for the free play of personality, and allowing nothing for differences of language, style, etc. This view is disproved, for example, by the varied wording of the superscription over the Cross: "This is Jesus, the King of the Jews": Matt. 27.37; "The King of the Jews": Mark 15.26; "This is the King of the Jews": Luke 23.38; "Jesus of Nazareth, the King of the Jews": John 19.19.

4. Dynamical Theory.

This view, as the name suggests, concedes power sufficient for all the facts. While it maintains the superintendence of the Holy Spirit, rendering the writers of Scripture infallible in their communications of truth and thus making their writings inerrant, yet it leaves room for the freest and fullest play of personality, style, etc. This theory accords with the verbal, plenary view of inspiration.

V. PROOFS OF INSPIRATION.

These are twofold, viz: Internal and External.

A. Internal.

These are Direct and Indirect.

1. Direct.

a. II Tim. 3.16; II Pet. 1.20-21.

b. "Thus saith the Lord," occurring over 2,000 times.

c. The way Old Testament quotations are introduced into the New Testament. See Matt. 1.22; Acts 2.16, 17; Heb. 3.7.

d. The way Christ and the Apostles treat the Old Testament. See Matt. 8.16-17; John 10.35.

e. The expression: "It is written." See Matt. 4.7; Luke 4.10; Gal. 3.10; Heb. 10.7; II Pet. 3.2, 15-16; Rev. 2.7.

f. The claim of Old Testament and New Testament writers (considered above).

2. **Indirect.**

a. Supernatural character of the Bible.

b. Supernatural character of Christ.

c. Unity of Scripture.

d. Number of Scripture.

e. Chronology of Scripture.

f. Wonderful knowledge of Scripture: (1) Light before sun: Gen. 1.4; (2) Firmament, (expanse): Gen. 1.7; (3) Music of spheres: Job 38.7; Psa. 65.8; (4) Circulation of the blood: Eccle. 12.6; (5) Gravitation: Job 26.7; (6) Number of the stars: Jer. 33.22; (7) Order of creation in accord with science: Gen. 1; (8) Revolution of the earth on its axis: Job 38.13, 14; (9) Weight of atmosphere: Job 28.25. See "Many Infallible Proofs," by A. T. Pierson, Chapters 5-7.

B.   **External.**

1.   Questions of introduction.
2.   Attested miracle.
3.   Fulfilled prophecy.
4.   Spread of the Gospel.
5.   Preservation of the Bible.
6.   Character of Christ.
7.   Existence of the Christian **Church.**
8.   Testimony of Christian experience.

"Whatever finds me bears witness that it has pro-
ceeded from a Holy Spirit; in the Bible, there is more
that finds me than I have experienced in all other books
put together" (S. T. Coleridge). "Oh! taste and see
that the Lord is good; blessed is the man that trusteth in
him": Psa. 34.8.

TOPIC SEVEN: ULTIMATE AUTHORITY.

There are three, and three only, possible sources
of ultimate authority in Christianity, viz: the Church,
the Reason, and the Bible.   There are those who make
a fourth source of final authority, namely, Jesus
Christ.   But inasmuch as our historic and doctrinal knowledge of Christ and the entirety of His
teachings rest upon the Scriptures, this is not a
source distinct from and independent of the Bible.

I. THE CHURCH AS ULTIMATE AUTHORITY.

This is the position of the Roman Catholic Church which exalts tradition to a plane of equality with the Scriptures and claims to be the infallible interpreter of both. Moreover, that Church claims the power of special authoritative revelation in addition to the Scriptures, and it has used this power. See the dogmas of the Immaculate Conception of the Virgin, and the Infallibility of the Pope. But the Bible was before the Church, certainly before the Roman Catholic Church, enfolding its mystery in the Old Testament, and in the New Testament unfolding its history in the Present and its destiny in the Coming Age. Moreover, the Bible is the authority of the Christian Church, its divine constitution and charter.

II. THE REASON AS ULTIMATE AUTHORITY.

This is the position of Rationalism. By Reason is meant not the logical faculty or "Pure Reason," but the "Moral Reason" (intellect plus conscience); Reason "conditioned in its activity by holy affection and enlightened by the Spirit of God." The view held is that the Scripture is authoritative only so far as its revelations are agreeable to the conclusions of reason or can be rationally demonstrated. But the Bible is higher than man, revealing what he originally was—perfect; what he is now—a sinner;

and what he shall be hereafter—glorified, in Heaven,
or damned, in Hell, according as he accepts or re-
jects the Word of God.   Instead of man being the
judge of the Scriptures, the Scriptures are the judge
of man: Heb. 4.12-13.   Among rationalists, the reason means the unaided reason, the natural (psychical
or soulish) man who receiveth not nor comprehendeth
spiritual things: I Cor. 2.14.   Moreover, even man's
moral reason, illuminated by the Holy Spirit,
is variable, differing in each one according to tem-
perament, training, and doctrinal predilection.   Of
this, the Protestant denominations are witness.
Again, the carnal mind is enmity against God, Rom.
8.7, and would tear from the Bible its supernatural
and miraculous elements.   Of this, Destructive Criticism is witness.

III. THE BIBLE AS ULTIMATE AUTHORITY.

This is the position of Protestantism.   The view
held is that the Holy Scriptures are the ultimate
authority, the Supreme Court, so to speak, whose
decisions are final in all matters pertaining to Christian faith and practice.

Yet to the moral reason, enlightened by the
Holy Spirit, the Holy Scriptures make frequent
appeal: I Sam. 12.7, Job 13.3; Isa. 1.18; Acts 17.2;
18.4, 19; 24.25; Rom. 12.1.   Indeed, the reason has

an important function. With reference to the Scriptures, this is threefold:

1. **To judge of man's need of a divine revelation.**

2. **To examine the credentials of Scripture.**

3. **To comprehend and interpret the Scriptures.**

Having done these things, reason stands aside, and makes room for faith. "Thus, reason prepares the way for a revelation above reason and warrants implicit faith in a divine revelation once given and properly attested" (Strong). The externals of revelation are for criticism; its internals are for faith. When we know God's will, we must do it. "If ye know these things, blessed are ye if ye do them": John 13.17.

QUESTIONS FOR STUDY.

1. Define Revelation.
2. What are the possible methods of Revelation?
3. Give reasons for believing in a special Divine Revelation.
4. Define Canon and Canonicity.
5. Give the law of Canonicity for the Old Testament; for the New Testament.
6. What is meant by Genuineness?
7. How is the Genuineness of the Old Testament settled? Of the New Testament?

8. What is meant by Authenticity?
9. How is Authenticity of a book established?
10. Discuss the Divine Authority of the Scriptures.
11. Distinguish between Revelation, Inspiration, and Illumination.
12. Describe the nature of Inspiration.
13. What is the extent of Inspiration?
14. Give the theories of Inspiration.
15. What are the proofs of Inspiration?
16. Name three possible sources of Ultimate Authority in Christianity.
17. Describe each position.

DOCTRINE TWO: THEOLOGY.

Part One: The Character of God.

Topics.

I. The Existence of God.

II. The Personality of God.

III. The Trinity of God.

IV. The Attributes of God.

V. The Perfections of God.

VI. The Names of God.

Part Two: The Works of God.

Topics.

I. The Decrees of God.

II. Creation.

III. Preservation

IV. Providence.

CHAPTER II.

THEOLOGY.

PART ONE.

THE CHARACTER OF GOD.

TOPIC ONE: THE EXISTENCE OF GOD.

I. SOME DEFINITIONS.

1. Theology.

In its restricted sense Theology means the Doctrine of God.

2. Theism.

Theism is the belief in the existence of a personal God, Creator, Preserver, and Ruler of all things.

3. Deism.

Deism is a denial of God's providence.

4. Atheism.

Atheism is a denial of God's existence.

5. Skepticism and Infidelity.

These two terms mean a doubt of or disbelief in the existence of God.

6. Agnosticism.

Agnosticism is a denial that God can be known.

NOTE: Etymologically, agnostic and ignoramus mean the same thing. The former is from the Greek, the latter from the Latin. However, an agnostic would be insulted were he to be called an ignoramus.

II. DEFINITION OF GOD.

A. Scriptural.

1. **God is Spirit:** John 4.24. The article before Spirit is not found in Greek or Hebrew.

2. **God is light:** I John 1.5.

3. **God is love:** I John 4.16.

4. **God is a consuming fire:** Heb. 12.29.

NOTE: These are perhaps not exact definitions so much as popular descriptions of God.

B. Theological.

1. "By God we understand the one absolutely and infinitely perfect Spirit who is the creator of all" (Catholic Dictionary).

2. "God is a Spirit, infinite, eternal, and unchangeable in His being, wisdom, power, holiness, justice, goodness, and truth" (Westminster Shorter Catechism).

3. "God is the infinite and perfect Spirit in whom

all things have their source, support, and end"
(Strong).

III. ORIGIN OF THE IDEA OF GOD.

The idea of God is an intuition of the moral reason;
that is, it is innate in the human race. "The knowledge of God's existence is a rational intuition.
Logically, it precedes and conditions all observation
and reasoning. Chronologically, only reflection upon
the phenomena of nature and of mind occasions its
rise in consciousness" (Strong). **Intuition** simply
means direct knowledge; it is to be distinguished
from observation and reasoning, which give knowledge by indirect means.

1. **The belief in a personal God is called a primary
or first truth.**

"A **First Truth** is a knowledge which, though developed upon occasion of observation and reflection, is not derived from reflection and observation; a knowledge on the contrary which has such
logical priority that it must be assumed or supposed
in order to make any observation or reflection possible. Such truths are not, therefore, recognized first
in order of time; some of them are assented to somewhat late in the mind's growth; by the great majority of men they are never consciously formulated at
all. Yet they constitute the necessary assumptions

upon which all other knowledge rests, and the mind has not only the inborn capacity to evolve them as soon as the proper occasions are presented, but the recognition of them is inevitable as soon as the mind begins to give account to itself of its own knowledge" (Strong). Other rational intuitions or first truths are: (1) intuitions of relations, as time and space; (2) intuitions of principles, as substance, cause, final cause, right, etc.; (3) intuitions of absolute Being, Power, Reason, Perfection, Personality, as God.

2. **Primary or first truths, which may be taken as synonymous with rational intuitions, have three unfailing marks, viz: universality, necessity, and logical independence and priority.**

a. By **universality** is meant "not that all men assent to them or understand them when propounded in scientific form, but that all men manifest a practical belief in them by their language, actions, and expectations" (Strong). The belief in God as a first truth meets this test: no race or tribe has ever been found without at least a rudimentary conception of the existence of a Supreme Being.

b. By **necessity** is meant "not that it is impossible to deny these truths, but that the mind is compelled by its very constitution to recognize them upon the occurrence of the proper conditions, and to employ them in its arguments to prove their non-exist-

ence" (Strong). The belief in God as first truth
meets this test: infinity is the inevitable correlative
of finiteness; the race has an innate capacity for religion; the denial of God's existence involves logical
processes whose validity rests upon the assumption of
His existence.

c. By **logical independence and priority** is meant
"that these truths can be resolved into no others, and
proved by no others; that they are presupposed in
the acquisition of all other knowledge, and can therefore be derived from no other source than an original
cognitive power of the mind" (Strong). The belief in God as a first truth meets this test: "the intuition of an absolute reason is (1) the necessary
presupposition of all other knowledge, so that we cannot know anything else to exist except by assuming
first of all that God exists; (2) the necessary basis
of all logical thought, so that we cannot put confidence in any one of our reasoning processes except
by taking for granted that a thinking Deity has constructed our minds with reference to the universe and
to truth; (3) the necessary implication of our primitive belief in design, so that we can assume all things
to exist for a purpose, only by making the prior assumption that a purposing God exists, can regard
the universe as a thought, only by postulating the
existence of an absolute Thinker; and (4) the necessary foundation of our conviction of moral obligation,

so that we can believe in the universal authority of
right, only by assuming that there exists a God of
righteousness who reveals His will both in the individual conscience and in the moral universe at large.
We cannot prove that God is; but we can show that,
in order to the existence of any knowledge, thought,
reason, conscience in man, man must assume that
God is" (Strong).

3. **By reflection and careful analysis it is learned
tha. the belief in God's existence as a rational intuition or first truth has a fourfold content, viz:**

a.   A Reason, in which man's mental processes are
grounded.

b.   A Power, awakening a sense of dependence.

c.   Perfection, imposing law upon the moral nature.

d.   A Personality, recognized in forms of worship
and prayer.

4. **There are some mistaken sources of the idea of
God:**

a.   The Bible.

We cannot attempt to prove from the Scriptures that
God exists, and then try to prove that the Scriptures are from God.   This would be reasoning in a
circle.   "A revelation takes for granted that he to
whom it is made has some knowledge of God, though
it may enlarge and purify that knowledge" (H. B.

Smith). The sun-dial calls for the sun without which it has no significance or use.

b. Experience.

Individual experience comes from sense-perception followed by reflection; but God is supersensible, and hence does not come within the range of experience. If by experience is meant "the accumulated results of the sensations and associations of past generations of the race," it may be asked, How did the original generation or first man at the head of the series acquire the belief in God to transmit, except as a rational intuition?

c. Reason.

Reason often brings into consciousness the belief in God but cannot cause it. "The actual rise of this knowledge in the great majority of minds is not the result of any conscious process of reasoning. . . . The strength of men's faith in God is not proportioned to the strength of the reasoning faculty. On the other hand, men of greatest logical power are often inveterate skeptics, while men of unwavering faith are found among those who cannot even understand the arguments for God's existence" (Strong).

IV. CORROBORATIVE EVIDENCE OF GOD'S EXISTENCE.

The Scriptures do not attempt to prove God's existence, but everywhere either assume or affirm it:

Gen. 1.1; John 1.1. The Scriptures declare that the knowledge of God is universal: Rom. 1.19-21, 28, 32; 2.15. God has inlaid the evidence of this fundamental truth in the very nature of man, so that nowhere is He without witness. The preacher may confidently follow the example of Scripture by assuming it. But he must explicitly declare it, as the Scripture does. "For the invisible things of him since the creation of the world are clearly seen" (that is, spiritually viewed); the organ given for this purpose is the mind; but then—and this forms the transition to our next division of the subject—they are "perceived through the things that are made": Rom. 1.20.

The fact is, the existence of God is incapable of direct proof. There is, however, a fivefold line of indirect proof which corroborates our rational intuition. By **indirect proof** is meant evidence which points to God's existence as the necessary ground and condition of the existence of anything else. The five arguments for the divine existence are as follows: the Cosmological Argument, the Teleological Argument, the Anthropological Argument, the Ontological Argument, and the Christological Argument.

Says Dr. Strong: "These arguments are probable, not demonstrative. For this reason they supplement each other, and constitute a series of evidence which is cumulative in nature. Though, taken singly, none of them can be considered absolutely decisive, they together furnish a corroboration of our primitive conviction of God's existence which is of great practical value, and is in itself sufficient to bind the moral action of men. A consideration of these arguments may also serve to explicate the contents of an intuition which has remained obscure and only half conscious for lack of reflection.

"The arguments, indeed, are the efforts of the mind that already has a conviction of God's existence to give to itself a formal account of its belief. An exact estimate of their logical value and of their relation to the intuition which they seek to express in syllogistic form is essential to any proper refutation of the prevalent atheistic and pantheistic reasoning."

A. The Cosmological Argument, or Argument from Change in Nature. (Cosmological comes from the Greek *kosmos,* world or orderly arrangement, i. e., of the universe.)

1. Statement.

"Everything begun, whether substance or phenomenon, owes its existence to some producing cause. The universe, at least so far as its present form is concerned, is a thing begun, and owes its existence to a cause which is equal to its production. This cause must be indefinitely great" (Strong). The same author continues: "This is not properly an argument from effect to cause; for the proposition that every effect must have a cause is simply identical and means only that every caused event must have a cause. It is rather an argument from begun existence to a sufficient cause of that beginning."

2. Value.

This argument proves that the cause of the universe must be indefinitely great. But it cannot prove:

a. Whether this cause is a cause of matter or of phenomenon only.

b. Whether it is a cause apart from the universe or one with it.

c. Whether it is a caused or an uncaused cause.

d. Whether it is finite or infinite.

e. Whether it is intelligent or unintelligent.

f. Whether it is one cause or many causes.

B. The Teleological Argument, or Argument from Order or Useful Collocation in Nature. (Teleological comes from the Greek *telos,* end or design.)

1. Statement.

"Order and useful collocation pervading a system respectively imply intelligence and purpose as the cause of that order and collocation. Since order and collocation pervade the universe, there must exist an intelligence adequate to the production of this order, and a will adequate to direct this collocation to useful ends" (Strong). The argument as above expressed is in syllogistic form.

The major premise expresses a primitive conviction, not invalidated (1) by the objection that the order and useful collocation of a system may exist without being purposed; or (2) by the objection that they may be the result of physical laws and forces.

The minor premise is the working principle of physical science, not invalidated (1) by the objection that we do not always understand the end subserved by the order and collocation pervading the universe; or (2) by the objection that we recognize in many things an imperfect order and collocation—due undoubtedly to sin.

2. Value.

The teleological argument proves that there exists an intelligence and will adequate to the contrivance of the universe in its present form. "But," as Dr. Strong says, "whether this intelligence and will is personal or impersonal, creator or only fashioner, one or many, finite or infinite, eternal or owing its being to another, necessary or free, this argument cannot assure us."

C. The Anthropological Argument, or Argument from Man's Mental and Moral Nature. (Anthropological comes from the Greek *anthropos,* man.)

NOTE: This is sometimes called the "Moral Argument."

but moral is too restricted a term, since man's mental constitution is considered as well as his moral nature.

1. Statement.

The argument may be represented in three parts:

a. Man's intellectual and moral nature requires for its author an intellectual and moral Being. Mind cannot evolve from matter, nor spirit from flesh. Consequently, a Being having both mind and spirit must have created man.

b. Man's moral nature proves the existence of a holy Lawgiver and Judge. Otherwise, conscience cannot be satisfactorily explained.

c. Man's emotional and volitional nature requires for its author a Being, who, as Dr. Strong says, "can furnish in Himself a satisfying object of human affection and an end which will call forth man's highest activities and ensure his highest progress." This author continues: "Only a Being of power, wisdom, holiness, and goodness, and all these indefinitely greater than any that we know upon the earth, can meet this demand of the human soul. Such a Being must exist. Otherwise man's greatest need would be unsupplied, and belief in a lie be more productive of virtue than belief in the truth."

2. Value.

In the words of Dr. Strong: "It assures us of the existence of a Personal Being, who rules us in righteousness, and who is the proper object of supreme affection and service. But whether this Being is the original creator of all things, or merely the author of our own existence, whether He is infinite or finite, whether He is a Being of simple righteousness or also of mercy, this argument cannot assure us."

D. The Ontological Argument, or the Argument from Our Abstract and Necessary Ideas. (Ontological comes from the Greek *on*, being.)

NOTE: The three arguments we have just considered are called *a posteriori* arguments, that is, from effect to cause. This one is called *a priori* argument, that is, from cause to effect.

1. Statement.

This is the most difficult of all the corroborative proofs of God's existence. Indeed, it is obscure—so obscure that many keen minds confess their inability to comprehend it. It has been likened to the Scotchman's definition of metaphysics: "one man talking about something of which he knows nothing to another man who does not understand him!" The argument has three forms:

First. That of Samuel Clarke, an English metaphysician of the 18th century:

"Space and time are attributes of substance or being. But space and time are respectively infinite and eternal. There must therefore be an infinite and eternal substance or Being to whom these attributes belong." Gillespie, a Scotch theologian, put it this way: "Space and time are modes of existence. But space and time are respectively infinite and eternal. There must therefore be an infinite and eternal Being who subsists in these modes." To all this it can be replied: space and time are not attributes of substance nor modes of existence. The argument would prove, if the reasoning were valid, that God is not mind but matter, for, according to the argument, space and time are attributes or modes of matter.

Second. That of Descartes, a French metaphysician of the 16th century:

"We have the idea of an infinite and perfect Being. This idea cannot be derived from the imperfect and finite things. There must, therefore, be an infinite and perfect Being who is the cause." But to this it may be replied: the argument confounds the idea of the infinite with an infinite idea; "man's idea of the finite is not infinite but finite, and from a finite effect we cannot argue an infinite cause" (Strong).

Third. That of Anselm, a schoolman of the Middle Ages:

"We have the idea of an absolutely perfect Being. But existence is an attribute of perfection. An absolutely perfect Being must, therefore, exist." To this the answer is: the argument confounds ideal existence with real existence. "Our ideas are not the measure of external reality" (Strong). This author continues: "A Being indefinitely great, a personal Cause, Contriver, and Lawgiver, has been proved by the preceding arguments. . . . To this one Being we may now ascribe infinity and perfection, the idea of which lies at the basis of the Ontological Argument—ascribe them, not because they are demonstrably His, but because our mental constitution will not allow us to think otherwise. Thus clothing Him with all perfections which the human mind can conceive, and these in illimitable fulness, we have One whom we may justly call God."

E. The Christological Argument. (Christological comes from the Greek *Christos,* the Anointed, i. e., the Messiah.)

This argument rests on the following pillars:

1. The Bible must be accounted for.
2. The fulfilment of prophecy must be accounted for.
3. Miracles must be accounted for.
4. The supernatural character and divine mission of Christ must be accounted for.
5. The influence of Christianity in the world must be accounted for.
6. The fact of conversion must be accounted for.

And these things, severally or together, cannot be accounted for apart from the existence of God.

"While not one of the above arguments taken by itself can be called decisive, yet taken together they constitute a series of evidences cumulative and conclusive. A whole bundle of rods cannot be broken, though each rod might be broken separately" (Farr).

TOPIC TWO: THE PERSONALITY OF GOD.

I. THE DEFINITION OF PERSONALITY.

Personality may be defined as sentient existence possessed of self-consciousness and the power of self-determination in view of moral ends.

NOTE: The distinguishing difference between a human being on the one hand and a plant or animal on the other hand is understood to be that while a human being has self-consciousness (that is, the capacity for self-knowledge) a plant and an animal have not.

II. THE CONSTITUENT ELEMENTS OF PERSONALITY.

The constituent elements of personality are three: intellect, or the power of thinking; sensibility, or the power of feeling; and volition, or the power of willing. Associated with these are conscience and the freedom of choice.

III. THE DIVINE PERSONALITY.

If it can be proved that to God are ascribed operations of intellect, sensibility, and will, then we may affirm His personality.

QUERY: Has God a conscience?

1. Intellect.

The following passages, to cite only a few of many, ascribe to God operations of intellect: Prov. 15.3; Jer. 29.11; Acts 15.18; Heb. 4.13.

2. Sensibility.

The following passages, to cite only a few of many, ascribe to God the power of feeling: Psa. 33.5; 103. 8-13; Heb. 12.29; Jas. 5.11.

3. Volition:

The following passages, to cite only a few of many, ascribe to God the power of will: Psa. 115.3; Isa. 46.10, 11; Dan. 4.35; Matt. 19.26.

TOPIC THREE: THE TRINITY OF GOD.

I. DEFINITION OF TRINITY.

The Trinity of God is His tripersonal existence as Father, Son, and Holy Spirit.

NOTE: It is not certain by whom the term trinity was invented as applied to the Godhead. Theophilus, Bishop of Antioch (A. D. 168-183), seems to have been the first one to use it. Trinity is from the Latin *trinus*, threefold.

II. CONTENTS OF DOCTRINE.

The trinity of the Godhead involves two elements, namely:

1. **The unity of God**: Ex. 20.3-7; Deut. 6.4, 5.

2. **The distinction of persons in the Godhead**: Matt. 28.19; Jno. 14.16, 17, 20-23; II Cor. 13.14.

NOTE: With reference to the Godhead the word "person" must be understood in a somewhat modified sense, namely, to signify that the distinctions between the Father, Son, and Holy Spirit are of a personal nature. Thus, the Scriptures reveal:

1. The deity of each member of the Godhead: John 1.1; Acts 5.3, 4.

2. Their mutual knowledge and love: Matt. 11.27; I Cor. 2.10; Matt. 3.17; John 3.35; 4.34; 5.30; Rom. 8.27.

3. Their distinct yet relative offices: I Cor. 12.4-6; Eph. 2.18-22.

III. ORTHODOX FORMULA.

The orthodox formula of the doctrine of the trinity is: "Three in One and One in Three."

NOTE: By maintaining the two elements of the trinity as above stated and by holding fast to the orthodox formula we are preserved from several serious errors, namely:

1. *Sabellianism*, or a modal trinity which holds that there are but three aspects or manifestations of one person.

2. *Arianism*, which holds that the Son is subordinate to the Father.

3. *Swedenborgianism*, which holds that "the Father, Son,

and Holy Spirit are three essentials of one God, which make one, just as the soul, body, and spirit make one in man."

4. *Tritheism,* which holds to three Gods. Midway between Sabellianism and Tritheism, which holds to three Gods, is Trinitarianism, which is the orthodox position. The Athanasian Creed reads: "We worship one God in trinity and trinity in unity, neither confounding the persons nor dividing the substance." The Century Dictionary well says: "The received doctrine of the Christian Church among trinitarians may be fairly stated to be that we are taught by the Scriptures to believe that there is but one God and yet three equal subjects in the Godhead, who are described as persons, but that we are unable to determine in what sense these three are separate and in what sense they are united in one."

IV. SCRIPTURE PROOF OF TRINITY.

As to statement the Scripture revelation of the doctrine of the trinity is not definite and explicit. It is generally admitted that I John 5.7 is an interpolated passage. However, the proof of the trinity is none the less conclusive and satisfactory, because indirect and apparently incidental. Notice the following:

1. The plural noun *Elohim* (God) with a singular verb *bara* (created) in Gen. 1.1.

2. The expression "Let us make" in Gen. 1.26.

3. The priestly benediction, in Num. 6.24-27.

4. The *Tersanctus* or *Trisagion,* in Isa. 6.3 and Rev. 4.8.

5. The formula of baptism in Matt. 28.19.

6. The Apostolic benediction in II Cor. 13.14.

V. ILLUSTRATIONS OF THE TRINITY.

The trinity is purely a matter of revelation. Moreover, it is a profound mystery. Analogies to it in nature there are none, for it is above finite experience and human reason, though not contrary thereto. "All attempts therefore," says Dr. Farr, "to represent it are in vain, and while illustrations are sometimes useful in overcoming objections, it is unwise to press them too far." The following illustrations have been suggested:

1. The fountain, stream, and river.

2. The cloud, rain, and rising mist.

3. Color, shape, and size.

4. The actinic, luminiferous, and calorific elements in the ray of light.

5. The three infinite dimensions of space.

6. The union of intellect, sensibility, and will in personality.

7. The thinker, the thought, and the relation between them.

8. The thought, the breath, and the uttered word.

9. The three angles of a triangle.

10. The spirit, soul, and body in man.

11. The legislative, judicial, and executive functions of government.

NOTE: Of these the tenth in order would seem to be the best.

TOPIC FOUR: THE ATTRIBUTES OF GOD.

I. DEFINITION OF ATTRIBUTE.

An **Attribute** may be defined as an essential, permanent, and distinguishing quality or characteristic, which may be affirmed of a subject; as, the color and fragrance of a rose.

NOTE: In thought an attribute is separable from its subject, but not so in experience; thus, we can think of the color or fragrance of a rose as an abstract quality, apart from the substance of the rose, but we could not take the color or fragrance away from the rose without thereby losing the rose.

II. DEFINITION OF DIVINE ATTRIBUTES.

The **Divine Attributes** are those essential, permanent, and distinguishing characteristics, which may be affirmed of the Triune God.

NOTE: The divine attributes may be considered by themselves, but they essentially inhere in God, in the sense that if we were to take them away from God we should thereby lose God Himself.

III. BASIS OF CLASSIFICATION.

This should be on the ground of that which is determinative in the subject. In God this is Personality.

NOTE: Theologians are not in agreement as to the classification or number of the divine attributes. Some include as attributes everything which may be predicated of God from the light of nature, the deduction of reason, and the revelation of Scripture. The alphabet could be exhausted more than once in this way. Dr. Strong makes two great classes: the Absolute, or Immanent, and the Relative, or Transitive attributes. The first class involve the mutual relations of the Godhead, as life, personality, self-existence, immutability, unity, truth, love, holiness. The second class involve God's relations to the universe, as eternity, immensity, omnipresence, omniscience, omnipotence, veracity and faithfulness, mercy and goodness, justice and holiness.

IV. THE DIVINE ATTRIBUTES.

There are three divine attributes corresponding to the three essential elements of personality. The three essential elements of personality are: Intellect, Sensibility, and Will. And the three divine attributes are: Omniscience, Goodness, or Benevolence, and Omnipotence.

A. Omniscience—Infinity of knowledge.

(The word omniscience comes from two Latin words, viz: *omnis* signifying all, and *scientia* signifying knowledge.) The following passages of Scripture reveal and prove the omniscience of God: I Sam. 16.7; I Kings 8.39; I Chron. 28.9; II Chron. 16.9; Job 26.6; 28.23, 24; 34.22, 25; 37.16; 42.2; Psa. 44.21; 94.11; 103.14; 119.168; 139 (whole psalm); 147.4; Prov. 3.19, 20; 5.21; 16.2; 24.12; Isa. 29.15; 40.13, 14, 27, 28; 41.4; 42.9; 44.7; 45.4; 46.10; 48.5, 6; Jer.

17.10; 23.24; 32.19; 51.15; Ezek. 11.5; Dan. 2.20, 22, 28; Amos 4.13; 9.2-4; Matt. 6.4, 18, 32; 10.29, 30; Acts 1.24; 2.23; Rom. 8.27-29; 11.33, 34; I Cor. 3.20; I Thess. 2.4; II Tim. 2.19; Heb. 4.13; I John 3.20.

NOTE 1. Calvin defined omniscience as "that attribute whereby God knows Himself and all other things in one eternal and most simple act."

NOTE 2. Wisdom may be classed under omniscience. It is that whereby God produces the best possible results by the best possible means.

B. Goodness, or Benevolence—Infinity of feeling.

Dr. Farr says: "Benevolence means that God desires the welfare of His creatures with a desire that is supremely powerful and pure."

Of the divine goodness, or benevolence, there are five modes or manifestations:

1. Holiness, or Righteousness.

Fundamentally and Scripturally, holiness and righteousness are the same. By many this is made to be the essential attribute of God. It is not altogether easy to define divine holiness. Thus Oehler, contrasting it with glory, says: "Holiness is glory concealed; glory is holiness revealed." But this is a description, not a definition. Dr. Strong says: "Holiness is self-affirming purity. In virtue of this attribute of His nature, God eternally wills and maintains His own moral excellence. In this definition are con-

tained three elements: first, purity; secondly, **purity**
willing; thirdly, purity willing itself." Dr. Clarke
says: "Holiness is the fulness of the glorious goodness of God, consistently held as the principle of His
own action, and the standard for His creatures."

The following passages reveal and prove the holiness of God: Ex. 15.11; Lev. 11.44; 19.2; 20.26; 21.8;
Deut. 32.4; Jos. 24.19; I Sam. 2.2; 6.20; Job 6.10;
34.10; Psa. 11.7; 22.3; 30.4; 47.8; 60.6; 89.35; 92.15;
99.3, 5, 9; 119.142; Isa. 5.16; 6.3; 43.14, 15; 47.4; 49.7;
57.15; Hos. 11.9; Hab. 1.12; Matt. 5.48; Luke 1.49;
John 17.11; I Pet. 1.15, 16; I John 1.5; 2.20; Rev. 4.8;
6.10; 15.4.

2. Justice.

Justice has been called transitive holiness; that is,
holiness dealing with moral beings. The term righteousness is frequently employed in this sense. Thus,
someone has said, "Justice is the execution of righteousness." Dr. Strong says: "By justice and righteousness we mean the transitive holiness of God, in
virtue of which His treatment of His creatures con-
forms to the purity of His nature, righteousness de-
manding from all moral beings conformity to the
moral perfection of God, and justice visiting non-conformity to that perfection with penal loss and suffering." The divine justice is both individual and public,
that is, it is visited upon an individual for his private
sins and upon a nation or a people for their corporate

sins: Matt. 22.12-14; 25.2-12; Amos 1.1-15; Matt. 11. 20-24; Rev. 20.11-15.

The following passages reveal and prove the justice of God: Gen. 18.23-33; Deut. 10.17; 32.4; Josh. 24.19; I Sam. 2.3; Job 37.23; Psa. 11.4, 7; 19.9; 33.5; 62.12; 84.11; 96.13; 103.6; 129.4; Isa. 30; Jer. 9.24; Ezek. 33.7-19; Acts 17.31; Rom. 1.32; 2.2-16; 11.22; II Thess. 1.5-9; Heb. 6.10; 12.22, 23, 29; I Pet. 1.17; II Pet. 2.9; I John 1.9; Jude 6; Rev. 11.18; 16.5-7; 19.2.

3. Mercy.

Mercy has been defined as that "eternal principle of God's nature which leads Him to seek the temporal good and eternal salvation of those who have opposed themselves to His will, even at the cost of infinite self-sacrifice."

Dr. Farr says: "The grace of God is His benevolence exercised toward the guilty or undeserving. The mercy of God is His benevolence exercised toward the miserable as well as guilty. The patience of God is His benevolence exercised in forbearing to punish the guilty without delay. The wisdom of God is His omniscience guided by His benevolence in securing the best ends by the best means."

The following passages reveal and prove the mercy of God: Gen. 18.26-32; Ex. 15.13; 20.2, 6; 22.27; 33.19; Num. 14.18-20; Deut. 7.9; I Kings 8.23; I Chron.

16.34; Neh. 9.17, 27-31; Job 33.14-30; Psa. 25.6; 36.5; 62.12; 69.16; 103.3-17; Isa. 55.7-9; Jer. 33.8-11; Lam. 3.22-33; Dan. 9.4; Joel 2.13; Jonah 4.2; Matt. 18.11-14; Luke 1.50, 77, 78; Acts 3.19; Eph. 2.4; I Tim. 1.13; Heb. 4.16; 8.12; Jas. 2.13; 5.11; I Pet. 1.3; II Pet. 3.9.

4. Love.

Like holiness, many make love to be the central attribute of God. It is indeed of the very essence of His being: I John 4.16. Dr. Strong makes love a composite of mercy and goodness, defining the latter thus: "Goodness is the eternal principle of God's nature which leads Him to communicate of His own life and blessedness to those who are like Him in moral character. Goodness, therefore, is nearly identical with the love of complacency; mercy, with the love of benevolence." The author quotes these passages: Rom. 2.4; Titus 3.4; Matt. 5.44, 45; John 3.16; II Pet. 1.3; Rom. 8.32; I John 4.10.

The following passages, in addition, reveal and prove the love of God: Deut. 4.37; 7.7, 8, 13; 33.3; Job 7.17; Psa. 42.8; 63.3; 103.13; 146.8; Isa. 43.4; Jer. 31.3; Hos. 11.1; Mal. 1.2; John 3.16; 14.21; 16.27; 17.23, 26; Rom. 1.7; 5.8; Gal. 2.20; Eph. 2.4; Heb. 12.6; I John 3.1; 4.8-16; Jude 20, 21.

5. Truth.

The divine truthfulness takes two forms, namely, veracity and faithfulness. Dr. Strong says: "By veracity and faithfulness we mean the transitive (that is, active) truth of God in its twofold relation to His creatures in general and to His redeemed people in particular. . . . In virtue of His veracity, all His revelations to creatures consist with His essential being and with each other. In virtue of His faithfulness, He fulfils all His promises to His people, whether expressed in words or implied in the constitution He has given them." The author quotes these passages: Psa. 138.2; John 3.33; Rom. 3.4; 1.25; John 14.17; I John 5.6; I Cor. 1.9; I Thess. 5.24; I Pet. 4.19; II Cor. 1.20; Num. 23.19; Titus 1.2; Heb. 6.18; I John 1.9; Psa. 84.11; 91.4; Matt. 6.33; I Cor. 2.9 (the order is that of Dr. Strong).

The following passages in addition reveal and prove the veracity of God: Deut. 32.4; I Sam. 15.29; Psa. 25.10; 33.4; 43.3; 100.5; Isa. 25.1; Jer. 10.10; John 17.17; Titus 1.2. The following passages, in addition, reveal and prove the faithfulness of God: Gen. 9.16; 28.15; Deut. 7.8, 9; I Kings 8.23, 24, 56; Psa. 36.5; 89.1; 92.1, 2; Isa. 42.16; 51.6; Jer. 29.10; 33.14; Heb. 6.10-19; 10.23; II Pet. 3.9; I John 1.9.

C. Omnipotence—Infinity of Power.

(The word omnipotent comes from two Latin words, viz: *omnis* signifying all, and *potentia* or *potens* signifying power.) The following passages reveal and prove the omnipotence of God: Gen. 17.1;

18.14; Job 42.2; Isa. 26.4; Matt. 19.26; Luke 1.37; Acts 26.8; Rev. 19.6; 21.22.

NOTE: "The omnipotence of God must be explained in such wise as not to contradict either the nature of God or the nature of things. It is morally impossible for God to lie or to die, and is naturally impossible for God to make two parallel lines meet, or to create two mountains without a valley between them" (Farr).

TOPIC FIVE: THE PERFECTIONS OF GOD.

There are several modes of the divine existence, usually classed as divine attributes, which are better regarded as divine perfections. They are: spirituality, unity, independence, immutability, eternity, and omnipresence.

I. SPIRITUALITY.

Like personality, spirituality is fundamental to the Being of God: John 4.24. It is not an attribute but rather a mode of God's complete and tripartite existence. Says Dr. Farr: "God is something more than a condition of being like space or time. He acts as well as exists. He is an Agent, an Actor, a Living Being, and Spirit Life: John 6.63; Gen. 1.3; Psa. 139.7; John 4.24; Ex. 20.4; Isa. 40.26; Rom. 1.20; Col. 1.15; I Tim. 1.17. In Psa. 139.7 and John 4.24, God's omnipresence seems to be accounted for by His spirituality. Matter presupposes the existence of space as a condition of its existence, but spirit does not. There is no evidence that spirit fills any part of space, or that the Infinite Spirit is dependent on space."

II. UNITY.

There is but one God. The trinity must be held in harmony with the singleness of the divine essence or substance: Deut. 6.4; II Sam. 7.22; Psa. 86.10; Isa. 43.10; Matt. 19.17; I Cor. 8.6; Gal. 3.20; I Tim. 2.5.

III. INDEPENDENCE.

Independence may be affirmed of God with respect to four things:

1. His existence, which is underived and absolute: Ex. 3.14; John 5.26.

2. His knowledge: Heb. 4.13.

3. His action: Gen. 1.1; Acts 17.24.

4. His happiness: Eph. 1.3; I Tim. 6.15, 16, R. V.

IV. IMMUTABILITY.

Immutability means unchangeableness. "God always remains what He is without development or change. He cannot change for the better, because He is best; nor for the worse, because He would thereby cease to be perfect" (Farr): Psa. 102.27; Isa. 40.28; Mal. 3.6; Jas. 1:17; Heb. 1.12.

V. ETERNITY.

Eternity means existence without beginning or end: Psa. 90.2. See also Deut. 32.40; Isa. 41.4; I Tim. 1.17; II Pet. 3.8; Rev. 10.6. "Some suppose that the idea of timeless being is also involved in the word (i. e., eternity). It seems implied in John 3.13, 8.58, and Jas. 1.17, and existence in time also seems inseparable from imperfections and limitations. On the other hand, the Scriptures generally speak of God as if His life were divisible into periods of past and future, and our minds are unable to conceive of real existence independent of time. Eternity is infinity in duration" (Farr).

VI. OMNIPRESENCE.

"The Scriptures represent God as filling immensity. He is present everywhere and there is no point in the universe where He is not" (Farr). God is omnipresent both in His works and in His personality: I Kings 8.23; II Chron. 6.18; Isa. 43.2; 66.1; Jer. 23.24; Amos 9.2; Psa. 139.7-12; Acts 17.27, 28; Matt. 28.20.

NOTE: The atheist wrote, "God is nowhere." But his little daughter read it, "God is now here." And it converted him. The omnipresence of God must be held in harmony with His transcendence and immanence. Divine transcendence means that God is *above* His works; divine immanence means that He is *within* them. Again, immanence must be distinguished from pantheism. One who holds to the divine immanence *separates* God from His works; but the pantheist *identifies* God with His works.

TOPIC SIX: THE NAMES OF GOD.

In our modern occidental life, proper names, particularly names of persons, have no special significance, except perhaps Indian names and those of some other primitive tribes. But in the ancient East (and to some extent in the modern East) it was otherwise. In the Bible, proper names are invested with peculiar significance. Thus, the Lord appears unto Jacob, and he calls the place "Bethel," "the house of God": Gen. 28.16-19. Rachel dies and calls her son "Benoni," "the son of my sorrow": Gen. 35.18. Again, the same person or place often had two names. Thus, the ancient name of Bethel was Luz, signifying "almond tree." And Jacob called Benoni, Benjamin, meaning "son of my right hand": Gen. 28.19; 35.18.

In His names God reveals His character and His manifold relations to His creatures. New crises or peculiar needs among His people called forth fresh names; and there can be no emergency among believers to which some name of God does not apply. "Even human nature and sin but evoke new and fuller revelations of the divine fulness."

The principal names of God are nine, falling into three classes of three names each and suggesting, many think, the trinity.

FIRST.

There are three primary names: God, LORD, and Lord.

I. God.

The Hebrew is *El, Elah,* or *Elohim.* See Gen.
1.11. *El* means strength or the Strong One. *Alah,* the
verb from which *Elah* and *Elohim* come, means to
bind oneself by an oath, i. e., faithfulness. *Elohim*
is a plural noun with singular meaning; in it the
trinity is latent. See Gen. 1.26, 27; 3.22.

II. LORD.

The Hebrew is *Yahwe,* English form Jehovah.
See Genesis 2.4 where *Yahwe Elohim* occurs. *Yahwe* comes from the verb *havah* signifying both to be
and to become, and means "the self-existent One who
reveals Himself," or, "the Coming One." See Ex.
3.13-17. Also Gen. 4.16. *Elohim* is the creation name
of God, and *Yahwe* the covenant-keeping or redemptive
name; accordingly, *Elohim* occurs in Gen. 1 and *Yahwe*
in Gen. 2. LORD, representing *Yahwe,* is printed in
capitals.

NOTE: Jehovah is a hybrid word, composed of the consonants
of the unpronounceable sacred name represented by *Yahwe* and
the vowels of the Hebrew word for master.

III. Lord.

The Hebrew is *Adon* or *Adonai.* See Gen. 15.2.
Adonai, master, is applied to both God and man; when
applied to man it is written with a small letter *l. Adonai*
means master, or husband. See Gen. 24.9, 10, 12; 18.12.

To us Christ is both Master and Husband. See Hos.
2.16, 20; John 13.13; II Cor. 11.2, 3.

SECOND.

There are three names compounded with *El*: Almighty God, Most High, or Most High God, and
Everlasting God.

I. Almighty God.

The Hebrew is *El Shaddai*. See Gen. 17.1. *El*
signifies, of course, the Strong One. The meaning of
Shaddai is uncertain. "The God who is enough,"
"the All-sufficient One," "the All-bountiful One"
have been suggested. It is quite probable that *Shaddai* comes from the Hebrew noun *shad* signifying
breast, and "invariably used in Scripture for a woman's breast": Gen. 49.25; Job 3.12; Psa. 22.9; Sol.
1.13; 4.5; 7.3, 7, 8; 8.1, 8, 10; Isa. 28.9; Ezek. 16.7.
"*Shaddai* therefore means primarily 'the breasted.'
God is *Shaddai* because He is the Nourisher, the
Strength-giver and so, in a secondary sense, the Satis-
fier, who pours Himself into believing lives. As a
fretful, unsatisfied babe is not only strengthened and
nourished from the mother's breast, but also is quieted,
rested, and satisfied, so *El Shaddai* is that name of God
which sets Him forth as the Strength-giver and Satis-
fier of His people." Both fruitfulness and chastening

are in this word: Gen. 17.1-8; 28.3, 4; Heb. 11.12; Ruth 1.20; John 15.2; Heb. 12.10.

II. Most High, or Most High God.

The Hebrew is *El Elyon, Elyon* signifying highest. See Gen. 14.17-24. The distinctive meaning of the name is given in verse 19, "the most high God, possessor of heaven and earth." *El Elyon* seems to be the name of God known by and in reference to the Gentile nations: Deut. 32.8; Dan. 3.26; 4.17, 24, 25, 32; 5.18, 21; see also Isa. 14.13, 14; Matt. 28.18; II Sam. 22.14, 15 Psa. 9.2-5; 21.7; 47.2-4; 57.2, 3; 82.6, 8; 83.18; 91.1-12.

III. Everlasting God.

The Hebrew is *El Olam.* See Gen. 21.33. *Olam* expresses eternal duration: Psa. 90.2. It is the equivalent of the Greek *aion,* signifying age or dispensation. *Olam* also expresses the idea of secrecy or hidingness. "The Everlasting God is therefore that name of Deity in virtue of which He is the God whose wisdom has divided all time and eternity into the mystery of successive ages or dispensations. It is not merely that He is everlasting, but that He is God over everlasting things": Eph. 1.9, 10; 3.3-6.

THIRD.

There are three names compounded with *Yahwe*: LORD God, Lord LORD, and LORD of Hosts.

I. LORD God.

The Hebrew is *Yahwe Elohim.* See Gen. **2.4.** **This**
divine name is used, first of God's relationship to man—
as Creator, Gen. 2.7-15; as Master, Gen. 2.16, **17; as**
Ruler, Gen. 2.18-24; 3.14-19, 22-24; and as Redeemer,
Gen. 3.8-15, 21; and second, of God's relationship to
Israel, Gen. 24.7; Ex. 3.15, 18; Deut. 12.1.

II. Lord LORD.

The Hebrew is *Adonai Yahwe.* See Gen. **15.2.** This
compound name emphasizes the first part rather than the
second part, that is, the thought of Master: Gen. **15.1, 8;**
Deut. 3.24; 9.26; Josh. 7.7.

III. LORD of Hosts.

The Hebrew is *Yahwe Sabaoth.* See I Sam. **1.3.**
Sabaoth signifies host or hosts. The word occurs
with special reference to warfare or service. It is
used of Jehovah as manifesting His power and glory:
Psa. 24.10. It occurs in the Old Testament mostly
in the crises of Israel's need. Thus, in his extremity
the psalmist cries out, "The Lord of hosts is with us;
the God of Jacob is our refuge": Psa. 46.7, 11. By
hosts, "primarily the angels are meant, but the name
gathers into itself the idea of all divine or heavenly
power as available for the needs of God's people."

Yahwe is compounded with seven names or words,
thus:

1. *Jehovah-jireh,* "the LORD will provide": Gen. 22.13, 14.

2. *Jehovah-rapha,* "the LORD that healeth": Ex. 15.26.

3. *Jehovah-nissi,* "the LORD our banner": Ex. 17.8-15.

4. *Jehovah-shalom,* "the LORD our peace," or "the LORD send peace": Judges 6.24.

5. *Jehovah-ro'i,* "the LORD my shepherd": Psa. 23.

6. *Jehovah-tsidkenu,* "the LORD our righteousness": Jer. 23.6.

7. *Jehovah-shammah,* "the LORD is present": Ezek. 48.35.

THEOLOGY.

PART TWO.

THE WORKS OF GOD.

TOPIC ONE: THE DECREES OF GOD.

I. DEFINITION.

The **Decrees of God** comprehend His eternal **purpose** which is worked out in time through the various ages or dispensations: Rom. 8.28; Eph. 1.11; 3.11. In I Tim. 1.17 Christ is called (lit. Greek) the *King of the ages.* Strong thus defines: "By the decrees of God we mean that eternal plan by which God has rendered certain all the events of the universe, past, present, and future."

II. EXTENT.

The divine decrees include creation, providence, and redemption. More particularly, they may be classified into two divisions, namely: first, decrees concerning nature—creation and preservation; and second, decrees concerning moral beings—providence and redemption, including grace.

NOTE: To our view the decrees are many, because they **are** worked out successively in time; but in their nature and from the divine standpoint they are *one*. What a plan is to an architect, that, so to speak, the decrees are to God.

III. SCRIPTURE PROOF.

Taking a comprehensive view, we may say that the Scriptures teach that all things, both great and small, are included within the divine decrees: Isa. 14.26, 27; 46.10, 11; Dan. 4.35; Eph. 1.11. But to particularize:

1. The stability of the physical universe: Psa. 119.89-91.

2. The outward circumstances of nations: Acts 17.26.

3. The length of human life: Job 14.5.

4. The mode of our death: Jno. 21.19.

5. The free acts of men, both good acts and evil acts: Isa. 44.28; Eph. 2.10; Gen. 50.20; I Kings 12.15; Luke 22.22; Acts 2.23; 4.27, 28; Rom. 9.17; I Pet. 2.8; Rev. 17.17.

6. The salvation of believers: I Cor. 2.7; Eph. 1. 3, 10, 11.

7. The establishment of Christ's kingdom: Psa. 2.7, 8; I Cor. 15.23.

8. The work of Christ and His people in establishing it: Phil. 2.12, 13; Rev. 5.7.

NOTE 1. The divine decrees are in harmony with God's fore-knowledge, wisdom, immutability, and benevolence. "A universe without decrees would be as irrational and appalling as would be an express train driving on in the darkness without head-light or engineer, and with no certainty that the next moment it might not plunge into the abyss" (A. J. Gordon).

NOTE 2. Objections are raised to the decrees:

1. That they are inconsistent with the free moral agency of man. But the same objection may be made to the divine fore-knowledge. Moreover, it confounds the decrees with their execution—quite a different thing.

2. That they take away all motive for human exertion. But the decrees are not fatalistic;.and they were framed, we may believe, in full view of man's cooperation in their execution.

3. That they make God the author of sin. This is true in a permissive sense. However, God is not the author of sin, but the author of beings who are themselves the authors of sin. Ingersol asked, "Why did God create the devil?" This answer was given him: "God did not create the devil—it was the devil who made the devil. God made a holy and free spirit who abused his liberty, himself created sin, and so made himself a devil."

Says Dr. Strong: "There are four questions which neither Scripture nor reason enables us completely to solve and to which we may safely say that only the higher knowledge of the future state will furnish the answers. These questions are: First, how can a holy God permit moral evil? Second, how could a being created pure ever fall? Third, how can we be responsible for inborn depravity? Fourth, how could Christ justly suffer? The first of these questions now confronts us. A complete theodicy *(theos,* God, and *dike,* justice) would be a vindication of the justice of God in permitting the natural and moral evil that exists under His government. While a complete theodicy is beyond our powers, we throw some light upon God's permission of moral evil by considering (1) that freedom of will is necessary to virtue; (2) that God suffers from sin more than does the sinner; (3) that, with the permission of sin, God provided a redemption; and (4) that God will eventually overrule all evil for good."

IV. PRACTICAL BEARINGS.

The doctrine of the divine decrees has practical bearings:

1. It inspires humility in the believer in the presence of God's sovereignty.

2. It teaches confidence in Him who works all things together for good to them that love God.

3. It warns the impenitent sinner that his punishment, though it be long delayed, will surely overtake him.

4. It invites the sinner to make his peace with God before it is too late.

NOTE: This doctrine of the divine decrees is often a stumbling-block to the beginner in the Christian life, because it is full of intellectual difficulties. But it proves to be of great comfort to the mature believer, particularly in times of trial and bereavement: Rom. 8.28. Here Arminians pray like Calvinists and Calvinists preach like Arminians, and both sing alike.

TOPIC TWO: CREATION.

I. DEFINITION.

Creation may be defined as "that free act of the triune God by which in the beginning and for His own glory He made, without the use of preexisting material, the whole visible and invisible universe" (Strong).

NOTE: The popular definition of creation as "production out of nothing" is open to objection: *nothing* is not a substance, nor an object of thought, nor a source of being. The better expression is "without the use of preexisting material."

II. PROOF.

Scripture proof of creation is both direct and indirect:

1. Direct.

This is found in two striking passages, viz: Gen. 1.1 and Heb. 11.3.

a. Genesis 1.1.

The Hebrew verb translated "created" is *bara*, which is found three times in chapter 1, viz: verse 1, of matter; verse 21, of animal life; and verses 26 and 27, of human life. This shows that there is an impassable gulf between plant life and animal life on the one hand, and between animal life and human life on the other hand.

NOTE: The Hebrew verb *bara* is to be distinguished from two other Hebrew verbs, viz: *asah,* to make, and *yatsar,* to form. *Bara* is used in Gen. 1.1 and *asah* in Gen. 2.4 of the creation of the heaven and earth. Of earth, both *yatsar* and *asah* are used in Isa. 45.18. In regard to man, in Gen. 1.27 we find *bara;* in Gen. 1.26 and 9.6, *asah;* and in Gen. 2.7, *yatsar.* In Isa. 43.7 all three are found in the same verse: "whom I have *bara* for my glory, I have *yatsar,* yea, I have *asah* him." In Isa. 45.12, "*asah* the earth, and *bara* man upon it"; but in Gen. 1.1 we read: "God *bara* the earth," and in 9.6 "*asah* man." Isaiah 44.2—"the Lord that *asah* thee (i. e. man) and *yatsar* thee"; but in Gen. 1.27 God "*bara* man." Gen. 5.2—"male and female *bara* He them." Gen. 2.22—"the rib *asah* He a woman"; Gen. 2.7—"He *yatsar* man"; i. e. *bara* male and female, yet, *asah* the woman and *yatsar* the man. *Asah* is not always used for *transform:* Isa. 41.20—"fir tree, pine, box-tree" in nature —*bara;* Psa. 51.10—"*bara* in me a clean heart"; Isa. 65.18— God "*bara* Jerusalem into rejoicing." This somewhat interchangeable use of these three verbs has led some to state that *bara* does not mean to *create.* But as Dr. Strong says, "If *bara* does not signify absolute creation, no word exists in the Hebrew language that can express this idea."

b. Hebrews 11.3.

This passage teaches that "the world was not made out of sensible and preexisting material, but by the direct fiat of omnipotence" (Strong). The following passages may also be consulted: Ex. 34.10; Num. 16.30; Isa. 4.5; 41.20; 45.7, 8; 57.19; 65.17; Jer. 31.22; Rom. 4.17; I Cor. 1.30; II Cor. 4.6; Col. 1.16, 17.

2. **Indirect.**

This is found in many passages:

a. The past duration of the world is limited: **Mark 13.19**; John 17.5; Eph. 1.4.

b. Each of the persons of the Godhead existed before the world began to be: Psa. 90.2; Prov. 8.23; John 1.1; Col. 1.17; Heb. 9.14.

III. AUTHOR.

God is the author of creation, acting through the twofold agency of the Word and the Spirit. More particularly the work of creation is ascribed to each of the three persons of the trinity:

1.   The Father: Gen. 1.1; I Cor. 8.6; Eph. 3.9.

2.   The Son: John 1.3; I Cor. 8.6; Heb. 1.2; 11.3; Col. 1.16.

3.   The Spirit: Gen. 1.2; Job 26.13; 33.4.

NOTE: In every work of God there is an agency of the Father, Son, and Spirit. Thus in creation the Father conceives, the Son executes, and the Spirit brings to completion. The illustration may be used of the architect planning, the builder erecting, and the decorator furnishing the interior of a house. In Gen. 1.1-3 we have the trinity: God the Father in verse 1; God the Spirit in verse 2; and God the Son in verse 3—"And God said" (Christ the spoken word; see John 1.1 and Heb. 11.3).

IV. SPHERES OF CREATION.

There are seven spheres of creation:

7

1. Angelic host: Col. 1.16.

2. Universe of matter: Gen. 1; on 1st, 2nd, and 4th days.

3. Vegetation: Gen. 1; on 3rd day.

4. Fish: Gen. 1; on 5th day.

5. Fowl: Gen. 1; on 5th day.

6. Animals—beast, cattle, reptile: Gen. 1; on 6th day.

7. Man: Gen. 1; on 6th day.

NOTE: Three interesting topics may be briefly noted:

First, the agreement between science and revelation. As to the order of creation, there is entire agreement, though the account of creation in Gen. 1 and 2 is in popular language. For example, light before the sun, inorganic matter before organic life, invertebrates before vertebrates, animals before man, etc. As to the time of creation, some scientists estimate 10,000 years; others 10,000,000 years. As to the creation of man, there is no good reason for putting it earlier than our accepted chronology, i. e., about B. C. 4,000 years.

Second, the meaning of the word "day" in Gen. 1. Two views are held, viz: that of 24 hours and that of an indefinite period. Both views seem to be sustained by Scripture. As to the latter, see Gen. 1 :5—a day before there was a sun; 1.8—evening and morning being a day; 2.2—a day that has not yet ended; 2.4; Isa. 2.12; Zech. 14.7; II Pet. 3.8.

Third, the method of interpretation. We reject the allegorical or mythical view and accept the literal view—the hyperliteral view. In other words, we accept without question the historicity of the early chapters of Genesis.

V. PURPOSE IN CREATION.

Scripture reveals a fourfold divine purpose in creation:

1. In God Himself: Prov. 16.4; Rom. 11.36; Col. 1.16.

2. In His own will and pleasure: Eph. 1.5, 6, 9; Rev. 4.11.

3. In His own glory: Isa. 43.7; 60.21; 61.3; Luke 2.14.

4. In the making known of His power, wisdom, and holy name: Psa. 19.1; Eph. 3.9, 10.

SUMMARY: "God's supreme end in creation is nothing outside of Himself, but is His own glory—in the revelation in and through creatures of the infinite perfection of His own being" (Strong).

TOPIC THREE: PRESERVATION.

I. DEFINITION.

Preservation may be defined as "that continuous agency of God by which He maintains in existence the things He has created together with the properties and powers with which He has endowed them" (Strong).

NOTE: Creation has to do with the origin of things; preservation with their continuance.

II. PROOF.

The following passages reveal and prove the divine preservation: Neh. 9.6; Psa. 36.6; 145.20; Acts 17.28; Col. 1.17; Heb. 1.2, 3.

NOTE: Psalm 105 has been called "a long hymn to the preserving power of God, who keeps alive all the creatures of the deep, both small and great."

III. METHOD.

How is preservation maintained? There are three views:

1. Deism.

"This view represents the universe as a self-sustained mechanism, from which God withdrew as soon as He had created it, and which He left to a process of self-development" (Strong). The illustration may be used of a clock, which one winds up and then lets it run of itself. The chief objection to this view is that logically it denies in full God's interposition in His universe, in the introduction of life, in incarnation, in regeneration, in history, in all providential occurrences, and in answers to prayer.

2. Continuous Creation.

"This view regards the universe as from moment to moment the result of a new creation" (Strong). The main objections to this view are: (1) it denies the testi-

mony of consciousness as to the sway of natural law;
(2) it exalts God's omnipotence at the expense of His
truth, love, and holiness; (3) it denies our own objective personal existence and thus destroys all responsibility for moral act.

3. Divine Power Operating through Natural Forces.

This view, which we hold to be the true one, may be
thus stated: Though God has established an order
of natural forces, yet He exercises a special and continuous activity in the upholding of the universe with
its powers. This activity is the activity of Christ,
who is the mediating agent in preservation as well
as in creation: Heb. 1.3. This passage gives warrant
for the view that natural law is only another name
for the exercise of God's personal will.

TOPIC FOUR: PROVIDENCE.

I. DEFINITION.

Providence may be defined as "that continuous
agency of God by which He makes all the events of
the physical and moral universe fulfil the original
design with which He created it" (Strong).

NOTE: While creation has to do with the beginning of
things and preservation with their continuance, providence
has to do with their development and fruition. Or, creation

concerns the existence, preservation the maintenance, and providence the care and control of all things. Providence here means both *prevision*, foreseeing, and *provision*, forecaring.

II. PROOF.

The Scriptures bear witness to:

1. **A general providential government and control:**

a. Over the universe at large: Psa. 103.19; Dan. 4.35; Eph. 1.11.

b. Over the physical world: Job 37.5, 10; Psa. 104.14; 135.6, 7; Matt. 5.45; 6.30.

c. Over the brute creation: Psa. 104.21, 28; Matt. 6.26; 10.29.

d. Over the affairs of nations: Job 12.23; Psa. 22.28; 66.7; Acts 17.26.

e. Over man's birth and lot in life: I Sam. 16.1; Psa. 139.16; Isa. 45.5; Jer. 1.5; Gal. 1.15, 16.

f. Over the outward successes and failures of men's lives: Psa. 75.6, 7; Luke 1.52.

g. Over things seemingly accidental and insignificant: Prov. 16.33; Matt. 10.30.

h. In the protection of the righteous: Psa. 4.8; 5.12; 63.8; 91.3; Rom. 8.28.

i. In the supply of the wants of God's people: Gen. 22.8, 14; Deut. 8.3; Phil. 4.19.

j. In the arrangement of answers to prayer: Psa. 68.10; Isa. 64.4; Matt. 6.8, 32, 33.

k. In the exposure and punishment of the wicked: Psa. 7.12, 13; 11.6; II Pet. 2.9; Rev. 20.11-15.

Still further the Scriptures bear witness to:

2. A government and control extending to the free actions of men:

a. To men's free acts in general: Ex. 12.36; I Sam. 24.18; Psa. 33.14, 15; Prov. 16.1; 19.21; 20.24; 21.1; Jer. 10.23; Phil. 2.13; Eph. 2.10; Jas. 4.13-16.

b. To the sinful acts of men: II Sam. 16.10; 24.1; Rom. 11.32; II Thess. 2.11, 12.

NOTE I. With respect to man's evil acts God's providence is:

1. Preventive—withholding from sin: Gen. 20.6; 31.24; Psa. 19.13; Hos. 2.6.

2. Permissive—refusing to withhold from sin: II Chron. 32.31; Psa. 17.13, 14; 81.12, 13; Isa. 53.4, 10; Hos. 4.17; Acts 14.16; Rom. 1.21, 28; 3.25.

3. Directive—overruling evil for good: Gen. 50.20; Psa. 76.10; Isa. 10.5-7; Acts 4.27, 28.

4. Determinative—prescribing its bounds and effects: Job 1.12; Psa. 124.2, 3; I Cor. 10.13; II Thess. 2.7; Rev. 20.2, 3.

NOTE 2. To the second class we may refer passages concerning Pharaoh: Ex. 4.21; 7.13; 8.15; Rom. 9.17, 18. God hardened Pharaoh's heart: first, by permitting him to harden his own heart; second, by giving him light and then leaving him to resist it; third, by abandoning him to the evil working of his will; and fourth, by causing his sin to be manifested in one direction more than another.

III. KINDS.

The providence of God is of two kinds, namely: unconditional and conditional.

1. Unconditional.

There is a providence of God which is in no wise dependent upon the meeting of conditions by its subjects. It is extended over:

1. The physical universe: Psa. 103.19; 135.6, 7; Dan. 4.35; Eph. 1.11; Heb. 1.3.

2. The vegetable world: Matt. 6.28-30.

3. The animal creation: Psa. 104.21, 27; Matt. 6.26; 10.29.

4. Man—as to certain general creature comforts: Matt. 5.45; Acts 14.17; 17.28.

2. Conditional.

There is a providence of God which is dependent upon the meeting of conditions in its subjects. These can be met only by true believers. They are: obedience, prayer, faith, and trust: Jno. 14.13, 14; 15.7; Mark 11.24; Phil. 4.6, 7; Jas. 5.14-16.

Note: Unconditional providence is sometimes called "General Providence"; conditional providence, "Special Providence."

QUESTIONS FOR STUDY.

1. What are the two general divisions of Theology?

2. Define: the restricted meaning of theology, theism, deism, atheism, skepticism, and agnosticism.

3. Give four Scriptural definitions of God.

4. Give a theological definition of God.

5. What is the origin of the idea of God?

6. What are the unfailing marks of a primary or first truth?

7. Can you show that the idea of God meets the unfailing marks of a primary or first truth?

8. What are the mistaken sources of a belief in God?

9. What is the attitude of the Scriptures towards the existence of God?

10. What are the five corroborative proofs of God's existence?

11. With the exception of the Christological proof, state any one of the corroborative proofs, pointing out its defects and value.

12. What is meant by "personality"?

13. What are the constituent elements of personality?

14. How may the personality of God be shown?

15. What is meant by the trinity of God?

16. What are the two elements of the doctrine of the trinity which must be carefully guarded?

17. How is the term "person" to be understood with respect to the trinity?

18. What is the orthodox formula of the doctrine of the trinity?
19. Can you give six Scripture proofs of the trinity of God?
20. Mention five illustrations of the trinity. Which satisfies you most?
21. Define attribute.
22. Define divine attributes.
23. What is the basis of classification of divine attributes?
24. Mention and give Scripture proof for the divine attributes.
25. Mention, define, and give Scripture proof for the divine perfections.
26. Show how Scripture proper names have special significance.
27. What do the names of God reveal?
28. Discuss briefly the significance of the name God.
29. Discuss briefly the significance of the name LORD.
30. Discuss briefly the significance of the name Lord.
31. Discuss briefly the significance of the name Almighty God.
32. Discuss briefly the significance of the name Most High God.

33. Discuss briefly the significance of the name Everlasting God.
34. Discuss briefly the significance of the names LORD God, Lord GOD, and LORD of Hosts.
35. What are the seven divine names compounded with Jehovah? Give references.
36. Define the decrees of God.
37. What do they include?
38. Give Scripture proof (the eight points).
39. What are the practical bearings of the doctrine?
40. Define creation.
41. Give the direct Scripture proof.
42. Give the indirect Scripture proof.
43. Who is the Author of creation?
44. What are several spheres?
45. What is the fourfold end?
46. Define preservation.
47. Give the Scripture proof of the doctrine.
48. State the three views as to method of preservation.
49. Define providence.
50. Give Scripture proof—any eight points.
51. State the fourfold providence of God as to man's evil acts.
52. What are the two kinds of providence? Give Scripture references.

DOCTRINE THREE: ANGELOLOGY.

Topics.

CHAPTER III.

ANGELOLOGY.

I. DEFINITION OF ANGELS.

Angels may be defined as an order of unembodied, finite, celestial beings: Psa. 8.5; Matt. 22.30.

Note: Both the Hebrew and the Greek word translated angel means literally *messenger*: Mal. 3.1. Malachi signifies *my messenger*.

II. NATURE.

1. As to their substance the Bible calls them spirits: I Sam. 16.14, 16, 23; 18.10; I Kings 22.21; Mark 9.20-25; Luke 7.21; 8.2; 24.39; Acts 19.12-15; I Tim. 4.1.

2. It represents them as above the known laws of matter: Num. 22.23; I Chron. 21.16-27; Acts 12.7.

3. In intelligence they are superior to man in his present state: II Sam. 14.17-20; Matt. 18.10; 24.36; I Tim. 3.16; 5.21; I Pet. 1.12.

4. In power they are superior to man in his present state: Psa. 103.20; II Thess. 1.7; II Pet. 2.11; Rev. 5.2; 10.1; 20.1-3.

5. They are distinct from man and were created before man; but when is not known: I Cor. 6.3; Heb. 1.14; 2.16; 12.22, 23; Gen. 2.1; Job 38.7.

6. They constitute a company in distinction from a race: Matt. 22.30; Luke 20.36; Heb. 2.16.

7. As created and finite intelligences, they are not omniscient, omnipotent, or omnipresent. We infer this from Scripture statements concerning them.

The Scriptures divide angels into two classes, viz: good angels and evil angels.

TOPIC ONE: GOOD ANGELS.

I. NATURE.

They are sinless. This we infer from the names given to them: "holy angels," Mark 8.38; "elect angels," I Tim. 5.21.

II. ABODE.

Heaven is their home: Matt. 18.10; Mark 12.25; Luke 1.19; 12.8, 9; 15.10. However, they sojourn upon earth: Gen. 28.12; John 1.51. In these passages the angels are seen ascending and descending, not descending and ascending.

III. NUMBER.

Though finite, yet their number is beyond computation: Deut. 33.2; Psa. 68.17; Dan. 7.10; Matt. 26.53; Luke 2.13; Heb. 12.22; Rev. 5.11.

IV. ORGANIZATION.

They seem to be organized in various ranks with correspondingly different authorities: Luke 2.13; Rom. 8.38; Eph. 1.21; 3.10; Col. 1.16; 2.10; I Pet. 3.22. Celestial intelligences have been classified thus: archangels, angels, principalities, authorities, powers, thrones, might, and dominion. This arrangement, however, is purely conjectural, since the ranking order is not clearly revealed.

NOTE: The names of two celestial beings are given in Scripture. These are Michael (Heb. *who is like God*), called an archangel: Jude 9. See also Dan. 10.13, 21; 12.1; Rev. 12.7. The other is Gabriel (Heb. *God's hero*) whom Milton calls an archangel: Dan. 8.16-26; 9.21, 22; Luke 1.19, 26. Michael seems to be the messenger of law and judgment; Gabriel of mercy and promise.

V. MINISTRY.

1. They stand in the presence of God and worship Him: Psa. 29.1, 2; 89.7; Matt. 18.10.

2. They rejoice in God's works: Job 38.7; Luke 15.10.

3. They execute God's will:

a. By working in nature: Psa. 103.20; 104.4; Heb. 1.7.

b. By guiding the affairs of nations: Dan. 10.12, 13, 21; 11.1; 12.1.

c. By watching over the interests of particular churches: Rev. 1.20. In this latter passage some take "the angels of the seven churches" to be the pastors.

d. By assisting and protecting individual believers: I Kings 19.5; Psa. 91.11; Dan. 6.22; Matt. 4.11; 18.10; Acts 12.15; Heb. 1.14.

NOTE: There are guardian angels, but it is probably not true that each one has a special guardian angel. At need, twelve legions of angels may be at the believer's disposal: Psa. 34.7; 91.11; Matt. 18.10; Acts 12.8-11. See also Gen. 48.16; Matt. 26.53.

e. By punishing God's enemies: II Kings 19.35; Acts 12.23.

NOTE: Some interesting facts concerning angels:

1. They do not marry or die: Matt. 22.30; Luke 20.35, 36.
2. They eat: Psa. 78.25, R. V.
3. They should not be worshiped: Col. 2.18.
4. They have been seen by men: Gen. 32.1, 2; Luke 2.9, 13; Jno. 20.12.
5. They bear God's servants to glory: Luke 16.22.
6. They will gather together God's elect: Matt. 24.31.
7. They gave the law: Acts 7.35; Gal. 3.19.
8. They will accompany Christ upon His return: Matt. 25.31, 32; II Thess. 1.7, 8.
9. They will carry out God's judgment against the wicked: Matt. 13.24-30, 39-42, 47-50, R. V.

The popular notion that angels have wings and sing seems

to be unscriptural. Dr. Henry Wilson used to take off, in his inimitable way, this popular notion by describing an angel as:

> "A beautiful creature with wings
> That sits up in heaven and sings."

VI. THE ANGEL OF THE COVENANT.

In the O. T., frequent mention is made of an august, celestial personage "who acts in the name of Jehovah, whose name is used interchangeably with that of Jehovah, and who receives divine honor and reverence." The names given to this Heavenly Being are: the Angel, or the Angel of Jehovah; the Angel of the Presence; the Angel, or Messenger, of the Covenant. He can be no other than a preincarnate manifestation (a Christophany) of the Logos—Christ Himself: Gen. 16.10-13; 18.16-22; 22.11, 12; 32.24-32; 48.16; Ex. 3.2; 23.20-25; 32.34; 33.2, 14; Josh. 5.13-15; Judges 2.1-5; 6.12-24; 13.3-21 (see verse 18, margin, and compare with Isa. 9.6, 7); Isa. 63.9; Zech. 1.11, 12; Mal. 3.1.

VII. SERAPHIM AND CHERUBIM.

The *seraphim* of Isaiah, the *living creatures* of Revelation, and the *cherubim* of Genesis, Exodus, and Ezekiel are probably to be regarded as "symbolic appearances intended to represent redeemed humanity, endowed by all the creature perfections lost by the

fall, and made to be the dwelling place of God."
Some hold the cherubim to be symbols of the divine
attributes; others, of God's government over nature.
Dr. Strong regards them as "symbols of nature per-
vaded by the divine energy and subordinated to the
divine purposes, but they are symbols of nature only
because they are symbols of man in his twofold capacity of *image of God* and *priest of nature.*"

NOTE: As to the cherubim:

1. They are not personal beings, but artificial, temporary,
symbolic figures.

2. While they are not themselves personal existences, they
are symbols of personal existence—symbols not of divine or
angelic perfections but of human nature: Ezek. 1.5.

3. They are emblems of human nature, not in its present
stage of development, but possessed of all its original perfections; for this reason the most perfect animal forms—the king-
like courage of the lion, the patient service of the ox, the
soaring insight of the eagle—are combined with that of man:
Ezek. 1 and 10; Rev. 4.6-8.

4. These cherubic forms represent not merely material or
earthly perfections, but human nature spiritualized and sanctified.

5. They symbolize a human nature exalted to be the dwelling place of God. Hence the inner curtains of the tabernacle
were interwoven with the cherubic figures: Ex. 26.1; 37.6-9. While
the flaming sword at the gate of Eden was the symbol of
justice, the cherubim were symbols of mercy—keeping the "way
of the tree of life" for man, until by sacrifice and renewal
Paradise should be regained: Gen. 3.24. (Condensed from
Strong).

TOPIC TWO: EVIL ANGELS.

I. NATURE.

They are sinful. This we infer from the names given to them: "the devil and his angels," Matt. 25.41; "wicked," Matt. 12.45; "unclean," Matt. 10.1; "evil," Acts 19.13.

II. ABODE.

The Scriptures assign them to various places: "hell," II Peter 2.4 (Greek *Tartarus*); "darkness," Jude 6; "deep," Luke 8.31 (lit. bottomless, Greek, abyss; see Rev. 9.1, 2, 11). But they also have access to the aerial regions, even the "heavenlies": Eph. 2.2; 6.12.

III. NUMBER.

Though limited, their number is unknown: Matt. 25.41; II Pet. 2.4; Jude 6.

IV. ORGANIZATION.

They seem to be of various ranks and authority, Satan being their leader: Eph. 6.12; Col. 2.15; Jno. 12.31; 14.30; 16.11.

V. MINISTRY.

1. They oppose God and strive to defeat His will:

Job 1.6; Zech. 3.1; Matt. 13.39; I Pet. 5.8; Rev. 12.10.

2. They hinder man's temporal and eternal welfare—"sometimes by exercising a certain control over
natural phenomena, but more commonly by subject-
ing man's soul to temptation": Job 1.12, 16, 19; 2.7;
Luke 13.11, 16; Acts 10.38; II Cor. 12.7; I Thess. 2.18;
Heb. 2.14. See also Gen. 3.1; Rev. 20.2; Matt. 4.3;
Jno. 13.27; Eph. 2.2; I Thess. 3.5; I Pet. 5.8.

NOTE: Temptation is both negative and positive—the good
seed is taken away and tares are sown: Mark 4.15; Matt. 13.38,
39. Satan has many angels and agents through whom he accom-
plishes his objects.

3. Yet, in spite of themselves, they execute God's
plans of punishing the ungodly, of chastening the
good, and of illustrating the nature and fate of moral
evil:

a. Punishing the ungodly: I Kings 22.23; Psa.
78.49.

b. Chastening the good: Job. chs. 1, 2; I Cor. 5.5; I
Tim. 1.20; Luke 22.31. As to I Cor. 5.5, being delivered
to Satan "for the destruction of the flesh," four things
seem to be involved: excommunication from the
church, authoritative infliction of bodily disease or
death, loss of protection of good angels who minister
only to the saints, and subjection to the buffetings
and tormentings of the devil.

c. Illustrating the nature and fate of moral evil: Matt. 8.29; 25.41; II Thess. 2.8; James 2.19; Rev. 12.9, 12; 20.10.

NOTE: The present condition of evil angels seems to have been due to a primitive apostasy—possibly at the time Satan fell: Matt. 25.41; II Pet. 2.4; Jude 6.

QUERY: Were they originally inhabitants of the earth and was the condition of the earth described in Gen. 1.2 as "without form and void" a judgment in consequence of their sin? In Isa. 45.18 we are told that God created the earth "not in vain" (R. V. *not a waste*: the same Hebrew word is used in Gen. 1.2 and is rendered "without form"). If this view be true, then Gen. 1.1 describes *creation*; Gen. 1.2a describes *desolation*; and Gen. 1.2b describes *restoration*. Or, we have FORMATION, DEFORMATION, and REFORMATION. See "Earth's Earliest Ages" by Pember.

TOPIC THREE: DEMONS.

I. NAME.

For the word *devils* of our English Bibles the term *demons* should be substituted. This has been done in the American Standard Revised Version (Nelson's): Matt. 8.16. "Devil" is the translation of the Greek *diabolos,* slanderer, a noun used in the singular number and applied exclusively to Satan: Matt. 4.1-5. "Demon" is the translation of the Greek *daimon* or *daimonion,* plural *daimonia.* The root signification of this word is uncertain; according to Plato it means "knowing" or "intelligent," pointing perhaps to the superior knowledge which it is believed these beings possess.

II. NATURE.

Whether demons are to be classed with evil angels or not is uncertain. What is certain, however, is:

1. They are personal intelligences: Matt. 8.29, 31.

2. They are unclean, sullen, vicious, and malicious spirits: Matt. 8.28; 9.33; 10.1; 12.43; Mark 1.23; 5.2-5; 9.17, 20; Luke 6.18; 9.39.

3. They are Satan's emissaries: Matt. 12.22-30.

4. They are so numerous as to make Satan practically everywhere present: Matt. 12.26, 27; 25.41.

III. ORIGIN.

The origin of demons is not revealed in the Scriptures. But it has been conjectured that they are disembodied spirits, perhaps of a pre-Adamic race or order of beings. If they are disembodied spirits, this would explain the fact that they seek embodiment, without which apparently they are unable to work evil: Matt. 12.43, 44; Mark 5.10-12.

IV. POWER.

1. They know Christ and recognize His supreme

authority: Matt. 8.29, 31; Mark 1.24; Acts 19.15; Jas. 2.19.

2. They know true believers and obey the authority of Jesus' name: Matt. 10.8; Mark 16.17; Luke 10.17-20; Acts 19.15.

3. They know their fate to be that of eternal torment: Matt. 8.29; Luke 8.31; Rev. 20.3, 10.

4. They enter and control the bodies of both human beings and beasts: Mark 5.8, 11-13.

5. They inflict physical infirmities: Matt. 9.33; 12.22; Luke 9.37-42.

6. They inflict mental maladies: Mark 5.4, 5.

7. They produce moral impurity: Matt. 10.1; Mark 5.2.

V. POSSESSION vs. INFLUENCE.

The New Testament warrants us in making a careful distinction between demoniacal possession and demon influence. To the former, we hold, unbelievers alone are exposed; to the latter, believers. Cases of demoniacal possession are: Matt. 4.24; 8.16, 28, 33; 9.32; 12.22; Mark 1.32; 5.15, 16, 18; Luke 8.36; Acts 8.7; 16.16. On the other hand, "Demon influence may manifest itself in religious asceticism and formalism, I Tim. 4.1-3, degenerating into uncleanness, II Pet. 2.10-12. The sign of demon influence in religion is departing from the faith, i. e., the body of revealed truth in the Scriptures, I Tim. 4.1. The demons maintain especially a conflict with believers who would be spiritual, Eph. 6.12; I Tim. 4.1-3. All unbelievers are open to demon possession, Eph. 2.2. The believer's resources are prayer and bodily control, Matt. 17.21, 'the whole armor of God,' Eph. 6.13-18" (Scofield Bible).

VI. POSSESSION vs. DISEASE.

Following the teaching of the Gospels, we should be careful to make a clear distinction between demoniacal possession on the one hand and purely physical sickness and mental disease on the other hand. Instances of the latter are: Matt. 4.24; 8.16; 9.20-35; 10.1; 14.35; Mark 1.32, 34; 3.15; Luke 4.40; 6.17, 18; 9.1. We need to be reminded that it is unkind, unchristlike, and unscriptural to attribute cases of ordinary physical and mental disease to demoniacal possession, oppression, or influence. We hold that a child of God who is fully yielded and wholly sanctified cannot be the subject of demoniacal possession in spirit, soul, or body: II Cor. 6.14-18; Eph. 5.18; I Thess. 5.23.

NOTE: Dr. Farr gives the following Scriptural tests for discovering demons: "They appear for the most part in darkness. They deny the personality of Satan. They hate the name of the Lord Jesus. They cast contempt on the inspiration of Scripture." The same writer adds: "Some of the disastrous effects of Spiritism are insanity, the squandering of fortunes, the breaking up of happy homes, and the making shipwreck of religious faith."

VII. DEMONOLOGY.

There are seven forms of demonology mentioned and condemned in the Word of God, viz:

1. Divination: Gen. 44.5; Hos. 4.12.
2. Necromancy: I Sam. 28.8; II Chron. 33.6.
3. Prognostication: Ezek. 21.21.
4. Magic: Gen. 41.8; Ex. 7.11; Dan. 4.7.
5. Sorcery: Isa. 47.9-13; Acts 19.19; Rev. 22.15.
6. Witchcraft: I Sam. 15.23; I Chron. 10.13; Gal. 5.20.
7. Ventriloquism: Isa. 8.19.

Read Deut. 18.9-14, where God has forbidden all these things. Then read verses 15-19, where we are shut up to Christ and to His supreme authority. With the following we fully agree: "Whatever of the phenomena of Spiritualism, or more properly Spiritism, may be of supernatural origin, has been regarded by some to be the direct work of evil spirits impersonating departed friends, or acting in other ways to arrest the attention, excite the wonder, and ensnare the souls of the foolish or unwary; others regard the entire system as fraud perpetrated by disreputable mediums to make money, and, doubtless, a considerable portion of it may be explained on this basis."

TOPIC FOUR: SATAN.

I. PERSONAL EXISTENCE.

That there exists a personal devil the clear teaching of Scripture leaves us no room to doubt: Job 1.6-12; 2.1-7; Zech. 3.1, 2; Matt. 4.1-11; Luke 10.18; Jno. 13.2; Acts 5.3; Eph. 6.11, 12; I Pet. 5.8; Rev. 20.1-3.

NOTE: The devil is not an impersonal force nor the principle of evil personified. Personal names and personal pronouns are used with reference to him, while personal attributes and acts are ascribed to him.

II. NAMES.

The principal Scriptural names applied to the devil are the following:
1. Abaddon, perdition: Rev. 9.11.
2. Apollyon, destroyer: Rev. 9.11.
3. Beelzebub, prince of demons: Matt. 12.24, 27.
4. Belial, vileness: II Cor. 6.15.
5. Devil, slanderer: Matt. 4.1.
6. Satan, adversary: Zech. 3.1; I Pet. 5.8.
7. Great Dragon: Rev. 12.9.
8. God of this world (age): II Cor. 4.4.
9. Liar and murderer: Jno. 8.44.

10. Lucifer, light-bearer: Isa. 14.12.
11. Prince of this world: Jno. 12.31.
12. Prince of the power of the air: Eph. 2.2.
13. Old Serpent: Rev. 12.9.
14. Tempter: I Thess. 3.5.
15. Wicked One: Matt. 13.19.

III. ORIGINAL CHARACTER, POSITION, AND APOSTASY.

It appears to be taught in the Scriptures that the devil was created perfect in his ways, of great beauty and brightness of person, and exalted in position and honor; that as a result of pride because of his own superiority, he directed to himself the worship due to God alone; and that in consequence of his sin he was degraded in person, position, and power, becoming the opponent of God and the enemy of man: Isa. 14.12-17; Ezek. 28.1-19; Col. 1.16; I Tim. 3.6; II Pet. 2.4; Jude 6, 9.

An interesting question concerns Ezek. 28.1-19. Is it a description of the original state of Satan? Two personages are in view: first the prince of Tyre, vss. 1-10; and second the king of Tyre, vss. 11-19. The prince of Tyre seems to refer primarily to Ethbaal II, and vss. 1-10 were fulfilled in the siege of Tyre by Nebuchadnezzar, which lasted thirteen years; B. C., 598-585. The king of Tyre and vss. 11-19 seem to refer in part to a worldly monarch and in part to a supernatural personage. It is generally believed by conservative and devout Bible students that the king of Tyre is to be regarded as a representative or re-incarnation (a type) of Satan, and vss. 11-19 a description of Satan's original character, position, and apostasy. Notice the following points:

1. Satan was full of wisdom, perfect in beauty, and "sealed up the sum" (perhaps of created perfection): vs. 12.

2. He was in Eden, the Garden of God: vs. 13. Some think an earlier mineral Eden is meant; others think these precious stones formed a kind of breast-plate, such as the high priest wore: Ex. 28.15; 39.8.

3. He was the anointed cherub that covereth: vs. 14a. *Covereth* probably refers to *outspreading wings*: Ex. 25.20; 37.9.

4. He was in the holy mountain of God: vs. 14b.

5. He walked up and down in the midst of the stones of fire: vs. 14c; Ex. 24.10.

6. He was perfect in his ways from his creation till his apostasy: vs. 15.

7. His heart was lifted up because of his beauty, and his wisdom was corrupted because of his bright-ness: vs. 17a.

8. He was cast forth from the mountain of God: vs. 16.

9. He was degraded in position and debased in character: vss. 17b, 18.

10. He became the enemy of man: vs. 19.

IV. ABODE.

According to the Scriptures Satan is not restricted to any one place:

1. He has access to heaven: Job 1.6; Zech. 3.1; Luke 10.18; Rev. 12.7-12.

NOTE: By many the last two passages are taken to refer to past events; we take them, however, to refer to future events.

2. He has access to the "heavenlies": Eph. 6.11, 12.

3. He walks up and down in the earth: Job 1.7; 2.2; I Pet. 5.8.

4. His proper place is hell: Rev. 9.11; Matt. 25.41.

V. POWER AND WORK.

1. Satan is the author of sin in the universe: Isa. 14.13, 14—"I will."

2. He is the author of sin in the world: Gen. 3.1-6.

3. He is the author of sickness: Luke 13.16; Acts 10.38.

4. He is the author of death: Heb. 2.14.

5. He tempts to sin: I Chron. 21.1 R. V.; Matt. 4.1, 3, 5, 6, 8, 9.

6. He ensnares people: I Tim. 3.7.

7. He puts wicked purposes into men's **hearts:** Jno. 13.2; Acts 5.3.

8. He blinds the heart: II Cor. 4.4 R. V.

9. He enters into men: Jno. 13.27.

10. He takes away the good seed of the Word: Mark 4.15.

11. He sows tares among the wheat: Matt. 13.25.

12. He will give power to Antichrist: II Thess. 2.9, 10 R. V.

13. He transforms himself into an angel of light: II Cor. 11.14, 15. Likewise his ministers.

14. He harasses God's servants: II Cor. 12.7.

15. He resists God's servants: Dan. 10.13; **Zech.** 3.1.

16. He hinders them: I Thess. 2.18 R. V.

17. He sifts them: Luke 22.31.

18. He accuses the brethren: Rev. 12.9, 10.

19. He holds the world—"like children asleep in his arms": I John 5.19. (R. V. "the evil one.")

NOTE: **Satan's favorite methods of attack are:**

1. Intimidations: I Pet. 5.8.

2. Seduction: II Cor. 11.3.

3. Destruction: Matt. 10.28.

He frightens, allures, or kills.

VI. LIMITATION.

Although a supernatural personage, Satan is finite: he is not omniscient, omnipotent, or omnipresent. Of course he is wiser and stronger than man, Jude 9, and, through his emissaries, seems to be in evidence in all places at the same time. It is doubtful whether anyone ever comes into personal conflict with Satan himself; temptations which come from Satan come, except in extraordinary instances, from the emissaries of Satan, that is, evil angels or demons. All Satan's power he exercises by permission of God; thus:

1. He cannot tempt a believer except by God's permission: Matt. 4.1.

2. He cannot inflict sickness except by God's permission: Job. 1.10, 12.

3. He cannot inflict death except by God's permission: Job 2.6; Heb. 2.14.

4. He cannot even touch us except by God's permission: Job 1.10-12; 2.6; Luke 22.31; I John 5.18.

5. He flees when resisted: James 4.7.

VII. DESTINY.

To our first parents the promise was made, Gen. 3.15, that the seed of the woman should bruise the serpent's head. The serpent is Satan: Rev. 12.9. Observe the following historic steps in the fulfilment of this promise:

9

1. Potentially, so to speak, this bruising of the serpent's head was accomplished by Christ on the cross: Jno. 12.31; Col. 2.15; Heb. 2.14; I Jno. 3.8. The devil is a defeated foe, and he knows it.

2. During the present age his power is restricted, being exercised (as we have seen) only by permission of God.

3. During the Millennium he will be confined in the abyss: Rev. 20.1-3.

4. After the Millennium he will be "loosed a little season": Rev. 20.3b, 7-9.

5. Finally he will be cast into the lake of fire and brimstone, there to be tormented day and night forever and ever: Rev. 20.10. Praise the Lord! Hallelujah!

VIII. DUTY OF CHRISTIANS.

The duty of Christians with reference to Satan is clearly set forth in the Scriptures:

1. We should be sober and watchful: I Pet. 5.8.

NOTE: There is no Scriptural warrant for defying the devil or for boasting over him. It is the part of wisdom neither to underestimate nor to overestimate, but to duly estimate an enemy's power.

2. We should not rebuke him, rail against him,

or speak evil of him: Zech. 3.1, 2; II Pet. 2.10; Jude 8, 9.

NOTE: It is the part of wisdom not to talk to the devil. When he speaks to us we should ignore him, or better still refer him to the Holy Spirit, our Advocate and Protector.

3. We should not be ignorant of his devices: II Cor. 2.11.

4. We should give him no place: Eph. 4.27.

5. We should resist him: Jas. 4.7; I John 2.13.

NOTE: Resist means, not to argue or fight, but to withstand, i. e., to stand one's ground: Eph. 6.13. Don't run; leave that to the devil! James 4.7. Mr. Lelacheur used to say, "Some people treat this verse as if it read, 'Resist the devil, and he will fly at you.'"

6. We can meet him victoriously only when clad in the "panoply of God": Eph. 6.13-18; I John 5.18.

NOTE 1. The devil, says Dr. Pierson, appears in many aspects, characters, and activities, such as the following:

1. A fowler, spreading his snares: Prov. 1.17.
2. A captor, binding and enslaving: Luke 13.11, 16; II Tim. 2.26.
3. A sower of tares in the field: Matt. 13.39.
4. A sifter with his sieve: Luke 22.31-34.
5. A deceiver, deluding and blinding his victims: I Kings 22.21-23; Matt. 24.24; II Cor. 11.14.
6. A destroyer with his scourge: Job. chs. 1, 2; II Cor. 12.7-10.
7. A warrior, arming sinners: Rev. 20.7-9.

Again, the same author enumerates these "devices" of Satan:

1. *Diversion,* turning the mind from things great to small, the unseen and eternal to the visible and temporal: II Cor. 4.4.

2. *Delusion,* by lies, wiles, denials, evasions, misrepresentations: Gen. 3.4; Ezek. 13.22; II Cor. 11.14; Eph. 6.11; II Thess. 2.11.

3. *Double-mindedness,* compromise, trying to serve God and mammon: Matt. 6.24; II Cor. 6.14, 15; 7.1.

4. *Doubt,* inducing hesitation: Rom. 14.23.

5. *Darkness,* enveloping the soul in gloom, either of imagination, difficulty, alienation from God, or despair: Isa. 50.10.

6. *Deadness,* substituting "dead works" for living godliness, etc.: Heb. 6.1; 9.14.

7. *Delay,* procrastinating all that is good, leading men to put off the time of decision and action: Acts 24.25; 26.28.

NOTE 2. Dr. Strong has the following remarkable contrast between the devil and the Holy Spirit:

1. The serpent and the dove.

2. The father of lies and the Spirit of truth.

3. Men possessed of dumb spirits and men given wonderful utterance in diverse tongues.

4. The murderer from the beginning and the life-giving Spirit who regenerate. the soul and quickens the body.

5. The adversary and the Helper.

6. The slanderer and the Advocate.

7. Satan's sifting and the Spirit's winnowing.

8. The organizing intelligence and malignity of the evil one and the Holy Spirit's combination of all forces of matter and mind to build up the kingdom of God.

9. The strong man fully armed and the Stronger than he.

10. The evil one who works only evil and the Holy One who is the author of holiness in the hearts of men.

QUESTIONS FOR STUDY.

1. Define angels.
2. Mention five points as to their nature.
3. Into what two classes are angels divided?
4. What is the abode of good angels?
5. What is their number?
6. How are they organized?
7. Mention five points as to their ministry.
8. Mention five interesting Scriptural facts concerning angels.
9. Who was "the Angel of the Covenant"?
10. Tell something about cherubim and seraphim.
11. What is the abode of evil angels?
12. What is their number?
13. How are they organiced?
14. What is their ministry?
15. Tell something about the meaning of the term demon.
16. Tell something about the nature of demons.
17. What is their conjectural origin?
18. Mention five points as to their power.
19. What Scriptural distinction should be made between demoniacal possession and demon influence?
20. What Scriptural distinction should be made between demoniacal possession and bodily and mental diseases?
21. What are the seven forms of demonology men-

tioned and condemned in the Bible? Give references.

22. Prove from Scripture that Satan is a person.
23. Mention ten Scriptural names of the devil, with references.
24. Discuss briefly but comprehensively the original character, position, and apostasy of Satan, giving an analysis of Ezekiel 28.11-19.
25. What is the abode of Satan?
26. Mention ten points, with references, as to his power.
27. Mention five points, with references, as to his limitation.
28. What is the destiny of Satan?
29. What is the duty of Christians with reference to Satan?

DOCTRINE FOUR: ANTHROPOLOGY.

Topics.

I. The Creation of Man.

II. The Essential Elements of Man.

III. The Moral Nature of Man.

IV. The Image of God in Man.

V. The Probation of Man.

VI. The Temptation of Man.

VII. The Fall of Man.

CHAPTER IV.

ANTHROPOLOGY.

TOPIC ONE: THE CREATION OF MAN.

I. THE FACT.

The Scriptures clearly and distinctly teach that man was created by God: Gen. 1.27; 2.7.

NOTE: Attention has been called to the occurrence of the Hebrew verb for create (*bara*) in Gen. 1.27, showing the absolute separation of mankind from the animal kingdom.

II. THE METHOD.

The Scriptures also clearly and distinctly teach that man is the result of an act of immediate divine creation: Gen. 2.7; Job 32.8; Eccles. 12.7; Zech. 12.1.

NOTE: There is no foundation in Scripture or science for the belief that the body of man, much less his moral and mental nature, is the result of evolution from lower forms of life. Dr. Strong says: "No single instance has yet been adduced of the transformation of one animal species into another, either by natural or artificial selection; much less has it been demonstrated that the body of the brute has ever been developed into that of man. All evolution implies progress and reinforcement of life, and is intelligible only as the immanent God gives new impulses to the process. Apart from the direct agency of God, the view that man's physical system is descended by natural generation from some ancestral simian form can be regarded only as an irrational hypothesis. Since the soul, then, is an immediate creation of God, and the creation of man's body is mentioned by the Scripture writer in direct connection with this creation of the spirit, man's body was in this sense an immediate creation also."

III. THE UNITY OF THE RACE.

The Scriptures teach that the whole human race is descended from a single pair—the first pair, Adam and Eve: Gen. 1.27, 28; 2.7, 22; 3.20; 5.2, 3; 9.19.

This Scriptural revelation finds a fourfold corroboration:

1. From History.

"So far as the history of nations and tribes in both hemispheres can be traced, the evidence points to a common origin and ancestry in Central Asia."

2. From Language.

"Comparative philology points to a common origin of all the more important languages, and furnishes no evidence that the less important are not so derived."

3. From Psychology.

"The existence, among all families of mankind, of common mental and moral characteristics, as evidenced in common maxims, tendencies, and capacities, in the prevalence of similar traditions and in the universal applicability of our philosophy and religion, is most easily explained upon the theory of a common origin. It is probable that certain myths common to many nations were handed down from a time when the families of earth had not yet separated. Among these are the accounts of the making of the world and man, a primitive garden, innocence, a serpent, a tree of knowledge, a temptation and fall, a flood, sacrifice, etc."

4. From Physiology.

"All races are fruitful one with another. The normal temperature of the body is the same. The mean frequency of the pulse is the same. There is liability to the same diseases. These facts are not true of other animals; and again, human blood can be distinguished by the microscope from that of any other animal."

IV. THE TWIN TRUTHS.

The origination of the race of mankind from one pair involves what we may call the twin truths:

1. The organic unity of mankind in the first transgression, and of the provision of salvation for the race in Christ: Rom. 5.12; I Cor. 15.21, 22; Heb. 2.16.

2. The natural brotherhood of mankind and, in consequence thereof, our obligation as believers to

bring the knowledge of Christ and the blessings of His salvation to every member of the race of Adam: Acts 17.26; Heb. 2.11; Luke 10.25-37; Matt. 28.18-20; Mark 16.15, 16; Luke 24.46-48; Acts 1.8; Romans 1.14-16.

NOTE: Conservative science estimates the time of man's appearance upon the earth at from 8,000 to 10,000 years B. C. Scripturally, there is nothing against this view, inasmuch as in the opinion of many "there is no fixed chronology before the time of Abraham." Archbishop Ussher's Chronology, adopted in our English Bibles, has no higher authority than an act of the British Parliament. This fixes the time of man's creation at B. C. 4004.

TOPIC TWO: THE ESSENTIAL ELEMENTS OF MAN.

I. GENERAL STATEMENT.

The Scriptures clearly and distinctly teach that man as constituted by creation has a material nature and an immaterial nature. The material nature is his body. The immaterial nature consists of his soul and spirit. This is proved by:

1. The record of man's creation: Gen. 2.7.

2. Passages in which the human soul or spirit is distinguished, on the one hand, from the divine spirit, and on the other hand, from the body, which it in-

habits: Num. 16.22; I Cor. 2.11; Heb. 12.9; Gen. 35.18; I Kings 17.21; Eccles. 12.7; James 2.26.

3. The mention of the body and soul (or spirit) as together constituting the whole man: Matt. 10.28; I Cor. 5.3; III John 2.

NOTE: The Hebrew word commonly rendered soul is *nephesh*, and the word commonly rendered spirit is *ruach*. The Greek word commonly rendered soul is *psuche;* and the word commonly rendered spirit is *pneuma*. The primary signification of these four words is practically identical, namely, wind, breath, the animating principle of a physical organism.

II. TRICHOTOMY vs. DICHOTOMY.

The question arises: Does the Bible teach that the soul and spirit of man are two separate entities, or two aspects of one and the same entity? (The term entity means thing.) Two views are held, namely: Trichotomy and Dichotomy.

NOTE: The root of these two words is Greek, namely: *temno,* cut; *dika,* in two; and *trika,* in three. Hence, trichotomy means the three-part nature of man; and dichotomy, the two-part nature of man.

III. THE TRICHOTOMOUS VIEW.

This view maintains that there are three essential elements of humanity; namely, body, soul, and spirit. The body is the material part; the soul, the principle of animal life; and the spirit, the principle of rational and immortal life. At death the body, it is held, disintegrates into dust; the soul ceases to exist; while the spirit alone abides, and at the resurrection is reunited to the glorified body. The spirit is peculiar to man and possesses reason, will, and conscience. The soul, which is possessed also by the brute creation, is endowed with understanding, feeling, and sense —perception. The body, alike of man and of brute, is, of course, pure materiality. The above is the common view of trichotomists. Some, however, hold that the soul is not a distinct entity, but a kind of resultant of the union of body and spirit. This is drawn from the language of Gen. 2.7. Others hold to a "dualism of being, but a trichotomy of substance." The "living soul" of Gen. 2.7 is described as a *tertium quid* (that is, a third something) attaching itself not to the body but to the spirit, from which it springs. "The soul is the effulgence of the spirit and its bond of union with the body."

Trichotomists adduce the following points in support of their position:

1. **The record of man's creation:** Gen. 2.7. Here there seem to be three things: the body formed from the dust of the ground, the breath of life (Hebrew, lives) breathed into the nostrils, and the living soul.

2. **The song of the virgin:** Luke 1.46, 47. Here

Mary seems to distinguish between her soul and spirit.

3. Paul's prayer for the Thessalonians. Here the apostle prays that their "whole body and soul and spirit" may be "preserved blameless unto the coming of our Lord Jesus Christ": I Thess. 5.23.

4. Description of the Word of God by the writer to the Hebrews: Heb. 4.12. It is characterized as "piercing even to the dividing asunder of soul and spirit."

NOTE: Consult also these references: I Cor. 2.14: "The natural (Greek, soulish) man receiveth not the things of the Spirit." I Cor. 15.44: a natural (soulish) body is contrasted with a spiritual body. Eph. 4.23: "That ye may be renewed in the spirit of your mind." And Jude 19: "Sensual (soulish) not having the Spirit."

IV. THE DICHOTOMOUS VIEW.

This view maintains that the soul and spirit are not two substances or parts, but that they designate the same immaterial principle from different standpoints. Dr. Strong thus states the dichotomous position: "The immaterial part of man, viewed as an individual and conscious life, capable of possessing and animating a physical organism, is called *psuche*; viewed as a rational and moral agent, susceptible of divine influence and indwelling, this same immaterial part is called *pneuma*. The *pneuma*, then, is man's

nature looking Godward, and capable of receiving
and manifesting the Holy Spirit; the *psuche* is man's
nature looking earthward, and touching the world of
sense.   The *pneuma* is man's higher part, as related
to spiritual realities and as capable of such relation.
Man's being is, therefore, not trichotomous but dichotomous, and his immaterial part, while possessing
a duality of powers, has unity of substance."

Dichotomists adduce the following points in support of their position:

1.   **The record of man's creation**: Gen. 2.7.   Here,
it is held, there are only two parts, viz: the material
body formed of the dust of the ground and the immaterial principle of life derived by the inbreathing
of God.

2.   **The interchangeable use of the terms soul and
spirit**: Gen. 41.8; Psa. 42.6; Matt. 20.28 *(psuche)*;
27.50; John 12.27; 13.21; Heb. 12.23; Rev. 6.9; 20.4.

NOTE: This is true both of the living and the dead.

3.   **Spirit as well as soul is used of the brute creation**: Eccles. 3.21; Rev. 16.3.   (In this latter passage
"soul" refers to fish.)

NOTE: The living principle in beasts (soul or spirit) is believed to be irrational and mortal; in man, rational and immortal.

4.   **Soul is ascribed to Jehovah**: Amos 6.8 (lit., by
His soul); Jer. 9.9; Isa. 53.10-12.

5. The highest exercises of religion are ascribed to the soul: Mark 12.30; Luke 1.46; Heb. 6.18, 19; James 1.21.

6. To lose the soul is to lose all: Mark 8.36, 37.

NOTE: The witness of consciousness corroborates the dichotomous position; when we look within ourselves, we can distinguish the material part (the body) from the immaterial part—but the consciousness of no one can discriminate between soul and spirit.

CONCLUSION: In view of these two classes of strong passages, it would seem that the teaching of the Scriptures as to the unity or duality of the soul and spirit of man is inconclusive. Accordingly, upon this question as upon all other questions which the Bible leaves in uncertainty, it is the wiser and safer course not to dogmatize. Moreover, as Dr. Miley well says: "The question, that is, as to trichotomy and dichotomy, does not seriously concern any important truth of Christian theology."

NOTE: As to the origin of the soul there are three theories, viz: preexistence, creationism, and traducianism. The first theory, which explains itself, is wholly without Scriptural foundation. In support of the second theory, which also explains itself, the following passages are adduced: Eccles. 12.7; Isa. 57.16; Zech. 12.1; Heb. 12.9. The traducian theory is that "the human race was immediately created in Adam, and, as respects both body and soul, was propagated from him by natural generation—all souls since Adam being only mediately (that is, indirectly) created by God, as the upholder of the laws of propagation which were originally established by Him '

This view accords best with Scripture, which "represents God as creating the species in Adam, Gen. 1.27, and as increasing and perpetuating it through secondary agencies, Gen. 1.22, 28. Only once is the breath of life breathed into man's nostrils, Gen. 2.7, 22; 4.1; 5.3; 46.26; Acts 17.21-26; I Cor. 11.8; Heb. 7.10, and after man's formation God rested from His work of creation, Gen. 2.2." Again, this view is favored by "the analogy of vegetable and animal life, in which increase of numbers is secured, not by a multiplicity of immediate creations, but by the natural derivation of new individuals from the parent stock. A derivation of the human soul from its parents no more implies a materialistic view of the soul and its endless division and subdivision, than the similar derivation of the brute proves the principle of intelligence in the lower animals to be wholly material." Again, this view finds support in the "observed transmission not merely of physical, but of mental and spiritual characteristics in families and races, and especially the uniform evil moral tendencies and dispositions which all men possess from their birth."

TOPIC THREE: THE MORAL NATURE OF MAN.

I. DEFINITION.

By the **moral nature of man** is meant those powers which fit him for right or wrong action. These powers are intellect, sensibility, and will, together with conscience and free agency.

Says Dr. Strong: "In order to moral action, man has intellect, or reason, to discern the difference between right and wrong; sensibility, to be moved by each of these; free will (or free agency), to do the one or the other. Intellect, sensibility, and will are man's three faculties. But in connection with these faculties there is a sort of activity which involves them all, and without which there can be no moral action, namely, the activity of conscience. Conscience applies the moral law to particular cases in our personal experience, and proclaims that law as binding upon us. Only a rational and sentient being can be truly moral."

II. ESSENTIAL ELEMENTS.

Assuming the threefold powers of intellect, sensibility, and will, as belonging to man's personality, the essential elements of his moral nature are two, viz: conscience and free agency.

A. Conscience.

1. Definition.

Conscience comes from the Latin *conscientia,* which is compounded of *con,* with, or together, and *scientia,* knowing skill, or science. The Greek word for conscience is *suneideesis,* signifying a coperception or coknowledge. *Sun* in *suneideesis* is the equivalent of *con* in *conscientia,* and is commonly expressed in English by the prefix *co,* meaning with, or together.

2. Nature.

Some regard conscience as a separate faculty—the faculty of moral obligation, which gives us the feeling of "I ought," or "I ought not." It has been called the voice of God in the soul of man. Others regard conscience as rather the response, so to speak, of the entire personality to an accepted and authoritative standard of duty. This latter view we take to be the correct one.

3. Contents.

A mental analysis of conscience discloses the following constituent elements:

a. Self-consciousness.

Primarily conscience is a knowledge of self—together with intellectual and emotional states and volitional acts. This is the meaning of Hebrews 10.2.

b. Knowledge of a standard of duty, or the moral law.

At this point conscience touches the moral reason. The working of conscience calls for some known objective standard of moral conduct, with reference to which the quality of states and actions may be discriminated and judged accordingly as right or wrong. This standard of moral conduct may be imperfect; but such as it is the conscience will respond to it in approval or disapproval. This we take to be the meaning of

Rom. 2.13-15. Again, the standard of moral conduct may be erroneous; but if accepted as authoritative the conscience will respond to it in approval or disapproval. Illustration: The Indian mother who from religious belief throws her babe into the river Ganges. For this reason the conscience, we say, needs enlightening; but what we mean is that the moral reason (that is, the reason controlled by the moral nature) needs enlightenment. The true standard of conduct, of course, is the moral law of God, in part engraved upon our hearts but revealed fully in the sacred Scriptures. Very many of the Lord's people lack full Scriptural enlightenment upon the question of Christian duty and privilege, and as a consequence their consciences are "weak" and easily become "defiled": I Cor. 8.7-13; Titus 1.15.

c. Knowledge of conformity or non-conformity to a standard of duty, or the moral law.

This is the exercise of self-examination. It is the correlation of the first two elements of conscience—the knowing of self in relation to a testing law of duty. Applying this accepted and authoritative law of duty to concrete cases in our own experience, we discern and pronounce our states and acts—past, present, and future—as right or wrong.

d. Remorse or complacency in view of conformity or non-conformity to a standard of duty, or the moral law.

This is the exercise of self-judgment. Having by self-examination discerned and pronounced our states and acts to be right or wrong with reference to the standard of the moral law, we commend or condemn ourselves accordingly. In the former case there is an instinctive sense of God's favor with a corresponding expectation of blessing; while in the latter case there is an instinctive sense of God's disfavor with a corresponding realization of being deserving of punishment. This is what is meant by having, on the one hand, a "good" or "pure" conscience, or a conscience "void of offense toward God and toward men": Acts 24.16; I Tim. 1.5; 3.9; and, on the other hand, an "evil" conscience or a conscience "seared with a hot iron": Heb. 10.22; I Tim. 4.2.

B. Free Agency.

1. Definition.

By **free agency,** or the freedom of the will, is meant the power of rational and responsible personal choice with respect to character and conduct.

2. Contents.

In free agency there are four constituent elements, viz: a purposive end, a motive state, a rational judgment, and an elective decision.

a. A purposive end.

All intelligent and responsible action is taken with

reference to some end in view—the attainment of a purpose through the use of appropriate means.

b. A motive state.

All action looking to a rational end or responsible purpose is influenced by motives, and motives produce states of mind and heart corresponding to them. Such are called motive states.

c. A rational judgment.

We have power over our motives and their corresponding motive states. Herein is the fundamental and essential fact of free agency. We can choose our course of action in accordance with the strongest motive or the weakest motive present to the mind at any given time; or we can suspend choice altogether, while by reflection and deliberation we bring into mental view other facts and considerations, having the force of new motives and producing corresponding new motive states, out of which in turn may spring personal choice and consequent action wholly different from what was at first contemplated. A denial of this power over or contrary to motives is a denial of free agency, or the freedom of the will.

d. An elective decision.

This is the actual exercise of the power of choice with respect to motives. Dr. Miley says: "The rational judgment does not include the elective decision. . . . In the judgment we estimate the value and character of the end, while in the elective decision we determine our action respecting its attainment. The act of judgment is complete before the elective decision is made. The judgment, however, is necessary to the rational character of the choice and, therefore, the choice itself, which in the very nature of it must have a reason for itself."

Dr. Strong thus states the question of free agency: "Free agency is the power of self-determination in view of motives, or man's power (1) to choose between motives, and (2) to direct his subsequent activity according to the motive thus chosen. Motives are never a cause, but only an occasion; they influence, but never compel; the man is the cause, and herein is his freedom. But it is also true that man is never in a state of indeterminateness; never acts without motive, or contrary to all motives; there is always a reason why he acts and herein is his rationality."

NOTE: Opposed to free agency, or the freedom of the will, are two theories which are forms of necessitarianism, or the doctrine of necessity. These are fatalism and determinism. *Fatalism* admits the certainty, but denies the freedom of human self-determination—thus substituting fate for providence. "Under the sway of fate," says Dr. Miley, "all things are absolutely determined; so that they could not but be, nor be other than they are. Fate binds in equal chains of necessity all things and events, all intelligences, thoughts, feelings, volitions, and even God Himself—if there be a God. Materialism and pantheism are fatalistic in character." *Determinism* holds that choice is always in accordance with the stronger or strongest motive present before the mind at any given time. Just as the heavier pan of the scales descends, so the weightier motive controls personal action. Determinism denies the power to suspend choice in the presence of motives, or to choose contrary to motives present at any time before the mind.

TOPIC FOUR: THE IMAGE OF GOD IN MAN.

I. GENERAL STATEMENT.

The Scriptures clearly and distinctly teach that man was created in the image and likeness of God: Gen. 1.26, 27; 5.1; 9.6; I Cor. 11.7; Col. 3.10. See also II Cor. 4.4; Col. 1.15; Heb. 1.3.

NOTE: The Hebrew word rendered "image" signifies *shadow* and the Hebrew word rendered "likeness" signifies *resemblance*. The Greek word rendered "image" means an *outline resemblance*, i. e., a *profile*. In Heb. 1.3 a different Greek word is used, meaning an *exact copy* or an *engraving*. Attempts to find an essential distinction in meaning between "image" and "likeness" must fail; they are substantially identical. Thus Dr. Strong stays: "Both (i. e. words) together signify 'the very image.'" And commenting on the force of both terms, Campbell Morgan writes: "Perhaps the simplest exposition of the thought would be gained by the co templation of the shadow of a man cast upon some white background, by the shining of a great light. What the shadow would be to the man, the man would be to God. Like and unlike, suggesting an idea, but by no means explaining the mystery, impossible apart from the substance, yet infinitely less in essence than the substance. Man no more perfectly expresses all the facts concerning God than does the shadow those concerning man. Nevertheless, the shadow is the image of the man, and indicates the truth concerning him." ("The Crises of the Christ," pp. 25, 26.)

II. CONSTITUENT ELEMENTS.

The image of God in man is twofold, namely: Natural likeness, or Personality; and Moral likeness, or Holiness.

1. Natural Likeness, or Personality.

Personality, as we have seen, consists of intellect, or the power of thinking; sensibility, or the power of feeling; and volition, or the power of willing. To complete the idea we must, however, add three other elements: self-consciousness, conscience, and free moral agency.

Dr. Strong says: "By virtue of this personality, man could at his creation choose which of the objects of his knowledge—self, the world, or God—would be the norm and center of his development. This likeness to God is *inalienable* (that is, it cannot be lost), and as constituting a capacity for redemption gives value to the life even of the unregenerate": Gen. 9.6; I Cor. 11.7; James 3.9.

NOTE: Dr. Farr says: "Man cannot lose this likeness (that is, the natural likeness or personality), or element of the divine image, without ceasing to be man. Insanity can only obscure it. Bernard said that it could not be burned out even in hell. The lost piece of money, Luke 15.8, still bore the image and superscription of the king, although it did not know it and did not know that it was lost. Human nature is, therefore, to be reverenced. He who destroyed human life was put to death: Gen. 9.6. Even men whom we curse are made after the likeness of God: Psalm 8.5; James 3.9."

2. Moral Likeness, or Holiness.

The Scriptures clearly and distinctly teach that by creation man was pure, upright, and holy: Eccle. 7.29; Eph. 4.24; Col. 3.10. This holiness, or righteousness, which constituted man's moral likeness to God, was *forfeitable* (that is, it could be lost) and it was forfeited or lost by the original sin: Eph. 4.23, 24; Col. 3.10.

a. Its Nature.

The nature of the original righteousness, or holiness, is to be viewed:

1. Not as constituting the essence, or substance, of human nature; for in that case, as Dr. Strong says, "human nature would have ceased to exist as soon as man sinned." "Nature" comes from the Latin *natura (nascor,* to be born). Sin can properly be called a nature only in the sense of its being *inborn,* i. e., in the race of Adam. "Disposition" would be a synonymous expression.

2. Not as a gift from without, foreign to human nature and added to it after man's creation; for man possessed the divine image by creation and not by

subsequent bestowal. Dr. Farr says: "Adam was created with a holy nature, i. e., tendencies toward God, as all men since are born with a sinful nature, i. e., tendencies away from God."

3. In distinction from these negative theories, the original righteousness, or holiness, consisted, in the language of Dr. Strong, in a "direction or tendency of man's affections and will, still accompanied by the power of evil choice, and so, differing from the perfect holiness of the saints as instinctive affection and childlike innocence differ from the holiness that has been developed and confirmed by experience of temptation." The same author continues: "It was a moral disposition, moreover, which was propagable to Adam's descendants, if it were retained, and which, though lost to him and to them, if Adam sinned, would still leave man possessed of a natural likeness to God which made him susceptible to God's redeeming grace."

NOTE: Another way of putting it would be that by creation man had a holy *nature* in distinction from a holy *character*. What is meant is that through birth (in the original instance through creation) a nature, or disposition, may be received, while character is the outgrowth and development only of moral probation, i. e., by the exercise of the power of free moral choice in the presence of good and evil. Two facts should be added: the first is that this holy nature was more than innocence; it was a positive likeness to God in rectitude and purity. The other fact is that righteousness, or holiness, both of nature and of character has two sides: it is a knowledge and perception as well as an inclination and feeling: Col. 3.10.

b. Two Erroneous Views.

Of man's original state two erroneous views are held:

1. The image of God included only personality.

"This theory," says Dr. Strong, "denies that any positive determination to virtue inhered originally in man's nature, and regards man at the beginning as simply possessed of spiritual powers, perfectly adjusted to each other."

There are three objections:

(a.) It really makes Adam the author of his own holiness. But this is contrary to analogy; for our sinful condition is not the product of our individual wills but rather the result of the first transgression; and our subsequent condition of holiness is not the product of our individual wills but rather the result of God's regenerating and sanctifying power.

(b.) Knowledge, which was an element of man's holy nature, logically presupposes "a direction toward God of man's affections and will; since only the heart can have any proper understanding of the God of holiness" (Strong).

(c.) A likeness to God in personality alone does not satisfy the demands of Scripture, in which "the ethical conception of the divine nature so overshadows the merely natural" (Strong).

2. The image of God consists simply of man's natural capacity for religion.

This is the view of the Roman Catholic Church. A distinction in meaning is made between image and likeness. The former alone was man's by creation; the latter was the product of his own acts of obedience. Dr. Strong thus elaborates the idea: "In order that this obedience might be made easier and the consequent likeness to God more sure, a third element was added—an element not belonging to man's nature —namely, a supernatural gift of special grace, which acted as a curb upon the sensuous impulses, and brought them under the control of reason. Original righteousness was therefore not a natural endowment, but a joint product of man's obedience and of God's supernatural grace."

There are three objections:

(a.) There is no real distinction in meaning between "image" and "likeness."

(b.) Whatever be denoted by "image" and "likeness," either singly or together, was conferred upon man in and by his creation. "Man is said to have been created in the image and likeness of God, not to have been afterwards endowed with either of them."

(c.) The theory is in direct contradiction to the Scriptures, in that it makes the first sin to have been a weakening but not a perversion of human nature, and the work of regeneration to be not a renewal of the affections but merely a strengthening of the natural powers. "The theory," says Dr. Strong, "regards the first sin as simply despoiling man of a special gift of grace and as putting him where he was when first created—still able to obey God and cooperate with God for his salvation, whereas Scripture represents man since the fall as 'dead through trespasses and sins,' Eph. 2.1; as incapable of true obedience, Rom. 8.7, 'not subject to the law of God, neither indeed can be'; and as needing to be 'created in Christ Jesus for good works,' Eph. 2.10."

III. RESULTS.

Man's possession of the divine image and likeness resulted in four things:

1. His physical form was a reflection of an original and heavenly type.

It is true that by His incarnation Christ took our nature: Jno. 1.14; Gal. 4.4; Heb. 2.14. But it is also true that by his creation man was moulded after a divine pattern even as to his body: Ezek. 1.26. In like manner the tabernacle was modelled after a heavenly pattern: Ex. 25.40; Num. 8.4; Heb. 8.1-5. Dr. Strong says: "Even in man's body were typified those higher attributes which chiefly constituted his likeness to God. A gross perversion of this truth, however, is the view which holds, upon the ground of

Gen. 2.7 and 3.8, that the image of God consists in bodily resemblance to the Creator. In the first of these passages, it is not the divine image, but the body, that is formed of dust, and into this body the soul that possesses the divine image is breathed. The second of these passages is to be interpreted by those other portions of the Pentateuch in which God is represented as free from all limitations of matter: Gen. 11.5; 18.1-5."

2. His sensuous impulses were in subjection to the spirit.

Dr. Strong says: "Here we are to hold a middle ground between two extremes. On the one hand, the first man possessed a body and a spirit so fitted to each other that no conflict was felt between their several claims. On the other hand, this physical perfection was not final and absolute, but relative and provisional. There was still room for progress to a higher state of being: Gen. 3.22."

3. He had dominion over the lower creation: Gen. 1.26, 28; Psalm 8.5-8.

Adam was the crown of creation. Having a perfect mind, he was not dependent upon the laborious processes of inductive and deductive reasoning in the acquisition of knowledge, but had immediate and intuitive insight into truth. Of this there are two proofs: first, his naming of the animals: Gen. 2.19, 20. Evidently, Adam had insight into the nature and habits of each animal and gave it a name corresponding to these. Second, his naming of his helpmeet: Gen. 2.23, 24; 3.20. Adam first called her woman because she was taken out of him. In English there is no connection between the words man and woman, but in Hebrew the connection is very close. In that language "man" is *ish*, and "woman" is *isha*. That is, literally, woman is the *manness*, or female man. Woman is not, as has been suggested, man's *woe*, but rather his *woo*. Next, Adam called his helpmeet Eve, because she was the mother of all living. "Eve" signifies *living*. Thus on the one hand, the name "woman" reflected her origin, and on the other hand, the name "Eve" reflected her destiny. Of the woman's creation Matthew Henry says: "Not out of his head to top him, nor out of his feet to be trampled on by him; but out of his side to be equal with him, under his arm to be protected by him, and near his heart to be beloved."

Note: Man's dominion over the lower creation involves his absolute separation from the animal kingdom—in origin, association, and destiny. A beast cannot ascend to the level of a man, but a man can easily descend to the level of a beast: Psalm 49.10; Prov. 30.2; Jer. 10.21; II Peter 2.12. By the law of Moses defilement with beasts was punishable by death: Lev. 20.15, 16.

11

4. **He had communion with God:** Gen. 3.8, 9.

Dr. Strong says: "Our first parents enjoyed the divine presence and teaching: Gen. 2.16. It would seem that God manifested Himself to them in visible form: Gen. 3.8. This companionship was both in kind and degree suited to their spiritual capacity, and by no means necessarily involved that perfected vision of God which is possible to beings of confirmed and unchanging holiness: Matt. 5.8; I John 3.2; Rev. 22.4."

TOPIC FIVE: THE PROBATION OF MAN.

I. GENERAL STATEMENT.

The Scriptures teach that after his creation God placed man in a garden in Eden and subjected him to a state of probation: Gen. 2.8-17.

NOTE: Eden signifies *pleasure, delight*. Its exact site cannot be determined. Speaking generally, its location must have been in the Mesopotamian valley, near the head-waters of the Tigris and Euphrates. The wildest theories have been advanced as to where the Garden of Eden was. There is a serious book written by a serious scholar, called "Paradise Found," claiming that the Garden of Eden was at the North Pole. However, unless revolutionary topological and climatic changes have occurred, Peary's discovery exploded this theory.

II. DEFINITION OF PROBATION.

Probation, from a Latin word signifying *to prove* or *test,* is a period of trial under a law of duty, which is the test of obedience and is enforced by the sanctions of reward for a right choice and good conduct, and punishment for a wrong choice and evil conduct.

Miley says: "Probation is a temporary economy. Its central reality is responsibility for conduct under a law of duty."

III. NECESSITY OF PROBATION.

While our first parents were created with holy natures, whose fluctuating emotions and spontaneous tendencies were wholly toward the good, yet they were susceptible to temptation from without. Consequently, a period of probation was essential in order to test their loyalty to God by obedience or disobedience to His command. Thus our divine Lord was likewise susceptible to temptation from without, from the reality and power of which He keenly suffered: Heb. 2.18; 9.14.

NOTE: Dr. Miley says: "With a holy nature, there were yet susceptibilities to temptation. In temptation there is an impulse in the susceptibilities adverse to the law of duty. This is true even where it finds no response in the personal consciousness. Yet, in the measure of it, such impulse is a trial to obedience. The proof of it is in a primitive constitution with susceptibilities which might be the means of temptation. These facts are en tirely consistent with the primitive holiness which we have maintained. In such a state primitive man began his moral life. The only way to confirmed blessedness was through temporary obedience. But obedience requires a law of duty, and, with the natural incidence of trial and the possibility of failure, such a law must be a testing law. It thus appears that a probationary economy was the only one at all suited to the state of primitive man."

IV. PURPOSE OF PROBATION.

The purpose of the probation of our first parents was, so to speak, to test their virtue—to transform their *holy natures* into *holy characters*. As has been pointed out, a moral nature is the result of creation, or birth; but moral character is produced only by probation, by the free personal choice of good in the presence of evil and with full power to choose evil. Now Adam and Eve were created with *holy moral natures.* A right choice—that is, obedience to God's command —would have transformed these holy moral natures into *holy moral characters.* As it was, however, their wrong choice—that is, disobedience to the command —transformed their holy moral natures into *sinful moral characters,* and involved both themselves and their posterity in the guilt of sin and the defilement of depravity.

V. THE PROBATIONARY LAW.

The probationary or testing law is recorded in **Gen.**

2.16b, 17: "Of every tree of the garden thou mayest freely eat; but of the tree of the knowledge of good and evil, thou shalt not eat of it: for in the day that thou eatest thereof thou shalt surely die."

In character this probationary or testing law was positive, not moral. The difference is that while "the obligation of a moral law is intrinsic and absolute, the obligation of a positive law arises from a divine commandment." In other words, a moral command carries its own reason for obedience, but a positive command does not. Thus, the ten commandments are moral in character, because we are so constituted as to understand their reasonableness and realize their necessity. For, the ten commandments are not right because they were given of God; they were given of God because they were right. On the other hand, God's call to Abraham to offer up Isaac (Gen. 22) was a positive command, because Abraham did not understand its reasonableness or realize its necessity. Another name for positive command is personal command. Now, it is of the very essence of moral probation that the testing law should be a positive or personal command, the reasonableness and necessity of which are not made known to the one who is subjected to the probation. In the case of our first parents, as we have seen, the probationary law was a positive or personal command. It was God's right to command: it was the duty of Adam and Eve to obey.

NOTE: Dr. Strong says: "Since man was not yet in a state of confirmed holiness, but rather of simple childlike innocence, he could be made perfect only through temptation. Hence the 'tree of the knowledge of good and evil': Gen. 2.9. The one slight command best tested the spirit of obedience. Temptation did not necessitate a fall. If resisted, it would strengthen virtue. In that case, the *posse non pecarre* would have become the *non posse pecarre*. (That is, the ability not to sin would have become the inability to sin.) The tree was mainly a tree of probation. It is right for a father   make his son's title to his estate depend upon the performance of some filial duty, as Thaddeus Stevens made his son's possession of property conditional upon his keeping the temperance-pledge. Whether, besides this, the tree of knowledge was naturally hurtful or poisonous, we do not know."

VI. REASONABLENESS OF PROBATION.

The reasonableness of the primitive probation is seen from the following facts:

1. In the love and wisdom of God, who could not and would not have subjected our first parents to any state of trial or probationary test which was not for their highest development and eternal welfare and consequently absolutely necessary. Therefore the prohibition of Gen. 2.17 must have been just, wise, and good.

2. In the manifold source of delight and satisfaction which were provided for Adam and Eve by their Maker: Gen. 2.9. They had everything.

TOPIC SIX: THE TEMPTATION OF MAN.

I. GENERAL STATEMENT.

The Scriptures clearly and distinctly teach that our first parents were tempted to sin by disobeying God's positive command: Gen. 3.1-6; II Cor. 11.3; I Tim. 2.14.

II. THE INSTRUMENT.

The instrument in the temptation of our first parents was the serpent: Gen. 3.1, 4, 5; II Cor. 11.3.

NOTE: The serpent is included among the beasts. He is described as being more *subtile* than them all. The Hebrew word translated *subtile* signifies *crafty* or *cunning*. It is not unlikely that originally the serpent was a very beautiful creature; and he seems to have possessed the power of upright locomotion: Gen. 3.14.

III. THE HIGHER AGENT.

The higher agent in the temptation of our first parents was Satan: Rev. 12.9.

NOTE: The devil used the serpent as an instrument in tempting Adam and Eve. Thus back of this "beast of the field" was a higher, even a supernatural intelligence. God's curse upon the serpent makes this fact unmistakable: Gen. 3.14, 15,—particularly the latter verse.

IV. THE THREEFOLD FORM.

Notice that the serpent approached the woman in two ways: first, by an affirmation followed by an interrogation, "Yea, hath God said," etc.: Gen. 3.1. So he approached Jesus with an insinuation, "If thou be the Son of God," etc.: Matt. 4.3. The writhing shape of the serpent is not unsuggestive of a question mark. Second, he made a flat contradiction of God's Word, "Ye shall not surely die": Gen. 3.4.

But in particular notice that in form the temptation of our first parents was threefold:

1. The Physical Nature.

Satan first attacked Eve through her body. He showed her that the tree was "good for food": Gen. 3.6a.

2. The Psychical Nature.

Satan next attacked Eve through her mind. He showed her that the tree was "pleasant (Heb. a desire) to the eyes": Gen. 3.6b.

3. Satan finally attacked her soul, or spirit. He showed her that the tree was "to be desired to make one wise": Gen 3.6c.

NOTE: In the wilderness Satan patterned his temptation of Jesus after his temptation of our first parent. See Matt. 4.1-11; Luke 4.1-13. We follow the order of Luke, whose Gospel is chronologically arranged. There we notice—as also in Matthew's account—that Christ's body was first attacked: in His intense hunger He was bidden to make bread of the stones at His feet. Next Christ's mind was attacked: the vision of all the kingdoms of the world was an appeal to His ambition to make Himself a universal ruler, as Alexander the Great, Cæsar, and Hannibal had aspired to be. Finally, Christ's soul, or spirit, was attacked: from the pinnacle of the temple He was bidden, as the favorite of heaven, to hurl Himself into the abyss in presumptuous defiance alike of gravitation and Providence. But again, Satan tempts the children of God today, as he tempted Eve and Jesus. In I John 2.16 we find the same threefold attack: (1) "The lust of the flesh": (2) "the lust of the eyes"; (3) "the pride, or vain glory, of life." We may call this the *trinity of evil.*

TOPIC SEVEN: THE FALL OF MAN.

GENERAL STATEMENT.

The Scriptures clearly and distinctly teach that Adam and Eve fell from their first estate, in sinning against God by disobeying His positive and personal command not to eat of the tree of the knowledge of good and evil: Gen. 3.6b; Rom. 5.12, 19; I Tim. 2.14. This was the first or "original sin."

NOTE: Dr. Torrey points out five steps leading to the first sin:
1. Listening to slanders against God.
2. Doubting His Word and love.
3. Looking at what God had forbidden.
4. Lusting for what God had prohibited.
5. Disobeying God's command.

As Dr. Strong says: "The first sin was in Eve's isolating her-self and choosing to seek her own pleasure without regard to God's will. This initial selfishness it was which led her to listen to the tempter instead of rebuking him or flying from him, and to exaggerate the divine command in her response: Gen. 3.3. . . . This was followed by positive unbelief, and by a conscious and presumptuous cherishing of desire for the for-bidden fruit as a means of independence and knowledge. Thus, unbelief, pride, and lust all sprang from the self-isolating, self-seeking spirit, and fastened upon the means of gratifying it: Gen. 3.6." In this connection we may notice the apostle James' account of the origin, development, and fruition of sin: Jas. 1.13-15.

The consequences of sin were manifold and varied; we may notice them under four topics as follows: The Immediate Effects of Sin; The Fourfold Divine Judgment; The Threefold Separation; and The Three-fold Death.

I. THE IMMEDIATE EFFECTS OF SIN.

The immediate effects of sin (Gen. 3.7-13) were six in number, viz:

1. A sense of shame.

This was due to the awakening of conscience.

2. The covering of fig leaves.

This was a bloodless covering. See Gen. 3.21; Phil. 3.9.

3. A feeling of fear.

This arose from their guilty conscience.

4. An attempt at concealment.

Foolishly Adam and Eve supposed that they could hide from the presence of God.

5. An effort at self-vindication.

Though guilty, yet Adam and Eve tried to justify themselves.

6. The shifting of blame.

Adam laid the blame for his sin upon Eve, and Eve laid the blame for her sin upon the serpent, i. e., Satan.

II. THE FOURFOLD DIVINE JUDGMENT.

After this painful scene the Lord God pronounced a fourfold judgment: Gen. 3.14-19. This was:—

1. Upon the serpent.

This was the curse of degradation: Micah 7.17.

NOTE: During the Millennium the curse upon the serpent will not be removed, for the serpent is the type of Satan: Isa. 65.25.

2. Upon the woman.

This was the judgment of sorrow and subjection: John 16.21.

NOTE: The blessing of the Gospel mitigates the rigor of the law: I Tim. 2.15.

3. Upon the man.

This was the judgment of sorrow and toil: Job 5.7; Eccle. 2.22, 23.

NOTE: Work is a blessing and not a curse: Gen. 2.9, 15. It is only the curse resting upon the ground which makes man's labor vexatious and unremunerative.

4. Upon the ground.

This was the curse of thorns and thistles.

NOTE: Like the serpent, the thorn is the natural enemy of man: Matt. 7.16. It is used in Scripture as a symbol of evil: Num. 33.55; II Cor. 12.7. Our Lord's mock crown was composed of thorns: John 19.2, 5. During the Millennium the curse upon the ground will be removed: Isaiah 55.13.

III. THE THREEFOLD SEPARATION.

The fourfold divine judgment resulted in a threefold separation: Gen. 3.22-24. Thus Adam and Eve were separated:—

1. From the tree of life.

NOTE: The tree of life represents wisdom: Prov. 3.18. Wisdom personified is Christ: I Cor. 1.24. So the tree of life was an emblem of Christ: Rev. 2.7; 22.14. Adam's body was mortal: Gen. 2.7; I Cor. 15.44, 45, 47. Science teaches us that physical life involves decay and loss. There was, however, a divine provision for checking this decay and loss, and preserving the body's youth. This was by means of the tree of life. It accomplished this through its sacramental value; that is, eating of this tree was symbolical of the communion of Adam and Eve with God and of their dependence upon Him. But this only because it had a physical efficacy. Physical immortality without holiness would have been unending misery. Accordingly, our first parents were shut out from the tree of life, until by redemption and resurrection such of their descendants as accept Christ can be prepared to partake thereof. Thus, our glorified bodies will be preserved throughout eternity by eating of the tree of life which is typical of our blessed Lord Himself: Rev. 2.7; 22.14. Physical decay and loss, which ended in the death of their bodies, began the instant Adam and Eve were denied access to the tree of life. The nine hundred and thirty years Adam lived, as also the extraordinary longevity of the antediluvians, is evidence of their wonderful natural vitality. "If Adam had maintained his integrity, the body might have been developed and transfigured without the intervention of death. In other words, the *posse non mori* (that is, able not to die) might have become a *non posse mori* (that is, not able to die)" (Strong). In his "Crises of the Christ" Campbell Morgan treats the transfiguration of Christ as the flowering of humanity; he regards it as God's demonstration of the fruition of the body—if there had been no sin.

2. From the Garden of Eden.

The only way to make the exclusion of Adam and Eve from the tree of life effective was to drive them from the Garden of Eden. And this the LORD God did, sending man forth "to till the ground from whence he was taken."

3. From the personal and visible presence of God.

Sin separates man from God,—and it is the only thing that can separate man from God. When Adam and Eve hid themselves from the presence of the LORD God, it was because their sin with its resulting guilt and shame had morally unfitted them for personal and face-to-face communion and fellowship

with their Maker. Separation from the Garden of Eden, therefore, simply sealed the spiritual separation of man from God which sin had already brought about. Henceforth, our first parents and their posterity had only a symbolical representation of Deity: the cherubim and the flaming sword placed at the east of the Garden of Eden were the visible manifestation of the LORD God. Thither the godly antediluvians came to worship and sacrifice: for there is no evidence that these primitive types of the presence and power, the mercy and redeeming grace of God, did not remain until swept away by the flood.

NOTE: The *flaming sword* (3.24) was the first appearance of that self-luminous flame which, as the Shekinah glory, rested over the mercy seat in the Holy of Holies in the tabernacle and the temple.

IV. THE THREFOLD DEATH.

In connection with the prohibition to eat of the tree of the knowledge of good and evil the LORD God said, "In the day that thou eatest thereof thou shalt surely die" (lit. dying thou shalt die) : Gen. 2.17.

This death, which was the result of sin, was threefold, viz: physical, spiritual, and eternal.

1. Physical death.

Physical death is the separation of the soul from the body. It includes, according to Dr. Strong, "all those temporal evils and sufferings which result from disturbance of the original harmony between soul and body, and which are the working of death in us": Num. 16.29; 27.3; Psalm 90.7-9, 11; Isa. 38.17, 18; Rom. 4.24, 25; 6.9, 10; 8.3, 10, 11; I Cor. 15.21, 22; Gal. 3.13; I Peter 4.6.

NOTE: Some regard physical death as a part of the penalty of sin, while others regard it as rather the natural consequence of sin. In either view, it seems to be clear that weakness and disease followed by death resulted primarily from the exclusion of Adam and Eve from the tree of life.

2. Spiritual death.

Spiritual death is the separation of the spirit from God. It includes, according to Dr. Strong, "all that pain of conscience, loss of peace, and sorrow of spirit, which result from the disturbance of the normal relation between the soul and God": Matt. 8.22; Luke 15.32; John 5.24; 8.51; Rom. 8.13; Eph. 2.1; 5.14; I Tim. 5.6; James 5.20; I John 3.14.

NOTE: Dr. Strong says: "It cannot be doubted that the penalty pronounced in the Garden and fallen upon the race is primarily and mainly that death of the soul which consists in its separation from God. In this sense only, death was fully visited upon Adam in the day on which he ate the forbidden fruit: Gen. 2.17. In this sense only, death is escaped by the Christian: John 11.26. For this reason, in the parallel between Adam and Christ, Rom. 5.12-21, the apostle passes from the thought of mere physical death in the early part of the passage to that of both physical and spiritual death at its close, verse 21: 'as sin reigned in death, even so might grace reign through righteousness unto eternal life through Jesus Christ our Lord'—where 'eternal life' is more than endless physical existence, and 'death' is more than death of the body."

3. Eternal death.

Eternal death is the result of spiritual death. It is, according to Strong, "the culmination and completion of spiritual death, and essentially consists of the correspondence of the outward with the inward state of the evil soul: Acts 1.25. It would seem to be inaugurated by some peculiar repellent energy of the divine holiness, Matt. 25.41; II Thess. 1.9, and to involve positive retribution visited by a personal God upon both body and soul of the evil-doer: Matt. 10.28; Heb. 10.31; Rev. 14.11." Eternal death is the same as hell, or *gehenna,* or the second death: Matt. 10.28; see II Kings 23.10; Rev. 20.14.

NOTE: Both spiritual and eternal death were arrested by grace through the institution of sacrifice: Gen. 3.21; 4.4; Heb. 9.22. Thus, the Coming One who was to "taste death for every man" saved those in the Old Testament age who through obedience and sacrifice believed in Him: Rom. 3.25; Heb. 2.9.

QUESTIONS FOR STUDY.

1. What do the Scriptures teach concerning the creation of man?
2. What do they teach concerning the method of his creation?

3. What do they teach concerning the unity of the race?
4. What fourfold corroboration have we of the unity of the race?
5. What twin truths are involved in the unity of the race?
6. What do the Scriptures teach concerning the constitution of man by creation?
7. What is the primary signification of the Hebrew words for *soul* and *spirit*? of the Greek words for *soul* and *spirit*?
8. What is the meaning of the terms *trichotomy* and *dichotomy?*
9. Give a general statement of the trichotomous view of man's nature.
10. Mention the Scriptural points which are believed to support the trichotomous view.
11. Give a general statement of the dichotomous view of man's nature.
12. Mention the Scriptural points which are believed to support the dichotomous view.
13. On which side of the question does the witness of consciousness stand?
14. In your judgment is the teaching of Scripture conclusive or inconclusive as to the matter? Is the subject vital to salvation?
15. State the three views as to the origin of the soul.
16. What is meant by the moral nature of man?

12

17. What are the essential elements of the moral nature?
18. Discuss the signification of the word conscience.
19. What is the nature of conscience? State the two views.
20. What are the constituent elements of conscience as given by mental analysis?
21. What is meant by free agency?
22. What are the constituent elements of free agency?
23. What is meant by Fatalism? by Determinism?
24. What do the Scriptures teach concerning the image of God in man?
25. What is the signification of the Hebrew words for *image* and *likeness*?
26. What were the constituent elements of the image of God in man?
27. In what does natural likeness consist? Why is it inalienable?
28. In what did moral likeness consist?
29. How is the original righteousness, or holiness, to be viewed?
30. Distinguish clearly between nature and character.
31. What two erroneous views are held as to man's original state?
32. What four things resulted from man's possession of the divine image and likeness?

33. What do the Scriptures teach concerning the probation of man?
34. What does the word Eden signify? Where was the Garden of Eden probably located?
35. Define probation.
36. Show wherein a period of moral probation for Adam and Eve was necessary.
37. What was the purpose of the primitive probation?
38. What was the probationary law?
39. Distinguish clearly between a moral law and a positive command.
40. Show wherein the primitive probation was reasonable.
41. What do the Scriptures teach concerning the temptation of man?
42. What was the instrument in the temptation?
43. Who was the higher agent?
44. In what two ways did the serpent approach the woman?
45. What was the threefold form of the temptation?
46. Trace the parallel between the temptation of our first parents and that of Jesus.
47. What Scripture passage teaches that Satan tempts Christians after the pattern of the Edenic and the wilderness temptations?
48. What do the Scriptures teach concerning the fall of man?

49. Point out five steps leading to the first sin.
50. Mention six immediate effects of sin.
51. What was the fourfold divine judgment in consequence of sin?
52. What was the threefold separation which resulted from sin?
53. What did the tree of life represent and what was its use?
54. What was the threefold death which sin caused?
55. How may the physical death of Adam and Eve be explained?
56. How do spiritual and eternal death stand related? What are some other Scriptural expressions for eternal death?

DOCTRINE FIVE: HAMARTIOLOGY.

Topics.

CHAPTER V.

HAMARTIOLOGY.

TOPIC ONE: THE ORIGIN OF SIN.

The origin of sin is wrapped in obscurity. It is one of the unrevealed mysteries of Scripture. We are, however, given a hint of the entrance of sin into the heart of Satan and also the introduction of sin into the human race.

I. THE ENTRANCE OF SIN INTO THE HEART OF SATAN.

1. In Isaiah 14.12-17, in the picture of the fall of Lucifer, son of the morning (the king of Babylon, vs. 4), we have an account, it is believed, of the rebellion of Satan against God. Notice the expression "I will," five times repeated—especially the last instance: "I will be like the most High," vs. 14.

2. Again in Ezekiel 28, in the prophet's lamentation upon the king of Tyre, we have a hint, it is believed, that Satan fell by reason of pride of heart, vs. 17.

II. THE INTRODUCTION OF SIN INTO THE HUMAN RACE.

The introduction of sin into the human race is recorded in the third chapter of Genesis and in other scriptures. It came about in a fourfold way.

1. Through deception. See I Tim. 2.14.
2. Through man's disobedience. See Rom. 5.19.
3. Through the serpent's enticement. See Gen. 3.1-6.
4. Through Satan's malignity. See Rev. 12.9.

TOPIC TWO: THE REALITY OF SIN.

Sin is a sad and terrible reality. This fact may be proved in three ways, namely: the teaching of Scripture, the testimony of mankind, and the witness of consciousness.

I. THE TEACHING OF SCRIPTURE.

As to the reality of sin the teaching of Scripture is clear and unmistakable. Among a multitude of passages take but three:

1. John 1.29: "Behold the Lamb of God, which taketh away the sin of the world."
2. Romans 3.23: "For all have sinned and come short of the glory of God."

3. Galatians 3.22: "But the Scripture hath concluded all under sin that the promise by faith might be given to all them that believe."

II. THE TESTIMONY OF MANKIND

The testimony of mankind as to the reality of sin has been enacted into government legislation, has found recognition in every false religion, and is reflected in secular literature.

Listen:

1. The Roman philosopher Seneca said: "We have all sinned, some more, and some less."

2. The Roman Ovid wrote: "We all strive for what is forbidden."

3. The German philosopher and poet Goethe confessed: "I see no fault in others which I myself might not have committed."

4. A Chinese proverb runs: "There are two good men: one is dead and the other is not yet born."

III. THE WITNESS OF CONSCIOUSNESS.

Consciousness gives no uncertain witness to the reality of sin. Everyone knows he is a sinner. No one of responsible years has ever lived free from the sense of personal guilt and moral defilement. Remorse of conscience for wrong-doing hounds all the sons and daughters of Adam; while the sad and terrible consequences of sin are seen in the physical, mental, and moral deterioration and degeneration of the race.

TOPIC THREE: THE NATURE OF SIN.

I. WHAT SIN IS NOT.

1. Sin is not an Accident.

There are those who hold that sin is an accident; but, as we have seen, the teaching of the Bible is that sin resulted from an act of responsible disobedience on the part of Adam: Rom. 5.19.

2. Sin is not Infirmity.

There are those who hold that sin is a kind of disease, because of which we are very unfortunate but in no wise culpable. But this, like the former view, is contrary to the revelation of the Bible.

3. Sin is not a Negation.

That sin is a negation is the teaching of Christian Science—that evil is the absence of good, and sin is the absence of righteousness. But the Word of God declares sin and evil to have a positive existence and to be an offense to the Lord: Psa. 51.4.

4. Sin is not "an Amiable Weakness."

In order to find excuse for their wicked indulgences,

there are those who hold that sin is "an amiable weakness." But sin is not pitiable but blameworthy, and the sinner is responsibly guilty before God.

5. Sin is not a Necessity.

Fatalism teaches that sin is a necessity and that while sin is of the nature of responsible personal guilt, yet we cannot escape it and consequently must make the best of it. There are indeed many Christians who practically maintain that sin is a means of grace. The old extreme Calvinistic view of sanctification was that death alone can free us from sin. Yet the clear and emphatic teaching of the New Testament is that the blood of Jesus Christ can cleanse us from all sin: I John 1.7.

II. WORDS FOR SIN IN THE OLD TESTA-MENT.

1. The most common word for sin signifies literally *to miss the mark*. In the original sense it is found in Judges 20.16: "Among all this people there were seven hundred chosen men left-handed; every one could sling stones at a hair breadth, and not *miss*." With its derivative forms this word means any moral deviation from the divine goal—a going beyond, a coming short, or a falling aside. Not only wilful and ignorant acts of sin but also evil states and wicked dispositions of the mind and heart are included with-

in the scope of this Hebrew word: Gen. 4.7; Ex. 9.27;
Lev. 5.1; Num. 6.11; Psalm 51.2, 4; Prov. 8.36; Isa.
42.24; Hosea 4.7.

2. Another word literally means *bent* or *twisted*,
or *crooked* (Isa. 21.3), and spiritually means moral
perverseness or iniquity,—"the distortion of nature
caused by evil doing." Our English word *wrong*,
i. e., that which is wrung out of its true course, exact-
ly expresses the idea. Not so much the act itself but
the character of the act is in the force of this Hebrew
word: Gen. 15.16; Psa. 32.5; Isa. 5.18.

3. Another word, whose root signifies stormy ex-
citement, means the *habit of evil;* that is, sin particularly in the disposition. It is the opposite of righteousness: Lev. 19.15, 35; Job 3.17; 16.11; 20.29; 34.8;
Psa. 82.2; Prov. 16.12; Isa. 57.20, 21; Mal. 2.6.

4. Another word is used for a revolt against rightful authority; that is, apostasy or rebellion. It is
commonly translated in the A. V. by *transgression*:
Psa. 51.3; Prov. 28.2.

5. Another word means to cross over a line, or go
beyond. It is usually rendered in the A. V. by *transgress:* Psa. 17.3; Hos. 6.7; 8.1.

6. Another word which literally signifies *to blow*,
represents sin in the aspect of vanity or nothingness:
Isa. 41.29.

7. Still another word refers to the hardness of the

heart—the highest degree of sin; stubbornness, or obduracy: Ex. 4.21.

But the Hebrew words that are translated sin, or mean sin in one form or another, are far too numerous to be considered separately. However, among those that remain these may be mentioned—following the A. V.—fault, Gen. 41.9; transgress, or sin through ignorance, Lev. 4.13; wander, Ezek. 34.6; err, Psa. 119.21; hate, Lev. 19.17; mischief, Psa. 94.20; misery, Prov. 31.7; etc., etc.

III. WORDS FOR SIN IN THE NEW TESTAMENT.

1. It is remarkable that in the New Testament Greek, as well as in the Old Testament Hebrew, the most common word for sin signifies *to miss the mark*. It is said to occur not less than 174 times, 71 times in the Pauline epistles. It expresses the state or disposition of evil as well as the act of sin: Rom. 3.23; 5.12.

2. Another word means the overpassing or overstepping of a line of duty. It is always used of the "violation of a positive law, an express precept with an express sanction": I Tim. 2.14.

3. Another word means a failure—a falling where one should have stood: Gal. 6.1. This Greek word is variously rendered in the A. V., viz: trespass, Matt. 6.14; sins, Eph. 1.7; faults, James 5.16.

4. Another word means lawlessness or anarchy: I John 3.4,

5. Another word means ignorance of what should have been known: Heb. 9.7.

6. Another word means the diminishing of that which one should have rendered in full: I Cor. 6.7.

7. Another word means disobedience to a voice: Heb. 2.2, 3.

8. Still another word means a debt or an offense: Matt. 6.12.

Instances of other words in the New Testament, which describe various forms of sin, are: ungodliness, unrighteousness, Rom. 1.18; lust, Rom. 1.24; fornication, wickedness, covetousness, maliciousness, envy, deceit, malignity, murder, Rom. 1.29, 30; enmity, Rom. 8.7; flesh, adultery, uncleanness, lasciviousness, idolatry, witchcraft, hatred, variance, emulations, drunkenness, revellings, Gal. 5.19-21; evil speaking, bitterness, wrath, anger, clamor, malice, Eph. 4.31, etc., etc.

IV. SCRIPTURE DEFINITIONS OF SIN.

There are in the Scriptures a number of descriptive definitions of sin, of which the following are the more striking:

1. Proverbs 21.4: "An high look, and a proud heart, and the plowing of the wicked, is sin."

2. Proverbs 24.9: "The thought of foolishness

is sin." R. V.: "The thought of the foolish is sin."
The word *thought* here has the force of premeditation.

3. John 16.8, 9: "And when he is come, he will re-
prove the world of sin and of righteousness, and of
judgment: of sin, because they believe not on me." R.
V.: "And he when he is come, will convict the world
in respect of sin, and of righteousness, and of judgment: of sin, because they believe not on me."

4. Romans 14.23: "For whatsoever is not of faith
is sin." R. V.: "And whatsoever is not of faith is
sin."

5. James 4.17: "Therefore to him that knoweth to
do good and doeth it not, to him it is sin." R. V.:
"To him, therefore, that knoweth to do good and doeth
it not, to him it is sin."

6. I John 3.4: "For sin is the transgression of the
law"—in *act, disposition,* or *state.*

7. I John 5.17: "All unrighteousness is sin." R.
V. The same.

V. THEOLOGICAL DEFINITIONS OF SIN.

The following definitions of sin are based on the
Scriptures:

1. Sin is the transgression of, or lack of conformity to, the law of God.

2. Sin is inordinate desire or concupiscence.

3. Sin is deficiency of love to God and man.

4. Sin is preference of self to God.

5. Sin is insubordination.

6. Sin is lack of conformity to God or His moral law in act, disposition, or state.

NOTE: In distinction from those who hold sin to be sensuousness or finiteness, Dr. Strong maintains that its essential principle is selfishness, i. e., selfness. This is in agreement with the fourth definition given above.

VI. SUMMARY OF SCRIPTURE TEACHING. CONCERNING SIN.

A careful review of the teaching of the Scriptures concerning the nature of sin discloses the fact that sin may be viewed in four aspects, namely: towards God, towards the divine law, towards man, and towards self.

A. Towards God.

Sin is either rebellion or failure to love God supremely.

1. Rebellion.

"For rebellion is as the sin of witchcraft, and stubbornness is as iniquity and idolatry": I Sam. 15.23.

2. Failure to love Him supremely.

"And thou shalt love the Lord thy God with all thine heart, and with all thy soul, and with all thy might": Deut 6.5. See Mark 12.30.

B. Towards the Divine Law.

Sin is either wilful transgression or violation through ignorance.

1. Wilful transgression.

"But the soul that doeth ought presumptuously (lit. with a high hand) whether he be born in the land, or a stranger, the same reproacheth the Lord; and that soul shall be cut off from among his people": Num. 15.30. See Psalm 19.13.

2. Violation through ignorance.

"And if any soul sin through ignorance, then he shall bring a she goat of the first year for a sin offering": Num. 15.27; Heb. 9.7.

C. Towards Man.

Sin is either injustice or failure to love him as one's self.

1. Injustice.

"Thou shalt not defraud thy neighbor, neither rob him; the wages of him that is hired shall not abide with thee all night until the morning": Lev. 19.13. See Micah 6.8; Rom. 1.18.

2. Failure to love him as one's self.

"But thou shalt love thy neighbor as thyself": Lev. 19.18. See Mark 12.31.

13

D.   Towards Self.

Sin is either selfishness (selfness) or corruption.

1.   Selfishness (selfness).

"If any man will come after me, let him *deny him-self*, take up his cross, and follow me": Matt. 16.24. See John 12.25.

2.   Corruption.

"Behold, I was shapen in iniquity, and in sin did my mother conceive me": Psalm 51.5. See Rom. 7.18.

TOPIC FOUR: THE EXTENT OF SIN.

As to the extent of sin, the Scriptures teach that it is universal; that is, it has affected some part of heaven and its inhabitants, and the whole of earth and its inhabitants.

I.   THE HEAVENS.

The sin and fall of Satan affected the heavens. As we have seen (see topic Satan under Angelology), the devil himself has access to heaven: Job 1.6; Zech. 3.1; Luke 10.18; Rev. 12.7-9. Moreover, the emissaries of Satan infest the heavenly places, where they make warfare with the believer: Eph. 1.3; 2.6; 6.11, 12.

II. THE EARTH.

The sin and fall of our first parents affected the whole of earth and its inhabitants.

1. The vegetable kingdom. This has been cursed because of man's sin, but will be restored in the Millennial age: Gen. 3.17, 18; Isa. 55.13.

2. The animal kingdom. This suffers in consequence of man's sin, but will be made to share in the peace and glory of the Millennium: Isa. 11.6-9.

3. The race of mankind. Sin has affected and infected the entire race of mankind. (For fuller treatment, see next topic: the result of sin, i. e. in man.) Dr. Farr says: "Both Scripture and experience justify the statement, that with the single exception of Jesus Christ all men are morally depraved at birth, and if they live long in the world, are found guilty of personal sin. By moral depravity is meant that state of the soul which naturally leads to sin."

NOTE: Speaking of the universality of sin Dr. Farr further says: "Sin and salvation both begin in heaven and come from heaven to earth. Much of Christ's work is performed in and for the heavens: Heb. 9.23. The intimate relation of heaven and earth is seen in Gen. 1.1. Man is destined for heaven as well as for earth: I Cor. 15.49. Christ comes from, ascends to, and returns from heaven. Heaven is always mentioned first, as ruling the earth. The new heaven and the new earth are the result of Christ's work of redemption: Isa. 65.17; II Peter 3.13; Rev. 21.1."

TOPIC FIVE: THE RESULT OF SIN.

Universal is the extent of sin, and likewise **universal** are its devastating and death-dealing **results.** Two spheres in particular may be mentioned, viz: **the** earth and man.

I. THE EARTH.

As to the result of sin in the earth, two things **may** be specified, namely:

1. The groaning of creation: Rom. 8.19-23.

In this passage Paul reveals the close connection between man and the lower creation. Sin has brought the lower creation into "the bondage of corruption," but full redemption for man will bring about its complete deliverance: vs. 21.

Note: It is said that every sound produced by nature is in the minor key, speaking of the tragedy of sin and suffering— the sighing of the wind, the rustling of the leaves, the chirping of the birds, the murmuring of the brook, etc. On the other hand, the major key speaks of redemption and joy. It is struck now wherever and whenever the work of the Holy Spirit is unhindered, but it will be the dominant note during the Millennium and throughout the ages of the new heaven and the new earth.

2. The emptiness of creation: Num. 14.21; Psalm 90.13; Hosea 5.15; Rom. 8.20.

Dr. F. L. Chapell says: "Since the creation was

for the indwelling of God, angels and men, who are the higher forms of creation in heaven and earth, must be subordinate to God for His indwelling. But when they became insubordinate, or, in other words, when they sinned, the indwelling of God was withdrawn, and thus commenced the lost condition of the general world of the heavens and the earth. The light and the life and the love of God have departed from His creation because of sin, and thus the darkness and the death and the hate that rule instead. Therefore much is said in Scripture of the absence of God and the emptiness of creation, on the one hand, and the prayers and the outcries for His return, and the filling of creation with His presence, on the other hand. Compare Hosea 5.15 with Psalm 90.13; and Rom. 8.20-23 with Num. 14.21. Much of the Bible is occupied with the accounts of the departure of the Lord, on the one hand, and with prophecies and promises of His return, on the other hand. Thus there was a presence of the Lord on the earth before the flood (Gen. 4.16), but it must have departed in that dreadful reign of sin and judgment (Gen. 6.3-12). There was a presence of the Lord in the Shekinah light (Ex. 40.35; I Kings 8.11), but it departed in the reign of the wicked kings (Ezek. 11.23) and was not found in the second temple. There was preeminently the presence of the Lord in the person of the Lord Jesus, but He departed because of the sins of the Jews, and their temple was left empty and desolate (Matt. 23.38, 39). And on the other hand the constant cry of the faithful has ever been, 'Return, return, come, come,' till it is the chief refrain of the Revelation, as we read in the last chapter: 'The Spirit and the bride say, Come; let him that heareth say, Come,' and 'He which testifieth these things saith, Surely I come,' to which the seer replies, 'Even so, come, Lord Jesus.' The whole spirit of prophecy and of promise looks forward to the grand coming of the Lord, that the earth may be filled with His glory: Isa. 59.20; Zech. 8.3; Mal. 3.1; John 14.3."

II. MAN.

In the doctrine of Anthropology, under the topic of The Fall of Man, we have noted the threefold separation that has resulted from the disobedience of our first parents, viz: from the tree of life, from the Garden of Eden, and from the personal and visible presence of the Lord. We have further noted that physical death was the natural consequence of separation from the tree of life, and spiritual death the inevitable consequence of separation from the presence of the Lord. Sin in the form of disobedience was the one and only cause of both. We are now to look at the dark and desolate picture which the Scriptures draw of the devastating and death-dealing results of sin in man's spirit, soul, and body:

1. All have sinned: Psalm 14.2, 3; Isa. 53.6; Rom. 3.9, 10, 22, 23; I John 1.8-10.

2. Every mouth stopped: Psalm 130.3; 143.2; Rom. 3.19, R. V.

3. All under a curse: Gal. 3.10.

4. All children of the devil: John 8.44; I John 3.8-10.

5. Natural man a stranger to the things of God: I Cor. 2.14.

6. Natural heart deceitful: Jer. 17.9.

7. Alienated from the life of God—understanding darkened: Eph. 4.18.

8. Mental and moral nature corrupt: Gen. 6.5, 12; 8.21; Psalm 94.11; Rom. 1.19-31.

9. Outward behavior vile and detestable: Eph. 2.3; Titus 3.3; Col. 3.5, 7.

10. Slaves of sin: Rom. 6.17; 7.5, 7, 8, 14, 15, 19, 23, 24.

11. Controlled by prince of the power of the air: Eph. 2.2.

12. Carnal mind enmity against God: Rom. 8.7, 8.

13. Children of wrath: Eph. 2.3.

14. Dead in trespasses and sins: Eph. 2.1.

15. Body weakened and death-doomed: II Cor. 4.7; Rom. 8.11.

Thus we see that, as the result of sin, man's spirit

is alienated from and antagonistic to God, his mind deteriorated and darkened, and his body diseased and death-doomed. By nature, man is helpless and a hopeless sinner; HE IS LOST.

TOPIC SIX: THE PENALTY OF SIN.

I. DEFINITION OF PENALTY.

Penalty has been defined as, essentially, the re-action of divine holiness against sin. It is the inflic-tion of pain or suffering as punishment upon the law-breaker by the Law-giver because of his ill-desert.

NOTE: The object of penalty is not primarily the reforma-tion of the law-breaker nor the prevention of others becoming law-breakers, but the vindication of the character of the Law-giver.

Two kinds of penalty have been distinguished, namely, moral and positive.

II. MORAL PENALTY.

The term **moral penalty** is used of the natural consequence of sin, the results of the transgression and depravity which manifest themselves now in the spirit, soul, and body of all the sons of Adam and Eve.

NOTE: An illustration may make clear the difference intended between the terms moral and positive penalty. A father forbids his son to climb trees under threat of punishment, the punishment to be a diet of bread and water for three days. The boy disobeys his father's command and breaks his arm by falling from a tree. Now, the long confinement and intense suffering which the lad undergoes because of his broken arm may be called the *moral penalty* which he endures, i. e., the natural consequences of his disobedience. But in no true sense is this the punishment for his act of disobedience. After the son's recovery, the father, in order to uphold parental authority, and punish him for his ill-desert, must keep him on bread and water for three days. And this may be called *positive penalty,* i. e., the actual infliction of suffering by the father upon the son for the latter's transgression.

On this point Dr. Farr says: "The natural consequences of transgression, although they constitute a part of the penalty of sin, do not exhaust that penalty. In all penalty there is a personal element, the holy wrath of the Law-giver, which is only partially expressed by natural consequences. Sensual sins are punished by the deterioration and corruption of the body; moral and spiritual sins by the deterioration and corruption of the soul: Prov. 5.22; 11.21. This is only half the truth. Those who confine all penalty to the reaction of natural law forget that God is not only immanent in the universe, but also transcendent; and that to fall into the hands of the living God, Heb. 10.31, is to fall into the hands, not merely of the law, but also of the Law-giver. Distinctive moral punishment is remorse of conscience and the pains connected with it—a sense of shame, regret, blameworthiness, etc. Michael Angelo has done as much mischief in art as Dante and Milton have in literature, by giving the impression that physical punishment and suffering alone await the transgressor."

III. POSITIVE PENALTY, OR THE FUTURE PUNISHMENT OF THE IMPENITENT WICKED.

The term **positive penalty** is used in reference to the final destiny of the wicked: II Peter 3.9. This destiny is set forth in the Scriptures under a variety of expressions, some of the more striking being the following:

1. The resurrection of judgment: John 5.28, 29. R. V.

2. Indignation and wrath, tribulation and anguish: Rom. 2.8, 9.

3. Eternal destruction: II Thess. 1.9. R. V.

4. Lake of fire: Rev. 20.15. R. V.

5. The punishment of eternal fire: Jude 7. R. V.

6. Eternal punishment: Matt. 25.41.

7. The lake of fire that burneth with brimstone: Rev. 19.20. R. V.

8. The second death: Rev. 21.8.

9. Hell (Greek, *Tartarus*): II Pet. 2.4.

While the above expressions all refer to the same thing, yet the final destiny of the impenitent wicked is perhaps most commonly described as *death* and *destruction*. Consequently, upon a right understanding of the Biblical usage of these terms hinges the truth concerning future punishment. Let us, then, briefly study these words.

The Word DEATH—Greek: Thanatos.

The New Testament usage—in fact the Biblical usage of the word death—is threefold, namely: physical death, spiritual death, and eternal death.

1. Physical Death.

Physical death is, of course, the separation of the soul from the body—resulting in the corruption and destruction of the material frame: John 11.14; Acts 2.24; Rom. 8.38.

2. Spiritual Death.

Spiritual death may be defined as the separation of the spirit from God. Into this state everyone comes by natural birth. Thus, the prodigal son, Luke 15.24; sinners, Eph. 2.1; the pleasure-loving widow, I Tim. 5.6; the church of Sardis, Rev. 3.1.

3. Eternal Death.

Eternal death may be defined as spiritual death continued after physical death—the state of a soul through eternity dying impenitent in trespasses and sin: Rom. 1.32; James 5.20.

But eternal death is more than the perpetuation throughout eternity of the state of spiritual death. It is referred to as the "second death": Rev. 2.11; 20.6, 14; 21.8. Now, in Rev. 20.10, "the lake of fire" is described as a place of conscious and unending torment: for the devil is cast therein, where after a thousand years "the beast and false prophet are, and shall be tormented day and night forever." Therefore, "the second death" is a place of conscious and unending torment.

NOTE: Dr. Torrey says: "Life is defined in the Bible not merely as *existence,* but as *right existence*—knowing the true God and the life manifested in Christ: John 17.3; I John 1.1, 4. Death, then, is not mere non-existence, but wrong, wretched, debased, devilish existence. And 'the second death,' which is the final outcome of a life of sin, is defined in the New Testament as a portion in the place of torment: Rev. 21.8."

The Word DESTRUCTION—Greek: Apoleia.

In the New Testament the word destruction (or perdition) has a twofold meaning, namely: a general and a special meaning.

1. General Meaning.

In the New Testament, when anything is said to perish or be destroyed, it is not meant that it *ceases to exist,* but that it is *ruined,* so that it no longer subserves the purpose for which it was intended or designed.

Thus, Matt. 9.17: "Neither do men put new wine in old wine-skins: else the skins burst, and the wine is spilled and the skins perish: but they put new wine into fresh wine-skins and both are preserved." R. V. Here the burst wine-skins have not perished or been destroyed in the sense of ceasing to exist, but they can no longer hold wine, and hence as wine-skins are ruined.

Again, Matt. 26.8: "But when the disciples saw it, they had indignation, saying, To what purpose was this *waste*" (literally, destruction). Here the precious ointment poured from the alabaster cruse upon the head of the Master was not destroyed nor had not perished in the sense of ceasing to exist, but it was ruined as *ointment*—that is, like spilt milk it could not be recovered.

2. Special Meaning.

In the New Testament the specific meaning of destruction, or perdition, is in application to the future punishment or the final destiny of the impenitent wicked: Matt. 7.13; John 17.12; Rom. 9.22; Phil. 1.28; 3.19; II Thess. 2.3; I Tim. 6.9; Heb. 10.39; II Pet. 2.1 (translated "damnable" and "destruction"); II Pet. 2.2 (translated "pernicious way"); II Pet. 2.3 (translated "damnation"); II Pet. 3.7, 16; Rev. 17.8, 11.

With reference to future punishment note carefully the following points:

First. There is no evidence or indication that the specific meaning of destruction, or perdition, differs in any way from the general meaning: that is, whenever the impenitent wicked are said to perish or be destroyed, it is not meant that they cease to exist, but that they are ruined or lost: that is, they are banished from the presence of God and from the felicity and ministry of heaven.

Second. The specific meaning of destruction, or perdition, coincides with that of eternal or the second death. This point is established by the fact that "the second death" is synonymous with the "lake of fire." That is to say, if the *second death* is the same as the *lake of fire*, Rev. 20.14, and *perdition*, or *destruction*, is the same as the *lake of fire*, Rev. 17.8, 11; 19.20, then destruction, or perdition, and the second death must be the same thing. This follows because of the mathematical and logical axiom that, if two things are equal to a third thing, they are equal to each other.

Third. Destruction, or perdition, which is the final doom of the impenitent wicked, is described in the New Testament as the condition of beings in a place of conscious and unending torment.

This vital fact is established by combining the teaching of a number of passages. For example: Rev. 17.8, 11. Here "the beast" is said to go into "perdition." Again, Rev. 19.20. Here "the beast" is declared to have been "cast into a lake of fire burning with fire and brimstone." That is to say, "the lake of fire burning with fire and brimstone" is "perdition," or "destruction." Therein the false prophet was cast along with the beast. Again, Rev. 20.10. Here we are told that "the devil . . . was cast into the lake of fire and brimstone, where the beast and false prophet are, and shall be tormented day and night forever." Upon this last passage Dr. Torrey's comment is: "Here we find the beast still in the lake of fire and brimstone (that is, in perdition), being tormented after a thousand years have passed away." With this agree Rev. 14.10, 11, where we learn that those who worship the beast and receive his mark "shall be tormented with fire and brimstone in the presence of the holy angels, and in the presence of the Lamb; and the smoke of their torment ascendeth up forever and ever: and they have no rest day nor night." Finally Luke 16.19-31—the story of the rich man and Lazarus. This is commonly called a parable, but the term parable is not used by the Master. It is rather an unveiling of the future—a real portrayal of the state of the impenitent lost. Note these facts concerning the rich man. (1) He has memory, verse 25. (2) He has remorse, verse 24. (3) He has torment, verse 24. (4) He has concern for his living brothers, verse 28. (5) He has a vision of Lazarus "comforted," verse 25. (6) He pleads in vain for mercy and relief, verses 25, 26. (7) A "great gulf fixed" separates the impenitent wicked from the saints of God. Surely all this must mean that the future punishment of the wicked is conscious and unending.

Fourth. The everlasting, or eternity, of the torment of the impenitent wicked is expressed by the

phrase "day and night forever and ever": Rev. 20.10.
R. V. (Literally, day and night unto the ages
of the ages.) But it is objected that this
phrase refers to a period of limited but unknown
duration. In reply it may be said: As to the
expression "day and night" it seems to imply a
sense of time in the eternal state. See Rev. 4.8;
7.15; 12.10; 14.11; 20.10. As to the expression "forever and ever" (literally, unto the ages of the ages),
it occurs twelve times in Revelation, viz: 1.6; 4.9, 10;
5.13; 7.12; 10.6; 11.15; 14.11; 15.7; 19.3; 20.10;
22.5. Eight times it refers to the duration of the existence or reign of glory of God and Christ, once to
the duration of the blessed reign of the righteous,
and in the three remaining instances to the duration
of the torment of the devil, beast, false prophet, and
wicked.

NOTE: The Greek word *aion* signifies an *age*—an indefinitely endless succession of ages—"unto the ages of the ages."
A measuring yardstick infinitely extended would give in terms
of *space* the conception that the Greek phrase *eis tous aionas ton
aionon*, "unto the ages of ages," gives in terms of time. From
aion comes *aionios*, an adjective, signifying, literally, *age-long*,
and rendered in English by "everlasting or eternal." It has been
objected that *aionios* cannot mean eternal duration, because it
is sometimes applied to objects which have an end, e. g., the
everlasting hills: Gen. 49.26. To this objection, Dr. Farr replies thus: "It may be conceded that it (*aionios*) does not
etymologically necessitate the idea of eternity, and that sometimes it is used in the sense of age-long to express limited

duration. It does, however, express the longest possible duration of which the subject to which it is attributed is capable. So that if the soul is immortal, its punishment must be without end. It is used several times to express the life and duration of God Himself: Rom. 16.26; I Tim. 1.17; Heb. 9.14; Rev. 1.8. *Aionios* is used in the New Testament sixty-six times—fifty-one times for the happiness of the righteous; two times for the duration of God and His glory; six times where there is no doubt as to its meaning 'eternal,' and seven times of the punishment of the wicked. *Aion* is used ninety-five times for duration that has limit, nine times to denote the duration of future punishment. The most eminent Greek scholars have decided and declare that if these words do not teach the endlessness of the future punishment, to which they are applied, there are no words in the Greek language to express that meaning."

Fifth. The teaching of the Scripture is clear that the issues of eternity are settled *in this life*. See Luke 16.26; John 5.28, 29; 8.21; Heb. 9.27. R. V.

Sixth. There is absolutely no Scripture to warrant the hope entertained by many that those who die having never heard of Christ in this world will be given another opportunity for salvation. See Rom. 2.12-16. This passage is introduced by the apostle not to show how men are saved by the light of nature, but rather to show "how the Gentile is under condemnation by the written law in his heart just as the Jew is under condemnation by the Law of Moses." Rom. 3.19-22 is conclusive that both Jew and Gentile are saved only by faith in Christ. Says Dr. Torrey: "The future state of those who reject the redemption offered to

14

them in Christ is plainly declared to be a state of conscious, unutterable, endless torment and anguish.
The conception is an awful and appalling one. It is,
however, the Scriptural conception and also a reasonable one when we come to see the appalling nature
of sin, and especially the appalling nature of the sin
of trampling under foot God's mercy toward sinners,
and rejecting God's glorious Son, whom His love
has provided as Saviour. Shallow views of sin
and of God's holiness, and of the glory of Jesus
Christ and His claim upon us, lie at the bottom
of weak theories of the doom of the impenitent.
When we see sin in all its hideousness and
enormity, the holiness of God in all its perfection,
and the glory of Jesus Christ in all its infinity, nothing
will satisfy the demands of our own moral intuitions
but a doctrine that those who persist in the choice of
sin, who love darkness rather than light, and who
persist in the rejection of the Son of God, shall en-
dure everlasting anguish. Nothing but the fact that
we dread suffering more than we loathe sin, and more
than we love the glory of Jesus Christ, makes us re-
pudiate the thought that beings who eternally choose
sin should eternally suffer, or that men who despise
God's mercy and spurn His Son should be given over
to endless anguish."

Seventh. In view of this awful doctrine, what about
our impenitent friends and loved ones? Dr. Torrey,

to whose book "What the Bible Teaches" we express
our indebtedness in the treatment of this topic, thus
answers this question and concludes his general dis-
cussion: "It is better to recognize facts, no matter
how unwelcome, and try to save these friends from the
doom to which they are certainly hurrying, than to
quarrel with facts and seek to remove them by shut-
ting our eyes to them. You cannot avert a hurricane
by merely believing that it is not coming.

"Suppose one you love should commit some hid-
eous wrong against one you love more, and persist
in it eternally, would you not consent to his eternal
punishment?

"If, after men have sinned, and God still offers them
mercy, and makes the tremendous sacrifice of His
Son to save them,—if they still despise that mercy and
trample God's Son under foot, if then they are con-
signed to everlasting torment, I say: 'Amen! Hallelujah! True and righteous are Thy judgments, O
Lord!'

"At all events, the doctrine of conscious, eternal
torment for impenitent men is clearly revealed in the
Word of God, and whether we can defend it on philo-
sophic grounds or not, it is our business to believe it,
and leave it to the clearer light of Eternity to explain
what we cannot now understand, realizing that God
may have infinitely wise reasons for doing things for
which we, in our ignorance, can see no sufficient rea-

son at all. It is the most ludicrous conceit for beings so limited and foolish as the wisest of men to attempt to dogmatize how a God of infinite wisdom must act. All we know as to how God will act is what God has seen fit to tell us.

"In conclusion, two things are certain: First, the more closely men walk with God and the more devoted they become to His service, the more likely they are to believe this doctrine. Many men tell us they love their fellow-men too much to believe this doctrine; but the men who show their love in more practical ways than sentimental protestations about it, the men who show their love for their fellow-men, as Jesus Christ showed His, by laying down their lives for them, *they believe it,* even as Jesus Christ believed it.

"As Christians become worldly and easy-going, they grow loose in their doctrine concerning the doom of the impenitent. The fact that loose doctrines are spreading so rapidly and widely in our day is nothing for them, but against them, for worldliness is also spreading in the church: I Tim. 4.1; II Tim. 3.1; 4.2, 3. Increasing laxity of life and increasing laxity of doctrine go arm in arm. A church that dances and frequents theaters and lives in self-indulgence during the week enjoys a doctrine on the Lord's Day that makes the punishment not so awful after all.

"Second, men who accept a loose doctrine regarding the ultimate penalty of sin (Restoration or Univers-

alism or Annihilationism) lose their power for God.
They may be clever at argument and zealous in pros-
elyting, but they are poor at soul-saving. They are
seldom found beseeching men to be reconciled to God.
They are more likely to be found trying to upset the
faith of those already won by the efforts of others
than winning men who have no faith at all. If you
really believe the doctrine of the endless, conscious
torment of the impenitent, and the doctrine really gets
hold of you, you will work as you never worked before
for the salvation of the lost. If you in any wise abate
the doctrine, it will abate your zeal. Time and time
again the author has come up to this awful doctrine
and tried to find some way of escape from it, but when
he has failed, as he always has at last, when he was
honest with the Bible and with himself, he has returned to his work with an increased burden for souls
and an intensified determination to spend and be spent
for their salvation.

"Finally: Do not believe this doctrine in a cold, intellectual, merely argumentative way. If you do,
and try to teach it, you will repel men from it. But
meditate upon it in its practical, personal bearings, until your heart is burdened by the awful peril of the
wicked and you rush out to spend your last dollar, if
need be, and the last ounce of strength you have, in
saving these imperiled men from the certain, awful
hell of conscious agony and shame to which they are
fast hurrying."

QUESTIONS FOR STUDY.

1. What have you to say concerning the origin of sin?
2. What do the Scriptures appear to teach concerning the entrance of sin into the heart of Satan?
3. How was sin introduced into the human race?
4. What is the teaching of Scriptures concerning the reality of sin?
5. What is the testimony of mankind as to the reality of sin?
6. What is the witness of consciousness as to the reality of sin?
7. How would you show that sin is not an accident, not an infirmity, nor "an amiable weakness"?
8. How would you show that sin is not a negation nor a necessity?
9. Can you give the literal signification of the seven most prominent Hebrew words for sin? Give one reference for each word.
10. Can you give the literal signification of the eight most prominent Greek words for sin? Give one reference of each.
11. Can you give seven Scripture descriptive definitions of sin? State where they are found.
12. Can you give six theological definitions of sin?
13. Can you give the summary of Scripture teaching concerning sin? Give references.
14. What is the extent of sin as it affects the heavens?

15. What is the extent of sin as it affects the earth?

16. Can you describe two results of sin as it affects the earth?

17. Can you mention ten results of sin as it affects man?

18. Can you define penalty? What is its primary object?

19. Can you make clear two kinds of penalty?

20. Can you give five Scripture expressions for the final destiny of the impenitent wicked? Give references.

21. Can you give the threefold Scripture meaning of death? Give references.

22. Can you show from Revelation that spiritual or second death is a place of conscious and unending torment?

23. What is the general New Testament meaning of destruction, or perdition?

24. What is the specific New Testament meaning of destruction, or perdition?

25. Can you find any Scripture evidence or indication that, either in its general or specific meaning, destruction, or perdition, signifies cessation of being?

26. Can you show from Revelation that the specific meaning of destruction, or perdition, coincides with eternal or the second death?

27. Can you show from the New Testament that de-

struction, or perdition, is a condition of being in a place of conscious and unending torment?

28. What is the New Testament usage of the expression "day and night forever and ever"?

29. What is the New Testament usage of the words signifying "age" and "age-long," the latter being rendered in English by "eternal" or "everlasting"?

30. What passages of Scripture teach us that the issues of eternity are settled in this life?

31. Can you find any clear and unmistakable Scripture warrant for the hope that those who die having never heard of Christ will be given another chance for salvation hereafter?

32. If we believe the Word of God and are loyal to Christ, what attitude are we bound to take regarding our friends and loved ones who die impenitent?

33. How should the doctrine of future punishment be believed and preached?

DOCTRINE SIX: CHRISTOLOGY.

Part One: The Person of Christ.

Topics.

I. The Preexistence of Christ.

II. The Incarnation of Christ.

III. The Exaltation of Christ.

Part Two: The Work of Christ.

Topics.

I. Christ as Prophet.

II. Christ as Priest.

III. Christ as King.

CHAPTER VI.

CHRISTOLOGY.

PART ONE.

THE PERSON OF CHRIST.

TOPIC ONE: THE PREEXISTENCE OF CHRIST.

I. PROOF.

The Scriptures clearly and distinctly teach that, as the second person of the trinity, Jesus Christ existed before His incarnation: John 1.1-5; 8.58; 17.5, 24; Col. 1.13-17; Heb. 1.2, 8; 2.10.

II. NATURE.

This was twofold, viz: as to God, and as to creation.

1. As to God.

As to God, Jesus Christ was "the only begotten Son": John 1.14, 18; 3.16, 18; I John 4.9.

NOTE: As the Son, "the only begotten of (Greek, *para*,

from) the Father," Jesus Christ was begotten not in *time,* but in *eternity.* Theologically, this truth is called "the eternal genera-tion of the Son." In the historic development of the doctrine of the trinity in the Scriptures, not the Father, the first person, but Christ, the second person, is first revealed. As we have seen and shall see again, Christ is the Jehovah of the Old Testament, who made and preserves the universe, and re-vealed Himself in many ways to His ancient people. The revela-tion of Christ in the relation of Son, and the consequent revela-tion of the first person of the trinity in the relation of Father, comes out in connection with the doctrine of the Kingdom. See II Sam. 7.12-17; Psa. 2.7-9; 89.24-29.

2. As to Creation.

As to creation, Jesus Christ is "the firstborn": Rom. 8.29; Col. 1.15, 18.

Note: In Col. 1.15, Jesus Christ is declared to be "the firstborn of every creature" (R. V. of all creation); while in verse 18 He is declared to be "the firstborn from the dead." These, then, are the two relations in which He is "firstborn"; in creation and in resurrection. As applied to Christ, believers cannot share the title "only begotten"; but by spiritual sonship and resurrection we share with Him His title of "firstborn": Rom. 8.29; Heb. 12.23. In the latter passage, the Greek word "firstborn" is in the plural. See Rev. 3.14.

III. PRIMEVAL GLORY.

The character of the preexistence of Christ cannot be better expressed than that of *primeval glory*: John 17.5, 24; Phil. 2.6, 7; Col. 1.15; Heb. 1.3.

Note: Just what this primeval glory was we do not **know.**

Jesus speaks of being "in the bosom of the Father," John 1.18; and of being loved by the Father "before the foundation of the world," John 17.24. These and other phrases express ineffable relationships within the Godhead, which we cannot comprehend. On Phil. 2.6 Thayer's Greek Lexicon says: "Form (Greek, *morphe*) is that by which a person or thing strikes the vision, the external appearance." There is nothing in this passage which teaches that the Eternal Word (John 1.1) emptied Himself of either His divine nature or His attributes, but only of the outward visible manifestation of the Godhead. "He emptied, stripped Himself, of the insignia of Majesty" (Lightfoot). "When occasion demanded, He exercised His divine attributes" (Moorehead).

IV. OFFICE WORK.

In His preexistent state, a threefold office work, in particular, is ascribed to Christ, viz:

1. Creator.

In our study of the doctrine of God, under the topic of Creation, we have seen that the created universe is the work of Christ: John 1.3; Col. 1.16; Heb. 11.3.

2. Preserver.

Under the topic of Preservation (doctrine of God) we have also seen that the created universe is sustained and controlled by Christ: Col. 1.17; Heb. 1.3.

3. Framer of the Ages.

In Hebrews 11.3, we read that "the worlds were framed by the Word of God." (R. V. the worlds—

margin, ages—have been framed by the Word of God.) Literally, *the ages were framed* (or fitted together) *by the utterance of God.* This passage teaches us a stupendous and glorious truth, which we shall study more fully when we come to the doctrine of Eschatology, or the Last Things. It is that the dispensations, extending successively from creation to the new heavens and the new earth, have been planned and executed by Christ. As is well known, we are now in the Dispensation of Grace, which began at Pentecost and will end with the Parousia.

V. OLD TESTAMENT APPEARANCES.

From Genesis to Malachi there are frequent instances of Christophanies, or appearances of Christ to His ancient people. These were two kinds, namely: material symbols, and manifestations in human form. The latter were Theophanies or Christophanies proper. (**Theophany** means an appearance of God; **Christophany,** an appearance of Christ.)

1. Material Symbols.

From the days of the Garden of Eden till the time of the destruction of Solomon's temple there was a sensible representation of God upon the earth. Our first parents were permitted to see the face and hear the voice of Jehovah: Gen. 3.8. In this verse the word presence is literally *face.* Here there was a divine manifestation to both the eye and the ear. After the Fall, God placed at the entrance of Eden cherubim and a flaming sword, visible manifestations of His presence. It was before this presence of God that Cain and Abel brought their offerings, and from it that Cain fled. Moreover, the Lord spoke to Cain concerning his murderous deed: Gen. 4.4, 5-16. To the patriarchs, the Lord both appeared and spoke in a manner sensible to the eye and ear: Gen. 17.1; 18.1; Acts 7.2. Again, to Moses at the burning bush Jehovah both appeared and spoke: Ex. 3.1-6. Finally, in the pillar of cloud and fire and in the Shekinah glory in tabernacle and temple, Jehovah repeatedly appeared and spoke to His servants Moses and Joshua, and made known His will to Israel: Ex. 13.21; 14.15; 19.24; 20.1-26; 40.34-38; I Kings 8.10, 11; II Chron. 5.13, 14. There was no visible manifestation of the presence of Jehovah in the temple of Zerubbabel or in the temple of Herod.

2. Manifestations in Human Form.

In the Old Testament mention is made of an august, celestial Personage, "who acts in the name of Jehovah, whose name is used interchangeably with that of Jehovah, and who received divine honor and reverence." The more prominent names given to this heavenly being are: the Angel, the Angel of Jehovah, the Angel of the Presence (or, face), and the Angel, or Messenger, of the Covenant. He can be none other than the Jehovah of the Old Testament, or the Christ of the New Testament—He who became the incarnate Word, or *logos:* Gen. 16.10-13; 18.16-22; 22.11, 12; 32.24; 48.16; Ex. 3.2; 23.20-25; 32.34; 33.21-23; Josh. 5.13-15; Judges 13.3-20; Isa. 63.9; Dan. 10.13; Zech. 1.11, 12; Mal. 3.1.

NOTE: The identity of the material symbols of the preexistent Christ with His manifestations in human form is clear from such passages as Exodus 3.2 and 14.19. Nor is there any doubt that these symbols and theophanies were manifestations and appearances of the preexistent Christ. "The glory of the Lord" and "The Word of the Lord" are frequent Old Testament names for the sensible representations of God—the former describing them as they appealed to the eye, and the latter as they appealed to the ear. In the first chapter of John, these same descriptive expressions are applied to Christ. In verse 14 we read, "And the *Word* was made flesh, and dwelt (lit. tented) among us, and we beheld His *glory,* even the glory as of the only begotten of the Father, full of grace and truth." Corroboration of this fact is found in the targums, or Chaldee paraphrases of the Old Testament, which were made for the use of those who returned from the captivity in Babylon and could not understand Hebrew. There the expression *Word of the Lord* is commonly substituted for the name of Jehovah. Thus, "They heard the voice of the Word of the Lord walking in the garden": Gen. 3.8. Again, "And Jacob vowed a vow to the Word, saying, If the Word of the Lord will be my help," etc.: Gen. 28.20. Now, the Jews to whom John wrote his gospel were familiar with the Chaldee targums, and understood the expression "the Word of the Lord" or "the Word" to refer to Jehovah. Of course John himself so understood it. Accordingly, as Dr. Wickes says, referring to the *logos* or Word of John 1.1, 14: "It is not possible to vindicate the apostle's reputation as a man of common sense and honesty, if he employed this term out of its usual meaning, without giving any intimation of the fact. He of necessity used the term in its *commonly accepted meaning.*" Theologians are accustomed to trace John's of the term "Word" (Greek *logos*) back to Philo, an Alexandrian Jewish writer of an earlier date. B..t Philo used the term more in the sense of *reason,* or *utterance.* Moreover, such a connection cannot be established. It is not necessary to go so far afield. As we have shown, the Old Testament Scriptures clearly and satisfactorily explain the origin of the term, that by its use John meant to teach that Jehovah of the Old Testament became incarnate in the Christ of the New Testament. Modern Bible students feel the necessity of proving the Deity of Christ. Not so John; his contention was that He whom we now know as the second person of the trinity, Jehovah of Old Testament revelation, became incarnate in Jesus of Nazareth.

VI. THREE PROPHETIC PICTURES.

There are three pictures of the preexistent Christ, so striking and beautiful as to deserve special attention and emphasis:

1. The Slain Lamb.

This is a picture of the passover Lamb: Ex. 12. John the Baptist identified Christ as the sacrificial Lamb: John 1.29. John the seer on Patmos had a vision of our Lord as the bleeding Lamb: Rev. 12.11.

2. The Obedient Servant.

This is the picture of Christ portrayed in Psalm

15

40.6-8. See Heb. 10.5-10. Undoubtedly the primary reference of these passages is to Ex. 21.2-6, where we read of the Hebrew bond-slave, who, unwilling to claim rightful liberty because of his love for master, wife, and children, submitted to have his ear bored with an awl as the seal of voluntary and perpetual service. In Psalm 40.6, the word *opened* means *digged* or *bored,* a reference to Ex. 21.6. This picture of our Lord is fulfilled in the Gospel of Mark, which represents Him as the Servant of God.

3. The Beloved Son.

This is the picture presented in three passages we have already considered in a similar connection: II Sam. 7.14-16; Psalm 2.7; 89.26-29. At the baptism of Jesus, the Father identifies Him as His well beloved Son: Matt. 3.17; Mark 1.11; Luke 3.22. This was repeated at the transfiguration: Matt. 17.5; Mark 9.7; Luke 9.35. See Isa. 42.1; Eph. 1.6.

TOPIC TWO: THE INCARNATION OF CHRIST.

I. PROOF.

It is the clear and distinct teaching of Scripture, both by way of prophetic utterance and historic statement, that Jehovah of the Old Testament became incarnate in Jesus of Nazareth, the Messiah of God: Gen. 3.15; Deut. 18.18; Isa. 9.6; Matt. 1.18-25; Luke

1.26-35; John 1.14; Acts 10.38; Rom. 8.3, 4; Gal. 4.4; I Tim. 3.16; Heb. 2.14.

NOTE: *Incarnation* is a word from the Latin; it means, literally, *enfleshment,* i. e., the assumption of humanity. This is brought out particularly clear in such passages as Rom. 8.3, and Heb. 2.14.

II. PURPOSE.

It is the clear and distinct teaching of Scripture that the purpose of the incarnation was *redemption*: Gen. 3.15; Isa. 53.4, 5; Matt. 1.21; 20.28; Luke 1.68-75; John 3.16, 17; Gal. 4.4, 5; I Tim. 1.15; I John 3.8; 4.10.

NOTE: There are those who assert that, if our first parents had not sinned, Jesus Christ would have been born into the world just the same. This may be true, but we know no Scripture which proves it. On the contrary, the above and many similar passages unmistakably teach that *the incarnation was in order to the atonement.*

III. CONDESCENSION.

It was an act of condescension for Jehovah to assume human form. Says Dr. Farr: "As we have seen, we cannot say that Christ did not come to the race till it was 4,000 years old. The incarnate Logos, wherein we see the departed divinity reinstated in humanity, is the greatest mystery of the gospel: I Tim. 3.16; Matt. 11.27; Col. 2.2. It was an unspeak-

able act of condescension for the Son of God to stoop
and take into personal and perpetual union with Himself a nature infinitely lower than His own. It is
so represented in Scripture: Gal. 4.4; Phil. 2.5-8."

NOTE: Westminster Confession: "Christ's humiliation consisted in His being born, and that in a low condition; made under
the law; undergoing the miseries of this life, the wrath of God,
and the cursed death of the cross; in being buried, and con-
tinuing under the power of death for a time."

IV. PERPETUITY.

It is the unmistakable teaching of the Scriptures
that the Son of God assumed forever the humanity
which He assumed at His birth by the virgin. The
incarnation is in *perpetuity*. For this there are, princi-
pally, three reasons:

1. It is essential to the integrity of our Lord's manhood.

Jesus Christ is the God-man, possessing a divine-hu-
man person. According to the Nicene Creed, He is "very
God of very God and very man of very man." Before the virgin birth, we can speak, of course, of the
Son of God only; but after that miraculous historic
event we can speak also of the Son of man. Again,
the incarnation was voluntary; it was not by com-
pulsion that "the Word was made flesh, and dwelt
among us": John 1.14. But having voluntarily as-

sumed our humanity, Jesus Christ could not lay it aside without ceasing to be the Son of man. He is now and forever "the Man in the Glory." The post-resurrrection appearances of Jesus give indubitable evidence that He possessed a literal but glorified body: Matt. 28.9; Luke 24.3, 15, 30, 31, 40, 42, 50; John 20.17, 22-29; 21.7, 15. Further, the ascension appearances of Jesus represent Him with a literal but glorified body: Acts 7.56; 9.4-6; Rev. 1.9-18. Finally, the teaching of the epistles is conclusive as to the perpetuity of the incarnation: Rom. 4.25; 6.3-5; 7.4; 8.11; I Cor. 15.3-8, 20, 23; Eph. 5.30; Phil. 3.20, 21; I Thess. 4.14; Heb. 2.14-16; 13.8, etc.

NOTE: The glorified humanity of Christ is the source of our physical quickening by the Holy Spirit: Rom. 8.11; Eph. 5.30; the ground of His sympathy and succor: Heb. 2.17, 18; 4.14-16; 7.25; and the pledge and pattern of our own raised and glorified bodies: I Cor. 15.20-30; Phil. 3.20, 21; I Thess. 4.14-16; I John 3.2.

2. It is essential to our Lord's high-priestly intercession.

Without a literal but glorified body, Jesus Christ would be disqualified from exercising His high-priestly ministry of intercession: Rom. 8.34; Heb. 2.14-18; 3.1; 4.14-16; 6.20; 7.23-28; 9.24; 12.2.

Says Dr. Farr: "The essential condition in the exercise of that office, 'High Priest,' is the sharing of our nature; and, therefore, able, as one touched with, the feelings of our infirmities, to present our needs before the Father, and secure us grace to help in time of need."

3. It is essential to our Lord's return and millennial reign.

Without His body Jesus could not personally, literally, and visibly return to earth: Acts 1.11. Again, it is as David's Son and Heir that Jesus is to sit on the throne and establish His millennial reign of righteousness and peace: II Sam. 7.12-16; Psalm 89.2-4; 132.11; Isa. 9.6, 7; 55.3, 4; Hosea 3.5; Amos 9.11.

V. REVELATION.

The incarnation was a divine revelation in three principal aspects:

1. It brought God to man.

The incarnation was not only a necessary step to redemption; it revealed God *to* man and *in* man: Matt. 1 23; Col. 1.27.

NOTE: Says Dr. Farr: "The incarnation was at first not so much a revelation as an obscuration. Christ needed a witness to testify unto Him until He should be revealed in transfiguration and resurrection. This witness was John the Baptist. It was a new revelation of love: John 1.18; (literally, hath made an exegesis of the Father) John 3.16. The revelation in creation and providence is partial and incomplete; but in the Son, it is in the highest degree perfect and glorious.

2. It established a new communion.

The bond of union between God and man, which had been broken by sin, was, after 4,000 years, reestablished in Christ. "Then appeared the Son of God in the flesh; and an atonement, which could not possibly proceed from the creature, is brought about by the Creator Himself": Luke 19.10; John 6.33; II Cor. 5.19; Heb. 2.14.

3. It involved a new creation.

Christ became "the firstborn from the dead," in order that we, His "brethren" by nature and faith, might be transformed into His image: Rom. 8.29; Col. 1.18; II Cor. 5.17. As it has been put, "The Word became flesh, in order that flesh might be conformed to the Word."

VI. TWOFOLD NATURE.

The Scriptures clearly and distinctly teach that our Lord is both *human* and *divine*. Jesus Christ is both God and man—the God-man.

A. His Humanity.

This is attested by:

1. His birth, Matt. 2.1; Luke 2; John 1.14; Gal. 4.4.

2. His manifold experiences, as hunger, Matt. 4.2; thirst, John 19.28; weariness, John 4.6; temptation,

Matt. 4.1 (see James 1.13); suffering, Heb. 2.9, 18; etc. etc.

3. His death, Matt. 27.50; Mark 15.37; Luke 23.46; John 19.30-34.

B. His Deity.

This is attested by:

1. Prophetic utterance: Psa. 2.2-9; 45.6, 7; 110.1; Isa. 7.13, 14; 9.6, 7; Micah 5.2.

2. Christ's own claims: John. 8.56-58; 10.30-32.

3. The ascription of divine attributes: Matt. 28.20; John 3.13 (omnipresence); Mark 11.2, 4; John 11.11, 14 (omniscience); Matt. 28.18; Luke 7.14; John 5.21-23; 6.19 (omnipotence).

4. The employment of divine titles: John 1.1; 20.28; Acts 20.28; Rom. 1.4; 9.5; II Thess. 1.12; I Tim. 3.16; Titus 2.13; Heb. 1.8; I John 5.10.

NOTE: Jesus is the Jehovah of the Old Testament. In the Hebrew O. T. the name Jehovah occurs some 11,600 times; yet in the A. V. it is found only four times, viz: Ex. 6.3; Psalm 83.18; Isa. 12.2; 26.4. (The R. V. has very largely restored the name.) The reason of this is that the Jews superstitiously avoided the pronunciation of their sacred name for God, that is, *Jahwe,* substituting therefor *Adonai,* which signifies Master or Lord. The O. T. Greek translation (the LXX) rendered *Adonai* by *Kurios,* which is the Greek for Lord. And in this way the word "Lord" found its way into our English Bible as the rendering of the Hebrew name *Jahwe.* Capital letters indicate this connection, i. e. LORD. Dr. A. T. Pierson says: "Were this great name (that is, Jehovah) always reproduced in the English and especially in New Testament quotations from the Old, it would prove that our Lord Jesus Cnrist is absolutely equal and identical with the Father; for passages which, in the O. T. contain the name 'Jehovah' are so quoted and applied to Him in the New as to demonstrate Him to be JEHOVAH-JESUS, one with God of the eternal past, Himself manifested in the flesh, in the present, and the coming God of the future. This is the climax of all arguments and evidences touching our Lord's Deity." See Psa. 102.25-27 and Heb. 1.10-12; Isa. 40.3 and Matt. 3.3; Jer. 23.6 and Rom. 3.21-26, and I Cor. 1.30.

5. The homage of divine worship: Matt. 2.11; 15.25; 20.20; 28.9; Luke 24.52; John 20.28.

6. Forgiveness of sin: Mark 2.5-7; Luke 7.48; 24.47.

7. The possession of absolute holiness and the resurrection from the dead: John 8.46; Rom. 1.4.

VII. NAMES.

Some suggestive and striking names are applied to Christ. Such are the following:

1. Jesus.

This word means saviour or salvation, and links the Redeemer with humanity: Matt. 1.21.

2. Christ.

This word means anointed; it is the Messianic name, and links Him with prophecy, which He came to fulfil: John 1.41.

3. Lord.

This word means master; it is the Jehovah name, and links Him with Deity, which He came to represent and reveal: Acts 9.5.

NOTE: The historic order of these three names is given in Luke 2.11: "a Saviour, Who is Christ the Lord." During the days of His flesh it was preeminently Jesus; during His high-priestly ministry it is preeminently Christ; during His millennial reign it will be preeminently Lord. Thus, Jesus suggests His prophetic office; Christ, His priestly office; and Lord, His kingly office. "These three names likewise suggest man's relation and responsibility— obedience to Him as Prophet; faith in Him as Priest; surrender to Him as King" (Pierson).

4. The Alpha and Omega.

The beginning and the end, the first and the last, the Lord, Who is and was and is to come: Rev. 1.8; 4.8; 22.13. Says Dr. Pierson: "*Alpha* and *Omega,* first and last letters of the Greek alphabet, suggest literature—the written Scriptures; Beginning and End, the material creation; First and Last, the historic ages, or time-worlds; Who is and was and is to come, Jehovah's eternity. Thus He is here declared, declares Himself, the subject matter of all Scripture; the Creator of all worlds and creatures; the Controller of all history, and the eternal, unchangeable Jehovah."

VIII. PERSONAL ONENESS OR HYPOSTATIC UNION.

The human nature and the divine nature—each in its completeness—are organically and indissolubly united in the one unique person of Jesus Christ. This is called in theological language, "the hypostatic union," or personal union. In our thinking and preaching we must exercise extreme care neither to divide the person nor confuse or confound the natures of Christ. It is not Scriptural to say that Christ was God *and* man, but that He was the God-man. This is expressed by the Greek *theanthropic* (Greek *theos*—God, *anthropos*—man).

1. There is no interchange of personal pronouns, as "I" or "Thou," between the human and divine natures in speaking of or referring to Christ, as there is between the three persons of the trinity: John 14.26; 17.23. John 3.11 may be explained as referring to both Christ and His disciples.

2. Neither the human nor the divine nature acts independently of the other; but in every thought, word, and act both natures are so inseparably united that the thought, word, or act is the product of one single personality. Thus, we cannot say that as *man* Jesus was born, while as *God* He received divine titles and worship, wrought miracles, and forgave sin. But we must say that as the *God-man* He was born, suffered the manifold experiences of hu-

manity, died on the cross, received divine titles and worship, wrought miracles, and forgave sins. "The characteristics of the two natures are ascribed to the one Christ; and conversely, the works of the one Christ are ascribed to either of the two natures, in a way inexplicable except on the basis that they are united in one Person. This may explain many paradoxes of Scripture; i. e., we say that Christ existed before Abraham and yet was born in the reign of Augustus; that He is the same yesterday, today, and forever, and yet that He wept, was weary, suffered, bled, and died" (Farr).

3. The union of the two natures in one person is essential for Jesus Christ to be the Mediator between God and man: I Tim. 2.5. "Christ's twofold nature gives Him fellowship with both parties, since it involves an equal dignity with God and at the same time perfect sympathy with man. Being man, He can make atonement. Being God, His atonement has infinite value. A merely human saviour could never reconcile or reunite us to God": Heb. 2.17, 18; 4.15, 16; 7.25.

IX. CHRISTOLOGICAL ERRORS.

Beginning in the days of the apostles and extending into the present time, many errors have been held concerning our Lord. These errors may be traced to one of two causes: first, failure to make a clear distinction between His two natures; and second, failure to hold fast the unity of His person. This subject belongs properly to Church History; but we can treat its doctrinal aspects here. The principal Christological errors are the following:

A. Errors of the Early Centuries.

1. Ebionism.

Ebionism is supposed to come from a Hebrew word signifying *poor;* this error closed about the end of the first century. It was the denial of the reality of the divine nature of Christ. "It held our Lord to be merely man, whether naturally or supernaturally conceived. This man, however, held a peculiar relation to God, in that from the time of His baptism, an unmeasured fulness of the divine Spirit rested upon Him. Ebionism was simply Judaism within the pale of the Christian Church, and its denial of Christ's Godhead was occasioned by an apparent incompatibility of this doctrine with monotheism" (Strong).

2. Cerinthianism.

Cerinthianism comes from Cerinthus, a heretic who flourished in the days of the apostle John. It was an offshoot of Ebionism, holding that there was no real and essential union of the two natures of Christ prior to His baptism. This error founded the deity of Christ, not on His supernatural birth, but on His baptism and enduement of the Spirit.

3. Docetism.

Docetism comes from a Greek word signifying *to seem* or *appear;* this error flourished from the latter part of the first to the latter part of the second century. It was the denial of the humanity of Christ, and was attacked by the apostle John in his first epistle: 4.1-3. In denying the reality of Christ's body, Docetism showed its connection with Gnosticism and Manicheism. "This view was the logical sequence of their assumption of the inherent evil of matter. If matter is evil and Christ was pure, then Christ's human body must have been merely phantasmal. Docetism was simply pagan philosophy introduced into the church" (Strong).

B. Errors of the Fourth and Fifth Centuries.

1. Arianism.

Arius, a presbyter of the church of Alexandria, Egypt, in the fourth century denied the deity of Christ and also His eternal generation from the Father. Arianism was condemned at the Council of Nice in A. D. 325.

NOTE: "Arius denied the integrity of the divine nature of Christ. He regarded the Logos who united himself to humanity in Jesus Christ, not as possessed of absolute Godhead, but as the first and highest of created beings. This view originated in a misinterpretation of the Scriptural accounts of Christ's state of humiliation, and in mistaking a temporary subordination (i. e., of office) for original and permanent inequality (i. e., of nature)" (Strong).

2. Apollinarianism.

Apollinarius, bishop of the church of Laodicea, in the fourth century denied the completeness of our Lord's human nature. Accepting the threefold division of man, namely, into body (Greek, *soma*), soul (*psuche*), and spirit (*nous* or *pneuma*), Apollinarius denied to Christ a human soul (*psuche*) supplying its place by the divine Logos. In this way he made Jesus only two parts human. The good bishop's motive was a worthy one, but his reasoning was faulty and led him into most serious error. He regarded the human soul (*psuche*) as the seat of sin; Christ was sinless; therefore, Christ could not have possessed a human soul. Apollinarianism was condemned at the Council of Constantinople in A. D. 381.

3. Nestorianism.

Nestorius, bishop of the church of Constantinople, in the fourth century denied the unique personality of Christ by separating and erecting the two natures into distinct persons. Thus he made of our Lord two persons instead of one person. The motive of Nestorius, like that of Apollinarius, was praiseworthy; but, like the latter, he himself fell into most serious error. Indeed, it was in combating the Apollinarian heresy of mutilating our Lord's humanity that Nestorius evolved the equally unscriptural position that the two natures of Christ constituted separate and distinct personalities. In modern times, R. L. Stevenson in his book, "The Strange Case of Dr. Jekyll and Mr. Hyde," has given dramatic expression to the old Nestorian heresy of dual personality. Nestorianism was condemned at the Council of Ephesus, A. D. 431.

4. Eutychianism.

Eutyches, an abbot of Constantinople, in the fifth century denied the integrity of our Lord's two natures by confusing them (that is, running them together) so as to make a third nature separate and different from either the human or the divine nature. Out of Christ's two natures, Eutyches constructed what has been called a *tertium quid,* or third nature. Eutychianism, known also as Monophysitism (from *mono* —one, and *physis*—nature) was condemned at the Council of Chalcedon in A. D. 451.

5. Monothelitism.

In comparison with the above this was a minor but still a serious error. It alleged that while Christ had two natures, He had but one will (*mono*—one, and *thelema*—will). "In opposition to this the sixth Ecumenical Council of Constantinople (A. D. 681) adopted the doctrine of two wills in Christ (*duo*— two, and *thelema*) as the orthodox doctrine, but decided that the human will must always be conceived as subordinate to the divine": John 6.38, 39.

NOTE: Says Dr. Strong: "All controversies with regard to the person of Christ must, of necessity, hinge upon one of three points: first, the reality of the two natures; secondly, the integrity of the two natures; thirdly, the union of the two natures in one person. Of these points, Ebionism and Docetism deny the reality of the natures; Arianism and Apollinarianism deny their integrity; while Nestorianism and Eutychianism deny their proper union."

C. Modern Errors.

1. Unitarianism.

In short, this is the old Arian heresy revived—the denial of the deity of our Lord.

2. Christian Science.

In short, this is the old Docetic heresy revived—the denial of the humanity of Christ. Christian Science denies the reality of matter. As our Lord's body was material, it must have been phantasmal, that is, shadowy and unsubstantial.

3. Millennial Dawn.

"Russellism" seems to go farther than any or all of the ancient heresies. It virtually denies the present and personal existence of our Lord and Saviour Jesus Christ. It makes Him a myth, like Jack-the-Giant-Killer or Alice in Wonderland.

NOTE: "The orthodox doctrine (promulgated at Chalcedon,

451) holds that in the person, Jesus Christ, there are two natures, a human nature and a divine nature, each in its completeness and integrity; and that these two natures are organically and indissolubly united, yet so that no third nature is formed thereby. In brief, to use the antiquated dictum, orthodox doctrine forbids us either to divide the person or to confound the natures" (Strong).

TOPIC THREE: THE EXALTATION OF CHRIST.

I. PROOF

The Scriptures clearly and distinctly teach that at the conclusion of His work on earth, our Lord was exalted to the right hand of God in heaven: Acts 2.33; 5.31; Phil. 2.9; Heb.12.2.

II. STAGES.

Historically, the exaltation of Christ was accomplished in two stages, viz:

1. His resurrection: Acts 2.24, 31, 32; 4.10; 17.31; Rom. 1.4; 4.25; 8.34; I Cor. 15.4, 20, 23.

2. His ascension: Mark 16.19; Luke 24.51; Acts 1.9-11; 2.33; Eph. 4.8-10.

NOTE: In Philippians 2.5-11 we can trace seven steps in the humiliation and seven steps in the exaltation of Christ. The depth to which Jesus voluntarily descended measured the height to which He was exalted by God in honor and glory.

Upon verse 7, the doctrine of the *kenosis,* so called, is founded —that is, the self-emptying of Christ. The nature and extent of this act are controversial questions.

III. CHARACTER.

The exaltation of Christ is marked by the following characteristics, viz:

1. Restoration to primeval glory: John 17.5; Heb. 1.8, 9; Rev. 5.9, 10.

2. Session at God's right hand: Psalm 110.1; Acts 7.56; Rom. 8.34; Eph. 1.20; Col. 3.1; Heb. 1.3; 8.1; 12.2; Rev. 3.21.

3. Giver of the Holy Ghost: Luke 24.49; John 15.26; 16.7; 20.22; Acts 1.8; 2.32, 33; 5.32.

4. Dominion over creation: Matt. 28.18; I Cor. 15.27; Eph. 1.20-22; Phil. 2.9-11; Col. 1.17; Heb. 2.8.

5. Headship of church: I Cor. 11.3; 12.12-27; Eph. 1.22, 23; 5.23-33; Col. 1.18.

6. Ministry of intercession: Rom. 8.34; Heb. 7.25; 9.24; I John 2.1.

7. Expectancy of return: Psalm 110.1; Acts 3.20, 21; Heb. 1.1, 13; 10.13.

QUESTIONS FOR STUDY.

1. Give Scripture proof of the fact that Jesus Christ existed before His incarnation.

2. What was the twofold nature of Christ's pre-existence?

3. What was Christ's threefold office work in His preexistent state?

4. In what two forms did the Lord appear in the Old Testament times? Discuss one of them.

5. What are the three prophetic pictures of the preexistent Christ?

6. What are the principal Scripture passages that teach the incarnation of Christ?

7. What was the purpose of the incarnation?

8. Why was the incarnation an act of condescension?

9. Why is it perpetual?

10. How is it a revelation?

11. What are the proofs of Christ's humanity?

12. What are the proofs of His deity?

13. Discuss some of the N. T. names applied to Christ.

14. What is meant by "the hypostatic union"?

15. What was the error concerning Christ's person known as Ebionism?

16. Known as Cerinthianism?

17. Known as Docetism?

18. Known as Arianism?

19. Known as Apollinarianism?

20. Known as Nestorianism?

21. Known as Eutychianism?

22. Known as Monothelitism?

23. What are some present day Christological errors?
24. What Scripture passages set forth the fact of Christ's exaltation?
25. In what two stages was it accomplished?
26. What are some of its characteristics?

CHRISTOLOGY.

PART TWO

THE WORK OF CHRIST.

According to the Scriptures, Jesus Christ has a threefold office work, viz: a prophetic ministry, a priestly ministry, and a kingly ministry. As someone has said: "Christ must be a Prophet to save us from the *ignorance* of sin; a Priest, to save us from its *guilt;* and a King, to save us from its *power.*"

TOPIC ONE: CHRIST AS PROPHET.

I. PREDICTIVE ANNOUNCEMENT.

The predictive announcement that Christ should be a prophet is recorded in Deut. 18.18, 19. See Matt. 13.57; 16.14; 21.11; John 1.21; 4.19; 6.14; 7.40; 9.17; and especially Acts 3.22 and 7.37.

II. EXTENT.

Officially, the prophetic ministry of Christ began at

the river Jordan, when He was endued with the Holy Spirit, and ended at the cross of Calvary, when He offered Himself as a sacrifice for sin: Matt. 4.23-25; Luke 4.14-27; Acts 2.22, 23; Heb. 9.26-28.

III. TWOFOLD NATURE OF PROPHET.

The primary idea of the prophetic office is that of one who "brings things to light," or "makes manifest." The secondary idea is prediction of the future. The O. T. prophet, then, exercised two functions: first, *insight;* and second, *foresight.* The prophet had also, so to speak, "hindsight"; for by revelation of the Spirit he frequently knew things of the past. This was true of Moses, when he penned the panorama of creation: Gen. 1 and 2.

NOTE: The original name of the prophet was *seer:* I Sam. 9.9; II Kings 17.13. A seer is one who sees, i. e., who sees things not beheld by mortal eye. The word prophet comes from the Greek *pro,* before or forth, and *phemi,* to speak, signifying to speak forth or beforehand. Thus a prophet was one who spoke to the people as the mouthpiece of God: Ex. 4.15, 16. On the primary idea of the prophetic office, see Ex. 4.10-17.

IV. MANIFOLD CHARACTER OF PROPHETIC MINISTRY.

An O. T. prophet fulfilled his ministry in three ways: by teaching (Matt. 5-7), by predicting (Matt.

24), and by healing (Matt. 8, 9). Our Lord did all these. Or, more particularly, Christ fulfilled His prophetic office in the following ways:

1. By His gracious words: Matt. 5.2; 7.28, 29; John 6.63; Rev. 1.10, 11.

2. By His wondrous deeds: John 5.36; 10.25; 15.24; Acts 2.22.

3. By His matchless example: John 13.15; I Peter 2.21-23.

4. By His unparalleled silence: Matt. 27.13, 14; I Peter 2.23.

5. By His gift of the Spirit: John 14.26; 15.26; I Peter 1.10, 11; I John 2.20-27.

TOPIC TWO: CHRIST AS PRIEST.

PREDICTIVE ANNOUNCEMENT.

The predictive announcement that Christ should be a priest is recorded in Psalm 110.4. See Heb. 5.6; 6.20; 7.21.

NOTE: Our Lord's priesthood is not in the line of Aaron, but "after the order of Melchizedec"; that is, it is exercised not on earth but in heaven; and it is unchanging and eternal.

EXTENT.

Officially, the priestly ministry of Christ began at

the cross, when He offered Himself as a sacrifice for sin, and will end at His return, when as King He will sit on the throne of David: Heb. 8 and 9.

NATURE OF PRIESTLY OFFICE.

A priest is a *mediator*—one who intercedes with a just God on behalf of guilty sinners: Lev. 4.16-18.

NOTE: Says Dr. Wickes: "Soon after the deluge, a class of men was set apart and consecrated to this sacred office of mediatorship with God, which is the essential idea of a priest—one to whom the offering of sacrifices is specially committed, that he may intercede with heaven in behalf of the guilty, who themselves have no access into the divine presence. Thus not only must a bloody sacrifice, or sin offering, be made, but made by certain persons who have been clothed with this special authority to act for others. They are appointed mediators between God and man, through whose intercession, by the offering of blood, atonement is made and justification obtained for the transgressor." In Israel, by the law of Moses, the priesthood was lodged in the house of Aaron.

THREEFOLD SCOPE OF PRIESTHOOD.

The scope of the Old Testament priesthood was threefold, viz: first, to offer sacrifices before the people; second, to go within the veil to make intercession for the people; and third, to come forth and bless the people. Or, RECONCILIATION, INTERCESSION, and BENEDICTION. As the Great High Priest, our Lord fulfilled these three functions. The first, reconciliation, He accomplished at His first coming, when on the cross He offered Himself as a sacrifice for sin. The second, intercession, He is accomplishing now in heaven between His first and second advent. And the third, benediction, He will accomplish at and after His coming return: Heb. 9.27, 28; I Peter 1.18-20; 2.24; Rom. 8.34; Heb. 7.25; II Thess. 1.10; I Peter 1.4, 5; Rev. 11.15; 20.4.

NOTE: The priests had access to the Holy Place of the ancient tabernacle; but the high priest alone, and then but once a year on the great day of atonement, could enter the Holy of Holies: Heb. 9.6, 7. The formula of benediction, which the high priest used, on emerging from the Holy of Holies, is believed to be recorded in Num. 6.22-27.

THE ATONEMENT OF CHRIST.

I. THE FACT.

By predictions, types, witnessing terms, and explicit statements, the Scriptures clearly set forth the fact of the atonement.

A. Types.

The typology of the Old Testament is full of the atonement. We may instance a few of the more striking types:

1. Coat of skins, Gen. 3.21.
2. Abel's lamb, Gen. 4.4.

3. The offering of Isaac, Gen. 22.

4. The Passover lamb, Ex. 12.

5. The Levitical sacrificial system, Lev. chaps. 1-7.

6. The brazen serpent, Num. 21; see John 3.14; 12.32.

7. The slain Lamb, Isa. 53.7. See John 1.29; Rev. 13.8.

B. Predictions.

The Old Testament abounds in predictions concerning the Messiah, His character and career. Indeed, there are said to be 333 specific striking O. T. pictures of the sacrificial death of Christ.

1. The seed of the woman, Gen. 3.15.

2. The sin offering, Psalm 22.

3. The substitutional Saviour, Isa. 53.

4. The cut-off Messiah, Dan. 9.26.

5. The smitten Shepherd, Zech. 13.6, 7.

C. Witnessing Terms.

There are five Scriptural witnessing terms of the Atonement. They are:

1. Atonement.

The word atonement occurs only once in the A. V. of the New Testament, viz: Rom. 5.11. The Greek noun here is *katallage* which is more correctly rendered in the Revised Version *reconciliation* (see below). The root of the Hebrew word for atonement is *kaphar,* which literally signifies to cover, i. e., forgive sin. See Ex. 30.10. Psalm 32.1 gives us both the figurative and spiritual meaning of atonement.

NOTE: The lid of the ark, called the mercy seat, is in Hebrew the *kapporeth,* signifying *the place of the covering* (i. e., of sin). The way some teachers divide the word atonement, viz., at-one-ment, is of curious interest; but at best it is a mere verbal trick, and no Scriptural warrant can justly be claimed for it.

2. Reconciliation.

Reconciliation is the translation of the Greek noun *katallage,* which literally signifies an exchange, i. e., of equivalent value in money-changing, or an adjustment, i. e., of a difference. The enmity between God and man has been destroyed and amity has been restored. "The word is used in the N. T.," says Thayer, "of the restoration of the favor of God to sinners that repent and put their trust into the expiatory death of Christ": Rom. 5.11, R. V.; 11.15; II Cor. 5.18, 19.

3. Propitiation.

Propitiation is the translation of the Greek nouns *hilasmos* and *hilasterion,* literally signifying an appeasing, a placating, an expiation. Propitiation comes from the Latin and means that which renders one propitious or favorably disposed towards another.

Thus, the death of Christ is the ground whereby God is rendered propitious or favorably disposed towards the sinner. Christ, in other words, is the propitiation for sin: Rom. 3.25; I John 2.2; 4.10. See Heb. 2.17, R. V.

NOTE: Propitiation or propitiatory is the Greek equivalent of the Hebrew *kapporeth*, or mercy seat, the lid of the ark of the covenant.

4. Redemption.

Redemption is the translation of the Greek nouns *lutrosis* and *apolutrosis*, signifying a releasing, or liberation from captivity, slavery, or death by the payment of a price, called a *ransom*. Thus, Christ is the ransom, who delivers us from sin and death. Redemption is from the Latin and signifies a buying back: Luke 1.68; 2.38; Rom. 3.24; I Cor. 1.30; Eph. 1.7, 14; 4.30; Col. 1.14; Heb. 9.12, 15.

NOTE: The medieval schoolmen taught that Christ was the ransom-price which God paid to Satan to release sinners. But this is pressing the figure of speech too far. See I Peter 1.18-20.

5. Substitution.

Substitution is not a Biblical word but it is a Scriptural idea. It means that one person or thing is put in, or takes, the place of another person or thing. Thus, Christ took the place of sinners and died, thus suffering the penalty of sin, which they deserved.

This is the significance of the scape-goat, Lev. 16.
This is also the meaning of Isa. 53.6. And it is the
clear teaching of the New Testament: Matt. 20.28;
Mark 10.45; II Cor. 5.21; Gal. 2.20; I Peter 3.18.

NOTE: There are two Greek prepositions which express the
substitutional or vicarious idea, viz: *huper*—in behalf of, and
anti—instead of. Some regard them as equivalents: Matt. 20.28;
Gal. 2.20. The English preposition *for* is ambiguous; it means
both in behalf of, and instead of.

D. Explicit Statements.

The New Testament abounds in explicit statements
concerning the atonement. If it be carefully read and
all the passages bearing on this subject marked, and
these classified, something like the following will be the
result:

1. **The center and heart of the atonement of Christ
is declared to be:**

a. His death, Rom. 5.10; Phil. 2.8; Heb. 2.9-14;
9.16; Rev. 5.6, 9, 12.

b. His cross, I Cor. 1.23; Gal. 3.1; 6.12; Eph. 2.16;
Col. 1.20.

c. His blood, Matt. 26.28; Mark 14.24; Luke 22.20;
Eph. 1.7; 2.13; Col. 1.14; I John 1.7; Heb. 9.12, 15;
Rev. 1.5; 5.9.

2. **The atonement bears a relation to God:**

a. It is grounded in His love, John 3.16.

b. It manifests His righteousness, Rom. 3.25; II Cor. 5.21.

c. It measures the extent of His sacrifice, John 3.16; Rom. 8.32; II Cor. 5.21; I John 4.10.

d. It is the basis of our reconciliation, Rom. 5.11; II Cor. 5.18, 19.

3. The atonement bears a relation to the law.

a. Christ was born under the law, Gal. 4.4, 5.

b. Christ bore its curse, Gal. 3.13; Phil. 2.8.

c. Christ fulfilled its righteousness, Rom. 5.18, 19; 8.3, 4; 10.4.

4. The sacrifice of Christ was necessary: Luke 24.26; Gal. 2.21; 3.21; Heb. 2.10.

5. The sacrifice of Christ was voluntary: John 10.17, 18; Gal. 2.20; Eph. 5.2; Heb. 9.14; 10.7-9.

6. The atonement of Christ was the only sacrifice for sin: Acts 4.12; Rom. 3.20-28; Heb. 1.3; 9.22; 10.10, 12, 14, 26; I Peter 3.18.

7. The atonement of Christ was vicarious: Matt. 26.28; Rom. 5.6; II Cor. 5.14, 15; Gal. 3.13, 14.

8. The atonement of Christ was for sin: John 1.29; Rom. 3.25; 5.8; 6.10; 8.3; I Cor. 15.3; II Cor. 5.21; Gal. 3.13; Heb. 9.28; I Peter 2.24; 3.18; Rev. 1.5.

9. The atonement of Christ was for various classes:

a. For His own people, Matt. 1.21; John 10.

11; 15.13; Eph. 5.25; Heb. 2.13, 14; I John 3.16.

b. For the many, Matt. 20.28; Mark 10.45; Heb. 9.28.

c. For the lost Matt. 18.11; Mark 2.17; Luke 5.32; 19.10.

d. For the whole world, John 1.29; 3.16; 6.51; 12.47; II Cor. 5.14, 15; I Tim. 2.6; Heb. 2.9; I John 2.2.

10. **The atonement of Christ produces many beneficial effects:**

a. Thereby Jesus becomes the Saviour of men, Matt. 1.21.

b. Thereby justification is received, Acts 13.39.

c. Thereby cleansing is received, I John 1.7.

d. Thereby sanctification is received, Heb. 13.12.

e. Thereby healing is received, I Peter 2.24.

f. Thereby universal blessings are received, John 14.13; Eph. 1.3; Heb. 9.15.

II. THE NECESSITY.

So far as we can penetrate into the mystery of the atonement, its necessity was fourfold:

1. The Holiness of God.

The holiness of God was outraged by sin and demanded appeasement by punishment.

2. The Law of God.

The law of God was violated by sin and demanded that the penalty of death be inflicted.

Law has been called "the expression of *will*." While all law is of God, we may distinguish between Natural and Divine law. **Natural Law** underlies the physical constitution of the universe. It has been defined as the observed uniform action or tendency of the forces or powers of the physical universe, as gravitation, cohesion, chemical affinity, etc. Natural law implies four things: (a) a lawgiver or authoritative will; (b) persons and things whereon the law operates; (c) a command or expression of this will; and (d) a power enforcing the command. On the other hand, **Divine Law** underlies the moral constitution of the universe. It is twofold, viz: the *moral* law and the *ceremonial* law. The **Moral Law** is a transcript of the character of God, that is, it is His essential nature expressed in perceptive form, as the Decalogue, the ethical teaching of the Sermon on the Mount, and the new commandment of Jesus: John 15.12. The moral law, therefore, is elemental, universal, and permanent. It implies six things: (a) A divine lawgiver or ordaining *will;* (b) subjects, or moral beings upon whom the law terminates; (c) commands, or the expression of this will in the moral constitution of the subjects and in the form of written perceptive enactments; (d) power enforcing these commands; (e) duty, or obliga-

17

tion to obey; and (f) sanctions, or pains and penalties for disobedience. Now, it is the moral law which the sinner has transgressed and for which transgression the penalty of death is threatened: Ezek. 18.4; Rom. 6.23. The **Ceremonial Law** is the expression in written perceptive form of the will of God for a specific purpose, as the Levitical system of ablutions and the distinction between clean and unclean animals: Lev. chaps. 11-15. The ceremonial law, accordingly, was local in application and temporary in character. Indeed, in Christ and His gospel, the *moral law is fulfilled* but the *ceremonial law is abrogated*. Rom. 10.4; Acts 10.9-16; I Tim. 4.1-5.

3. The Guilty Conscience.

The guilty and defiled conscience of the sinner can be acquitted and cleansed only through punishment—the punishment of the sinner himself or of his Substitute, the Saviour. Peace and rest cannot come to the condemned heart till it is assured that its just penalty has been borne by the spotless Lamb of God: Heb. 10.1-8.

4. The Lost Sinner.

In the doctrine of Hamartialogy (see Topic 5: The Result of Sin) it has been shown that in consequence of sin man is both helpless and hopeless. HE IS LOST, "having no hope, and without God in the world": Eph. 2.12. For this reason "the Son of man came to seek and to save that which was lost": Luke 19.10.

NOTE: Heathen sacrifices bear witness to the necessity of atonement for sin. They are best explained as a perversion of an original divine revelation. This perversion is seen in the fact that while in heathen sacrifices the victim is offered to appease an offended deity, the truth as set forth in the Scriptures is that "God was in Christ, reconciling the world unto himself": II Cor. 5.19. That heathen sacrifices are a perversion of an original divine revelation is further seen in the fact that the idea of *substitution* is uppermost; that is, the worshiper, conscious of his sinfulness, brings his offering, by whose *innocent blood* he believes his guilt is expiated.

III. THE EXTENT.

As to the extent of the atonement, a distinction must be made between its sufficiency and its efficiency. In sufficiency the atonement in Christ is universal; that is, potential provision is made for all mankind. But in efficiency the atonement is limited; that is, actual provision is made only for those who accept God's gracious offer of salvation through Christ. Both aspects are presented in I Tim. 4.10: ... "we trust in the living God, who is the Saviour of all men, specially of those that believe."

1. **Passages bearing on the universality of the atonement:** Heb. 2.9; I Tim. 2.6; 4.10; Titus 2.11; I John 2.2; II Peter 3.9.

2. **Passages bearing on the limitation of the atone-**

ment: Eph. 1.4, 7; II Tim. 1.9, 10. See John 17.9, 20, 24.

NOTE: Christ is the Saviour of all men in the sense that: (1) His atonement acts as a stay in the execution of the sentence against sin, securing for all men a space for repentance, and the enjoyment of the common blessings of life, forfeited by transgression: II Peter 3.9; Matt. 5.45; Acts 14.17; (2) His atonement has made objective provision for the salvation of all, by removing from the divine mind every obstacle to the pardon and restoration of sinners, except their wilful opposition to God and refusal to turn to Him: Rom. 5.8-10; II Cor. 5.18-20; (3) His atonement has procured for all men the powerful incentives to repentance presented in the cross, together with the combined agency of the Christian Church and the Holy Spirit: Rom. 2.4; John 16.8; II Cor. 5.18-20; (4) His atonement provides for the removal of the curse from nature: Isa. 55.13; Rom. 8.21, 22; and (5) His atonement provides for the salvation of infants: Matt. 18.10; 19.13-15. On the other hand, Christ is the Saviour only of those who believe, because repentance and faith are the conditions of salvation: Acts 2.38.

IV. PHILOSOPHY.

The philosophy of the atonement seeks its rational explanation. It must be frankly admitted that a complete and satisfactory philosophy of the atonement is impossible, for at bottom it is a profound and impenetrable mystery. Indeed, the early church viewed the atonement as a fact more than as a doctrine; that is, as a historic event, not as a speculative problem. It was the central truth of the gospel. Forgiveness was offered freely through the blood of Christ on the simple condition of repentance from sin and faith towards God. It would have been well if this had continued to be the case. But with the scholasticism of the Middle Ages, the speculative element entered into the view of the atonement. It has been estimated that fully fifteen theories, so called, of the atonement have been formulated. Of these, six merit our attention: five, which we believe to be untrue to the Scriptures; and the last one, which we believe to be the true Biblical view.

A. The Socinian, or Example Theory of the Atonement.

1. Statement.

"This theory held that subjective sinfulness is the sole barrier between man and God. Not God, but only man, needs to be reconciled. This can be effected by man's own will, through repentance and reformation. The death of Christ is but the death of a noble martyr. He redeems us, only as His human example of faithfulness to duty has a powerful influence upon our moral improvement. This fact the apostles, either consciously or unconsciously, clothed in the language of the Greek and Jewish sacrifices" (Strong).

NOTE: This theory was fully elaborated by Laelius Socinus

and Faustus Socinus, of Poland, in the 16th century. Its moder.. representatives are Unitarians.

2. Objections.

a. Philosophically, it is based upon false principles; for example, that will is simply the volitional faculty; that utility is the basis of virtue; that law is the expression of arbitrary will; that penalty is a means of reforming the offender; and that righteousness, in either God or man, is only the manifestation of benevolence.

b. Historically, it is the outgrowth of the Pelagian view of sin, and "logically necessitates a curtailment or surrender of every other characteristic doctrine of Christianity—inspiration, sin, the deity of Christ, justification, regeneration, and eternal retribution" (Strong).

Note: Pelagianism was the denial of total depravity in man and the affirmation of "ability"—that is, that man by his own efforts, with divine help, is capable of salvation. The Socinian theory requires the abandonment of the doctrine of inspiration because throughout the Scriptures a vicarious and expiatory sacrifice is presented; the doctrine of sin, because sin as objective guilt and subjective defilement is denied; the doctrine of Christ's deity, because if man can save himself, he has no need of an infinite sacrifice by an infinite Saviour; the doctrine of justification, because it denies our being declared innocent before the law on account of anything Christ has done; the doctrine of regeneration, because it denies the necessity of the birth from above; and the doctrine of eternal retribution, because "this is no longer appropriate to finite transgression of arbitrary law, and to superficial sinning that does not involve nature" (Strong).

c. Scripturally, it contradicts the fact that sin involves objective guilt as well as subjective defilement; that God's holiness requires Him to punish sin; that the atonement was vicarious and substitutional; and that such vicarious and substitutional bearing of sin was necessary in order to furnish a ground whereby God might show favor to the guilty.

d. Again, "it furnishes no proper explanation of the sufferings and death of Christ. The unmartyrlike anguish cannot be accounted for, and the forsaking by the Father cannot be justified upon the hypothesis that Christ died as a mere witness to truth. See Psalm 22. If Christ's sufferings were not propitiatory, they neither furnish us with a perfect example, nor constitute a manifestation of the love of God" (Strong).

e. Once more, it makes the chief result of Christ's death what at most can only be a subordinate result; for neither Scripture nor Christian experience finds in Christ's example the principal motive of His death. "Mere example is but a new preaching of the law, which repels and condemns. The cross has power to lead men to holiness, only as it first shows a satisfaction made for sins. Accordingly, most of the passages which represent Christ as an example also contain references to His propitiatory work" (Strong). See I Peter 2.21.

f. Finally, it "contradicts the whole tenor of the New Testament in making the life, and not the death, of Christ the most significant and important feature of His work. The constant allusions to the death of Christ as the source of salvation, as well as the symbolism of the ordinances, cannot be explained upon a theory which regards Christ as a mere example, and considers His sufferings as incidents, rather than essentials, of His work" (Strong).

B. The Bushnellian, or Moral Influence Theory of the Atonement.

1. Statement.

"This theory holds, like the Socinian, that there is no principle of the divine nature which is propitiated by Christ's death; but that this death is a manifestation of the love of God, suffering in and with the sins of His creatures. Christ's atonement, therefore, is the merely natural consequence of His taking human nature upon Him; and is a suffering, not of penalty in man's stead, but of the combined woes and griefs which the living of a human life involves. This atonement has effect, not to satisfy divine justice, but so to reveal divine love as to soften human hearts and to lead them to repentance; in other words, Christ's sufferings were necessary, not in order to remove an obstacle to the pardon of sinners which exists in the mind of God, but in order to convince sinners that there exists no such obstacle" (Strong).

NOTE: This theory was held by Horace Bushnell, of New England, and by Robertson, Maurice, Campbell, and Young, of Great Britain, and by Schleiermacher and Ritschl, of Germany.

2. Objections.

a. It is open to the same objection as the example theory of the atonement, in that it magnifies a subordinate into the principal effect of Christ's death. Our Lord's sufferings do produce a moral effect upon men; but suffering *with* the sinner is one thing and suffering *in his stead* quite another.

b. Again, as Dr. Strong points out, like the example theory, it rests upon false philosophical principles: as, "that righteousness is identical with benevolence, instead of conditioning it; that God is subject to an eternal law of love, instead of being Himself the source of all law; that the aim of penalty is the reformation of the offender."

c. Again, it furnishes no proper reason for Christ's sufferings. "While it shows that the Saviour necessarily suffers from His contact with human sin and sorrow, it gives no explanation of that constitution of the universe which makes suffering the consequence of sin, not only to the sinner, but also to the innocent being who comes into contact with sin. The holiness of God, which is manifested in this constitution of things and which requires this atonement, is entirely ignored" (Strong).

d. Again, it contradicts the teaching of the Scriptures, like the example theory, in that it asserts that the atonement was necessary, not to satisfy God's justice, but merely to reveal His love; that Christ's sufferings were not propitiatory and penal; and that the human conscience does not need to be propitiated by Christ's sacrifice before it can feel the moral influence of His sufferings.

e. Again, "it can be maintained only by wresting from their obvious meaning those passages of Scripture which speak of Christ as suffering for our sins; which represent His blood as accomplishing something in heaven when presented there by our Intercessor; which declare forgiveness to be a remitting of past offenses upon the ground of Christ's death; and which describe justification as a pronouncing, not a making, just" (Strong).

f. And again, "this theory confounds God's method of saving men with men's experience of being saved. It makes the atonement itself consist of its effect in the believer's union with Christ and the purifying influence of that union upon the character and life" (Strong).

g. Finally, "the theory confines the influence of the atonement to those who have heard it,—thus excluding patriarchs and heathen. But the Scriptures represent Christ as being the Saviour of all men, in the sense of securing them grace, which, but for His atoning work, could never have been bestowed consistently with the divine holiness" (Strong).

C. The Grotian, or Governmental Theory of the Atonement.

1. Statement.

"The vicarious sufferings of Christ are an atonement for sin as a *conditional substitute* for penalty, fulfilling, on the forgiveness of sin, the obligation of justice and the office of penalty in moral government" (John Miley, of Drew).

"This theory holds that the atonement is a satisfaction, not to any internal principle of the divine nature, but to the necessities of government. God's government of the universe cannot be maintained, nor can the divine law preserve its authority over its subjects, unless the pardon of offenders is accompanied by some exhibition of the high estimate which God sets upon His law and the heinous guilt of violating it. Such an exhibition of divine regard for the law is furnished in the sufferings and death of Christ. Christ does not suffer the precise penalty of the law, but God graciously accepts His suffering as a substitute for the penalty. This bearing of substituted suffering on the part of Christ gives the divine law such hold upon the consciences and hearts of men, that

God can pardon the guilty upon their repentance, without detriment to the interests of His government" (Strong).

NOTE: This theory was originated by Hugo Grotius, the Dutch jurist and theologian (1583-1645). It is commonly known as Arminianism. It is held prominently by the Wesleyan and Methodist Churches.

2. Objections.

a. Like the example and moral influence theories, it has the fatal defect of substituting for the principal aim of the atonement a subordinate one, namely, the securing of the interests of God's government.

b. Like the two former theories, it rests upon false philosophical principles: "that utility is the ground of moral obligation; that law is an expression of the will, rather than of the nature, of God; that the aim of penalty is to deter from the commission of offenses; and that righteousness is resolvable into benevolence" (Strong).

c. Again, it "ignores and virtually denies that immanent holiness of God of which law with its threatened penalties, and the human conscience with its demand for punishment, are only finite reflections. There is something back of government, and if the atonement satisfies government, it must be by satisfying that justice of God, of which government is the expression" (Strong).

d. Again, it "makes that to be an *exhibition* of

justice which is not an exercise of justice; the atonement being, according to this theory, not an execution of law, but an exhibition of regard for law, which will make it safe to pardon the violators of law. Such a scenic representation can inspire respect for law, only so long as the essential unreality of it is unsuspected" (Strong).

e. Again, it makes the sufferings of Christ in the garden and on the cross inexplicable "upon the theory that the atonement was a histrionic (that is, a kind of theatrical) exhibition of God's regard for His government, and can be explained only upon the view that Christ actually endured the wrath of God against human sin" (Strong).

f. Again, "the actual power of the atonement over the human conscience and heart is due, not to its exhibiting God's regard for law, but to its exhibiting an actual execution of law, and an actual satisfaction of violated holiness made by Christ in the sinner's stead" (Strong).

g. Finally, "the theory contradicts all those passages of Scripture which represent the atonement as necessary; as propitiating God Himself; as being a revelation of God's righteousness; as being an execution of the penalty of the law; as making salvation a matter of debt to the believer, on the ground of what Christ has done; as actually purging our sins, instead of making that purging possible; as not simply assuring the sinner that God may now pardon him on account of what Christ has done, but that Christ has actually wrought out a complete salvation, and will bestow it upon all who come to Him" (Strong).

D. The Irvingian, or Theory of Gradually Extirpated Depravity.

1. Statement.

"This theory holds that, in His incarnation, Christ took human nature as it was in Adam, not before the Fall, but after the Fall,—human nature, therefore, with its inborn corruption and predisposition to evil; that, notwithstanding the possession of this tainted and depraved nature, Christ, through the power of the Holy Spirit, or of His divine nature, not only kept His human nature from manifesting itself in any actual or personal sin, but completely purified it through struggle and suffering, until in His death He completely extirpated its original depravity, and reunited it to God. This subjective purification of human nature in the person of Jesus Christ constitutes His atonement, and men are saved, not by any objective propitiation, but only by becoming through faith partakers of Christ's new humanity" (Strong).

NOTE: This theory was elaborated by Edward Irving, of England (1792-1834), and is held in substance by some German scholars.

2. Objections.

a. It recognizes an important truth in the fact of the new humanity of Christ, of which all believers are partakers by faith; but it denies the fact of an objective atonement, through which alone we can receive this new spiritual humanity.

b. It rests upon false fundamental principles, namely: that law is identical with the natural order of the universe, and as such, is an exhaustive expression of the will and nature of God; that sin is simply a power of moral evil within the soul, instead of also involving an objective guilt and desert of punishment; that penalty is the mere reaction of law against the transgressor, instead of being also the revelation of a personal wrath against sin; that the evil taint of human nature can be extirpated by suffering its natural consequences,—penalty in this way reforming the sinner" (Strong).

c. It contradicts the plain teaching of Scripture, namely: "with regard to Christ's freedom from all taint of human depravity; misrepresents His life as a growing consciousness of the underlying corruption of His human nature, which culminated at Gethsemane and Calvary; and denies the truth of His own statements when it declares that He must have died on account of His own depravity, even though none were to be saved thereby" (Strong).

d. Again, "it makes the active obedience of Christ

and the subjective purification of His human nature to be the chief features of His work, while the Scriptures make His death and passive bearing of penalty the center of all, and ever regard Him as One who is personally pure and who vicariously bears the punishment of the guilty" (Strong).

e. Finally, the theory requires the "surrender of the doctrine of Justification, as a merely declaratory act of God; and requires such a view of the divine holiness, expressed only through the order of nature, as can be maintained only upon principles of pantheism" (Strong).

Note: The theory rests upon three chief arguments: First, that Paul teaches it in Romans 8.3: "God having sent his own Son *in the likeness of sinful flesh.*" To this Dr. Farr replies: "If Paul's language were 'in sinful flesh,' the theory would be plainly taught, but it is not. His words signify that the flesh of Christ was like the flesh of sin, inasmuch as it was flesh, but unlike, inasmuch as it was not affected with sin. Paul could not have said 'in sinful flesh' without making Christ partaker of sin. He could not have said merely 'in flesh,' for then the bond between the manhood of Jesus and sin would have been wanting. He says, 'in likeness of flesh and sin,' meaning that Christ had a nature like sinful human nature but He had not Himself a sinful nature." Second, that it is clearly implied in the susceptibility of Christ to temptation and especially in knowing by experience how to succor those who are tempted, the latter being sinners. Again Dr. Farr replies: "This argument is plausible, but not conclusive. For if it be necessary to have a depraved nature in order to feel the force of temptation, then Adam and the angels must have been created with depraved natures. Also, if it be necessary to have been in the moral nature of sinners who are tempted, in order to succor them, Christ must have had not only a sinful nature but also a habit of sinning to qualify Him for His work." Third, that it is implied in a proper view of the atonement, because humanity in its fallen nature was summed up in the humanity of Christ and in that humanity paid the just penalty for all its sin. Once again Dr. Farr answers: "But the idea that the human nature of Christ was the whole human nature, in any other sense than that in which human nature is entire in any other, is a mere fiction and fancy. If He bore the penalty of sin at all, it was not the penalty of His own personal sin, or sinfulness, but the penalty due to others for their sins. Bearing the penalty of His own sinfulness would not help them, unless it were in turn to bear the penalty of their sinfulness. This is self-evident and if there were anything vicarious in His suffering it presupposes His holiness rather than His sinfulness."

E. The Anselmic, or Commercial Theory of the Atonement.

1. Statement.

"This holds that sin is a violation of the divine honor or majesty, and, as committed against an infinite being, deserves an infinite punishment; that the majesty of God requires Him to execute punishment, while the love of God pleads for the sparing of the guilty; that this conflict of divine attributes is eternally reconciled by the voluntary sacrifice of the God-man, who bears in the virtue of the dignity of His person the intensively infinite punishment of sin, which must otherwise have been suffered extensively

18

and eternally by sinners; that this suffering of the God-man presents to the divine majesty an exact equivalent for the deserved sufferings of the elect; and that, as the result of this satisfaction of the divine claims, the elect sinners are pardoned and regenerated" (Strong).

NOTE: This theory was first held by Anselm, of Canterbury, (1033-1109), who propounded it as a substitute for an earlier patristic view that Christ's death was a ransom paid to Satan, to deliver sinners from his power. Many Scotch theologians hold this view.

2. Objections.

a. It recognized an all-important truth in the fact that Christ's death satisfied a principle of the nature of Deity, but it errs in representing the majesty of honor as higher than the holiness of God; while it is seriously at fault in admitting a conflict between the divine attributes.

b. It overlooks entirely the value of the active obedience of Christ, and of His holy life.

c. It gives "disproportionate weight to those passages of Scripture which represent the atonement under commercial analogies, as the payment of a ransom or debt, to the exclusion of those which describe it as an ethical fact, whose value is to be estimated not quantitatively, but qualitatively" (Strong).

d. It limits the extent of the atonement to the

elect, thus ignoring the teaching of the Scripture that Christ died for all.

e. It is "defective in holding to a merely external transfer of the merit of Christ's work, while it does not clearly state the internal ground of that transfer, in the union of the believer with Christ" (Strong).

F. Substitutional, or Satisfaction Theory of the Atonement.

This theory, the first suggestions of which are found in the writings of Augustine (4th century), was elaborated by John Calvin (16th century), and is today held by the Reformed and Presbyterian theologies. It is commonly known as Calvinism; sometimes it is called the "Orthodox Theory," or "Ethical Theory." It is, we believe, the true Scriptural view.

a. Preliminary Points.

1. **The theory holds to a twofold element in Christ's substitution, namely:** a vicarious obedience (known theologically as "active obedience") for righteousness, and a vicarious punishment (known theologically as "passive obedience") for sin. Thus, Christ takes the place of sinners in both penalty and precept, and, as their substitute, endures the punishment which on account of sin they deserve, and in His obedience fulfils the righteousness required of them.

2. Two Kinds of Substitution.

There are two kinds of substitution, namely: **unconditional,** which grants full and absolute deliverance to those for whom substitution is made; and **conditional,** which grants deliverance to those for whom substitution is made only on the terms agreed upon between the one who makes the substitution and the one who accepts it. Christ's substitution was conditional, dependent upon the repentance and faith of sinners.

3. Two Kinds of Satisfaction.

"The **satisfaction of Christ** means all He has done to satisfy the demands of the holiness and law of God in the place of and in behalf of sinners." There are two kinds of satisfaction, namely: **pecuniary,** a money payment, which can be made by anyone, and **penal,** blood payment, which can be made only by the guilty. Christ's satisfaction was penal; the atonement was in His blood.

4. Three Kinds of Penal Satisfaction.

There are three kinds of penal (that is, vicariously penal) satisfaction. First, **identical.** Christ's death was not identical because the death of one could not be the same as the death of many: Mark 10.45. Second, **equal.** Christ's satisfaction was not equal, because the death of the entire race of finite beings would not be equal to the death of the Infinite Being,

Jesus Christ. Third, **equivalent**. Christ's satisfaction was equivalent, because one infinite factor, Jesus Christ, is inconceivably greater than all the finite factors making up the race of Adam. Illustration: a gold eagle ($10) weighs less than 500 pennies, but has double the value.

b. The Two Questions Stated.

There are two questions which conduct us into the heart of the atonement. And the answers to these questions give us its true philosophy. First: What did the atonement accomplish? Or, what was the object of Christ's death? Second: What were the means used? Or, how could Christ justly die? The answer to the former question views the atonement in its relation to God. The answer to the latter question views the atonement in its relation to man. Again, the answer to the first question is an unfolding of the meaning of Romans 3.25, 26. The answer to the second question is an unfolding of the meaning of II Cor. 5.21.

c. The First Question Considered.

What did the atonement accomplish? Or, what was the object of Christ's death? Briefly, the answer is threefold:

1. It satisfied the outraged holiness of God:

Psalm 22; Isa. 53; Rom. 3.25, 26; 4.25; 8.3; Gal. 1.4; 3.13; Heb. 9.15; I John 2.2; 4.10.

2. It avenged the violated law of God: Gen 2.17; Ezek. 18.4, 20; Rom. 6.23.

3. It exhibited the love of God, thereby furnishing man a motive for repentance from sin and faith towards Christ: John 3.16; 15.13; Rom. 5.8; I Pet. 2.21; I John 4.9, 10.

In viewing this aspect of the atonement Dr. Strong declares: "Its necessity is grounded in the holiness of God, of which conscience in man is a finite reflection. There is an ethical principle in the divine nature, which demands that sin shall be punished. Aside from its results, sin is essentially ill-deserving. As we who are made in God's image mark our growth in purity by the increasing quickness with which we detect impurity, and the increasing hatred which we feel toward it, so infinite purity is a consuming fire to all iniquity. As there is an ethical demand in our natures that not only others' wickedness, but our own wickedness, be visited with punishment, and a keen conscience that cannot rest till it has made satisfaction to justice for its misdeeds, so there is an ethical demand of God's nature that penalty follows sin." The same writer continues: "Punishment is the constitutional reaction of God's being against moral evil—the self-assertion of infinite holiness against its antagonist and would-be destroyer. In God this demand is devoid of all passion, and is consistent with infinite benevolence. It is a demand that cannot be evaded, since the holiness from which it springs is unchanging. The atonement is, therefore, a satisfaction of the ethical demand of the divine nature, by the substitution of Christ's penal sufferings for the punishment of the guilty. This substitution is unknown to mere law, and above and beyond the powers of law. It is an operation of grace. Grace, however, does not violate or suspend law, but takes it up into itself and fulfils it. The righteousness of law is maintained, in that the source of all law, the Judge and Punisher, Himself voluntarily submits to bear the penalty, and bears it in the human nature that has sinned. Thus the atonement answers the ethical demand of the divine nature that sin be punished if the offender is to go free. The interests of the divine government are secured as a first subordinate result of this satisfaction to God Himself, of whose nature the government is an expression: while, as a second subordinate result, provision is made for the needs of human nature—on the one hand the need of objective satisfaction to the ethical demand of punishment for sin, and on the other hand the need of a manifestation of divine love and mercy that will affect the heart and move it to repentance."

NOTE on Romans 3.25, 26. These verses expand the subject of the epistle—the revelation of the "righteousness of God," righteousness being that which God both provides and accepts. This righteousness is mentioned in 1.17, and in 1.18-3.20 it is shown to be the only means whereby both Jew and Gentile can be saved. The commentator Meyer points out that in verse 25 the phrase "in His blood" is to be taken with the verb "set forth." The purpose of this setting forth in Christ's blood he says is "for the display of God's judicial and punitive righteousness, which received its satisfaction in the death of Christ as a propitiatory offering, and was thereby practically demonstrated and exhibited." On the expression "for the remission (literally, passing over) of sins that are past," Meyer's comment is: "because He (God) had allowed the pre-Christian sins to go without punishment, whereby His righteousness had been lost sight of and obscured, and had come to need an exhibition to men." "Omittance," he says, "is not acquaintance; the passing over or passing by is intermediate between pardon and punishment. 'Through the forbearance of God' expresses the motive of the 'passing over or passing by.' Before Christ's sacrifice, God's administration was a scandal—it needed vindication. The atonement is God's answer to the charge of freeing the guilty." On verse 26 Meyer says that it presents the final purpose of God's act as set forth in verse 25, namely, "God's *being just* and His *appearing just* in consequence of this." On the whole passage Strong's comment is that it shows: (1) That Christ's death is a propitiatory sacrifice; (2) That its first and main effect is upon God; (3) That the particular attribute of God which demands the atonement is His justice, or holiness; (4) That the satisfaction of this holiness is the necessary condition of God's justifying the believer.

d. The Second Question Considered.

With respect to the atonement, what were the means used: or how could Christ justly die?

Briefly, the answer is threefold:

1. He took our flesh: John 1.14; Rom. 8.3; Gal. 4.4; Heb. 2.14-18.

2. He assumed our guilt: II Cor. 5.21; Gal. 3.13.

3. He bore our penalty: Isa. 53.4, 5; Matt. 20.28; II Cor. 5.21; Gal. 2.20; 3.13; I Pet. 2.24.

The consequences of Adam's sin, both to himself and to his posterity, are:

1. Depravity, or corruption of human nature.

2. Guilt, or obligation to make satisfaction for sin to the holiness and the law of God.

3. Penalty, or actual endurance of loss or suffering as punishment for sin. If Christ had entered the world in the natural way, He would have had depravity; but through His virgin birth He escaped it: Luke 1.35; II Cor. 5.21; Heb. 7.26. However, together with His partaking of our common humanity Christ assumed guilt with its consequent penalty. The guilt which our Lord assumed was not of course the guilt of personal sin. It could not be. This is proved by the transfiguration. The transfiguration marks the close to a sinless life, a life having taken on humanity immaculately conceived, and having passed through the course of human existence without the least taint of sin. God's voice, "This is my beloved Son in whom I am well pleased," assures us of Christ's absolute sinlessness. "The Lord hath laid on him

the iniquity of us all," Isa. 53.6, but it was *our* iniquity, not His that was laid upon Him. It was not in His birth, but in His death on the cross that the assumption of our guilt took place.

In attempting to explain how Christ could justly suffer, the innocent for the guilty, we must keep in mind that it is not the act of the cross which is to be justified primarily, but God who is to be justified by the act of the cross (Rom. 3.25, 26). Moreover, the solution does not lie in making human comparisons (such as, the innocent for the guilty) but in seeing Infinity *voluntarily* bearing the guilt of the finite. This was done "through the obedience of one" (Rom. 5.17-19). The cross is in God's *eternal* plan (both before and after time) and is a necessary and adequate expression of a God of holiness, justice, righteousness, love, and mercy.

The *ground* of His substitutional death is His voluntary reception of our guilt, and God's act in laying it upon Him. The death was *just* in that it was *voluntarily* assumed: "I lay it down of myself," John 10.18. It was *vicarious* in that it was voluntarily assumed by a perfect, righteous One. It was *complete* and *acceptable* in that God raised Him (the Sacrifice) from the dead.

The suffering of Christ, according to Dr. Strong, "was the enduring of the reaction of the divine holiness against sin and so was a bearing of penalty (Isa. 53.6; Gal. 3.13); but it was also the voluntary execution of a plan that antedated creation (Phil. 2.6, 7), and Christ's sacrifice in time showed what had been in the heart of God from eternity (Heb. 9.14; Rev. 13.8)."

NOTE on II Corinthians 5.21. This verse gives us the scriptural support for the view that Christ assumed our guilt and so justly bore our penalty. Notice these three points:

1. Our Lord had no depravity. "Him who knew no sin"; this expression teaches us Christ's sinlessness.

2. Our Lord incurred our guilt. "He was made to be sin for us." Since Christ had no depravity of nature, sin here must mean guilt, that is, obligation to suffer for sin. Indeed, Meyer calls attention to a parallel of meaning between "sin" here and "righteousness" a little later in the verse. He says that if *righteousness* means *holiness,* then *sin* must mean *depravity;* but if *righteousness* means *justification,* then *sin* must mean *condemnation.* Of course, the latter is the true meaning; that is, Christ was constituted a condemned person in order that the believer might in Him be constituted a justified person.

3. Our Lord bore our penalty. "He was made to be a sin offering for us." The term sin here must carry the double meaning of guilt and penalty: Heb. 10.18.

TOPIC THREE: CHRIST AS KING.

NOTE: The third topic under the work of Christ, namely His Kingship, belongs more properly to Eschatology, and in particular to the study of the Millennium. Accordingly, its treatment will be presented there.

QUESTIONS FOR STUDY,

1. What was the extent of Christ's prophetic ministry?

2. What was the twofold nature of the prophetic office?

3. In what five ways did Christ fulfil His prophetic ministry?

4. What is the extent of Christ's priestly ministry?

5. State clearly the idea of the priestly office.

6. What was the threefold scope of the Old Testament priesthood?

7. Trace the parallelism between the three steps in the work of the atonement in the Old Testament and in the ministry of Christ.

8. Mention five types of the atonement in the Old Testament. Give references for all and discuss one of the types.

9. Mention five predictions of the atonement in the Old Testament. Give references and discuss one of the predictions.

10. Mention five New Testament witnessing terms of the atonement. Give references for all and discuss one of the terms.

11. Show the fourfold necessity of the atonement.

12. What is the extent of the atonement?

13. What is the Socinian, or Example Theory of the atonement? What facts, Scriptural and otherwise, refute it?

14. What is the Bushnellian, or Moral Influence Theory of the atonement? What facts, Scriptural and otherwise, refute it?

15. What is the Grotian, or Governmental Theory of the atonement? What facts, Scriptural or otherwise, refute it?

16. What is the Irvingian, or Theory of Gradually Extirpated Depravity? What facts, Scriptural or otherwise, refute it?

17. What is the Anselmic, or Commercial Theory of the atonement? What facts, Scriptural or otherwise, refute it?

18. What, briefly, is the Satisfaction Theory of the atonement? (a) What are the two kinds of substitution? (b) What are the two kinds of satisfaction? (c) What are the three kinds of penal satisfaction?

19. What two questions conduct into the heart of the atonement?

20. What is the threefold answer to the first question?

21. Give a brief exposition of Romans 3.25, 26.

22. What is the threefold answer to the second question?

23. Give a brief exposition of II Corinthians 5.21.

DOCTRINE SEVEN: PNEUMATOLOGY.

Part One: The Person of the Holy Spirit.

Topics.

I. Personality.

II. Deity.

III. Names.

IV. Symbols.

Part Two: The Work of the Holy Spirit.

Topics.

I. The Holy Spirit in Creation.

II. The Holy Spirit in Christ.

III. The Holy Spirit in the Scriptures.

IV. The Holy Spirit in the Old and New Dispensations.

V. The Holy Spirit in the Church.

VI. The Holy Spirit in the World.

VII. The Holy Spirit in the Believer.

CHAPTER VII.

PNEUMATOLOGY.

PART ONE.

THE PERSON OF THE HOLY SPIRIT.

TOPIC ONE: PERSONALITY.

I. STATEMENT.

That the Holy Spirit is not an impersonal force, nor a mere influence, but possesses full, distinct personality, is the clear and unmistakable teaching of Scripture.

Note: "A person is that which, when speaking, says 'I'; when spoken to, is called 'thou'; and when spoken of, is called 'his' or 'him'" (Farr).

II. PROOF.

That the Holy Spirit possesses personality the following facts prove:

19

A. Personal pronouns are used in relation to Him:
John 14.16, 17; 15.26; 16.7-14.

NOTE: The Greek noun for Spirit, literally signifying breath or wind, is *pneuma*, and is in the neuter. Yet in John 16.14 the masculine demonstrative pronoun *that one* (*ekeinos*) is employed, and in Eph. 1.14 (according to the best MSS.) the masculine relative pronoun *who* (*os*) is used.

B. Personal qualities are ascribed to Him:
1. Knowledge, I Cor. 2.10-13; 12.8.
2. Love, Rom. 15.30.
3. Will, I Cor. 12.11.

C. Personal acts are attributed to Him:
1. Searches deep things of God, I Cor. 2.10.
2. Speaks, Acts 13.2; 21.11; Rev. 2.7, 11, 17, 29.
3. Intercedes, Rom. 8.26.
4. Testifies, John 15.26.
5. Teaches, John 14.26.
6. Guides, Acts 16.6.
7. Commands and appoints, Acts 13.2, 4; 20.28.
8. Communes, II Cor. 13.14.
9. Works miracles, Acts 8.39; 10.38.

D. Personal treatments are accorded Him:
1. Grieved and rebelled against, Gen. 6.3; Isa. 63.10; Acts 7.51; Eph. 4.30.
2. Done despite to, Heb. 10.29.
3. Lied unto, Acts 5.3.

TOPIC TWO: DEITY.

I. STATEMENT.

That the Holy Spirit is a divine person is the clear and unmistakable teaching of the Scripture.

NOTE: The word *person* in relation to the Trinity must not be understood in the exact sense in which it is applied to human beings. This is true because the Three Persons, so-called, of the Godhead constitute but one God: Deut. 6.4. As used of the Trinity, the term *person* simply means that there are personal distinctions in the Godhead.

II. PROOF.

That the Holy Spirit possesses essential Deity, the following facts prove:

A. Divine attributes and perfections are ascribed to Him:

1. Eternity, Heb. 9.14.
2. Omniscience, John 14.26; 16.12, 13. (R. V.); I Cor. 2.10.
3. Omnipotence, Luke 1.35
4. Omnipresence, Psa. 139.7-10.

B. Divine works are ascribed to Him:

1. Creation, Job 33.4; Psa. 104.30.
2. Life-giving, Gen. 2.7; John 6.63; Rom. 8.2.
3. Prophecy, II Sam. 23.2, 3; II Peter 1.21.

C. The name of the Holy Spirit is coupled in equality with the names of God and Christ.

1. Apostolic Commission, Matt. 28.19.
2. Apostolic Benediction, II Cor. 13.14.
3. Administration of the Church, I Cor. 12.4-6.

Note: In Eph 4.4-6 the name of the Holy Spirit occurs first and in Rom. 15.30 it occurs second.

D. The Holy Spirit is identified with Jehovah of the Old Testament: Isa. 6.8-10 with Acts 28.25-27; Jer. 31.31-34 with Heb. 10.15-17; Ex. 16.7; Heb. 3.7-9; Gen. 1.27; Job 33.4; Psa. 95.8-11.

E. The Holy Spirit can be blasphemed: Matt. 12.31.

F. The Holy Spirit can be worshiped: II Cor. 13. 14.

G. The Holy Spirit is called God and Lord: Acts 5.3; II Cor. 3.17, 18, R. V.

TOPIC THREE: NAMES.

The following are the principal Scriptural names of the Holy Spirit:

1. The Spirit, Psa. 104.30; John 3.6-8; I Cor. 2.10 (R. V.).
2. The Spirit of God, I Cor. 3.16.

3. The Spirit of Jehovah, Isa. 11.2; 61.1.

NOTE: When the word "Lord" in the Old Testament is written in capitals, the meaning is always "Jehovah."

4. The Spirit of the Living God, I. Cor. 3.3.
5. The Spirit of Christ, Rom. 8.9.
6. The Spirit of His Son, Gal. 4.6.
7. The Spirit of Jesus Christ, Phil. 1.19.
8. The Spirit of Jesus, Acts 16.7 (R. V.).
9. The Holy Spirit, Luke 11.13.

NOTE: The word Ghost is an old English word for Spirit.

10. The Spirit of Burning, Isa. 4.4.
11. The Spirit of Holiness, Rom. 1.4.
12. The Holy Spirit of Promise, Acts 1.4, 5; Eph. 1.13.
13. The Spirit of Truth, John 14.17; 15.26; 16.13.
14. The Spirit of Life, Rom. 8.2.
15. The Spirit of Grace, Heb. 10.29.
16. The Spirit of Glory, I Peter 4.14.
17. The Eternal Spirit, Heb. 9.14.
18. The Comforter, John 14.26; 15.26.

NOTE: A better translation of the Greek word would be Paraclete, which literally signifies "one called to the side," i. e., for help.

All these names have spiritual significance, and we may know the Holy Spirit experimentally in the various relationships expressed by His names.

TOPIC FOUR: SYMBOLS.

The principal symbols of the Holy Spirit are the Dove, Water, Fire, Wind, Wine, and Oil.

NOTE: The term "symbol," from two Greek words *sun*, together, and *ballo*, to throw, signifies, literally, something thrown alongside of another, that is, to represent and explain it. In other words, a symbol is a material emblem portraying and unfolding a spiritual reality.

I. THE DOVE.

The scene at Jesus' baptism, when the Holy Spirit descended upon Him "like a dove," shows clearly that the Dove is a symbol of the Holy Spirit: Matt. 3.16; Mark 1.10; Luke 3.22; John 1.32.

The following traits of the Dove in Scripture may be noted:

1. Love, Song of Songs 5.2; Rom. 5.5; 15.30; Gal. 5.22, 23.

2. Purity, Song of Songs 5.2; 6.9.

NOTE: In Leviticus the dove is a sacrificial bird and hence clean.

3. Peace, Gen. 8.8-12; Psa. 55.6; Song of Songs 2.12 (R.V. turtle dove); Gal. 5.22.

4. Modesty, Song of Songs 2.14; John 16.13. See also Isa. 42.1, 2.

5. Harmlessness and Innocence, Matt. 10.16.

NOTE: The dove has no gall. The Holy Spirit can be grieved, but not angered: Eph. 4.30.

6. Beauty, Psa. 68.13; Song of Songs, 1.15; 2.14.

7. Tenderness and Gentleness, Isa. 38.14; 59.11.

NOTE: "The dove possesses a special fondness for a home, Isa. 60.8, and it is a bird that instincts the change of seasons, Jer. 8.7. (R. V.) See also Song of Songs 2.12" (Schultz).

II. WATER.

Water is a double symbol—of the Word and of the Spirit.

1. As a symbol of the Word it represents cleansing: Psa. 119.9; John 15.3; 17.17, 19; Eph. 5.26.

2. As a symbol of the Spirit it represents refreshment, satisfaction, and fulness: Psa. 72.6; Isa. 41.18; 43.19; 44.3; John 4.14; 7.37-39; Rev. 21.6; 22.17.

NOTE: "This water comes out of the rock, Psa. 105.41; I Cor. 10.4; out of the well, John 4.14; out of the clouds, Acts 2.33; 3.19; out of the Word, Isa. 55.10, 11. Moreover, it is like a well springing up, John 4.14; like a bucket pouring out, Num. 24.7; like clouds showering down, Joel 2.28, 29; Mal. 3.10; Acts 2.33; like rivers flowing, Ezek. 47; and like the dew silently dropping, Deut. 33.28; Prov. 3.20" (Schultz).

III. FIRE.

Like water, fire is also a double symbol—of the Word and of the Spirit.

A. As a symbol of the Word it signifies searching and purification, Jer. 23.29.

B. As a symbol of the Spirit it represents three things, namely:

　1. The presence of God, Ex. 3.2-6; I Kings 18.38; Isa. 63.9-14; Acts 2.3.

　2. The power of God (same references as above).

　3. The purging of God, Isa. 4.4; 6.6, 7; Mal. 3.3; Matt. 3.11; Heb. 12.29.

NOTE: "This symbol does not so much suggest consumption and combustion as the subtle electric energy. It is an all-prevailing mighty force, energizing, illuminating, beautifying, and working all manner of wonders. . . . Fire is the great purifying and cleansing agent in nature. What fire is to the natural world, the Holy Spirit is to the supernatural world" (Farr).

IV. WIND.

This symbol denotes life and activity. It refers particularly to two aspects of the Spirit's work in man, namely:

　1. Born of the Spirit, Gen. 2.7; Ezek. 37.5-10; John 3.3-8; Titus 3.5.

　2. Baptized with the Spirit, Matt. 3.11 (*with* in the R. V. is rendered *in*); Mark 1.8; Luke 3.16; Acts 1.5.

NOTE: Dr. Farr says, "This symbol suggests the idea of universal expansion, life, and activity. Air is everywhere, touching, penetrating, and sustaining all things. Wind is air in motion; gently, in a breeze, swiftly, in a gale; and by the circulation of air currents, healthfulness and purity are carried over the earth. The Holy Spirit is likewise the source and producer of natural, intellectual, and spiritual life, purity, and power."

V. WINE.

As a symbol of the Spirit, wine stands for stimulation, exhilaration, and hence, rejoicing: Psa. 104.15; Prov. 31.6; Isa. 55.1; Luke 5.37-39; John 2.1-11; Acts 2.13; Eph. 5.18.

NOTE: Dr. Farr says, "In Eph. 5.18, two possible sources of stimulation are indicated—drunkenness and Deity; full of wine or full of the Spirit. Satan was called by Augustine *Simius Dei,* the ape of God, because he counterfeits the work of God. Human nature needs a stimulus of some kind. Doubtless, the Holy Spirit was intended to be the only original stimulus of humanity, but Satan has invented alcohol as a substitute, stealing the nomenclature of the truth to mask the lie, i. e., *aqua vitae, eau de vie."*

VI. OIL.

The name Messiah in both Hebrew and Greek signifies the anointed one: Isa. 61.1-3; Luke 4.14-18. The key to the meaning of oil as a symbol of the Spirit is I Sam. 16.13. It signifies:

1. Enduement of gifts for ministry, Isa. 61.1; Acts 10.38; I Cor. 12.7-11.

2. Bestowment of graces for living, Psa. 23.5; Gal. 5.22, 23.

3. Healing for the body, Isa 1.6; James 5.14.

4. Illumination and revelation, John 16.12-15; I Cor. 2.9-16; Eph. 1.17-18; I John 2.20, 27.

PNEUMATOLOGY.

PART TWO.

THE WORK OF THE HOLY SPIRIT.

In taking up the work of the Holy Spirit, a popular misconception needs to be removed. This is the result of the teaching of Sabellius, namely: that in creation, God the Father works; in redemption, God the Son works; and in salvation, God the Spirit works. Another way of putting it is, that the Old Testament dispensation was the dispensation of the Father; the New Testament dispensation, the dispensation of the Son; and the present dispensation, the dispensation of the Spirit. Quite to the contrary, the Scriptures teach that in every manifestation of the works of God, the Father, the Son, and the Spirit are alike active. Thus, to use the classification of Sabellius, in creation, in redemption, and in salvation, we trace the working of each member of the Trinity. And in general, the working of each member of the Trinity is this: in every divine activity, the power to bring forth proceeds from the Father; the power to arrange proceeds from the Son; and the power to perfect proceeds from the Spirit: Rom. 11.36; I Cor. 8.6. Consequently, the office work of the Holy Spirit in every phase and sphere of the divine activity is to bring forward to completion that which has been conceived by the Father and executed by the Son.

NOTE: The works of God have been divided theologically into His *indwelling* and *outgoing* works. The hidden or indwelling works concern God's invisible operations; the manifest or outgoing works concern His visible works or operations. The indwelling works belong to Eternity; the outgoing works belong to Time. From another point of view, the indwelling works relate to God's Being; the outgoing works relate to His Activities. For example, the question of the Trinity, the eternal generation of the Son, and the procession of the Spirit (whether from the Father alone or from the Father and the Son) refer to the indwelling works of God, which have not been fully revealed, and therefore cannot be clearly understood.

TOPIC ONE: THE HOLY SPIRIT IN CREATION.

I. AS THE WORK OF THE TRINITY.

In the Scriptures, creation is ascribed to each member of the Trinity:

1. The Father, Gen 1.1.
2. The Son, Col. 1.16; Heb. 11.3.
3. The Holy Spirit, Psa. 33.6; 104.30.

NOTE: In the work of creation, three forces are manifestly operating: a causative force proceeding from the Father; a constructive force, proceeding from the Son; and a perfective force, proceeding from the Holy Spirit.

II. AS THE WORK OF THE HOLY SPIRIT.

The special work of the Holy Spirit in creation is, as Dr. Kuyper, the Dutch theologian, expresses it, "To lead creation to its destiny, which is the glory of God." In other words, the particular work of the Holy Spirit is to sustain and mature life and to bring order and beauty into the universe. We note the following points:

1. Bringing order into the universe, Gen. 1.2.

2. Creating and garnishing the heavens, Job 26.13; Psa. 33.6; Isa. 40.12, 13.

3. Renewing the face of the earth, Psa. 104.30.

4. Sustaining vegetation, Psa. 104.10-13.

5. Sustaining the animal creation, Psa. 104.11, 12, 14, 21, 27.

6. Giving life to man, Gen. 2.7; Job 33.4.

7. Sustaining and controlling man's life, Gal. 5.22, 23; Eph. 5.18.

TOPIC TWO: THE HOLY SPIRIT IN CHRIST.

With respect to our Lord, the Holy Spirit fulfils a distinct office work. We may trace the following stages:

1. In the prediction of His coming, I Pet. 1.10-12.

2. In His birth of the virgin, Matt. 1.20; Luke 1.35.

3. In His symmetrical development, Luke 2.40, 52.

4. In His official consecration, Matt. 3.16, 17; Mark 1.9-11; Luke 3.21, 22; John 1.31-34. See Isa. 61.1-3 and Luke 4.16-22.

5. In His wilderness temptation, Matt. 4.1-11; Luke 4.1-13.

6. In His ministry of preaching and healing, Matt. 12.28; Luke 4.16-22; Acts 10.38.

7. In His death on the Cross, Heb. 9.14.

8. In His resurrection, Rom. 1.4; 8.11; I Tim. 3.16.

9. In His post-resurrection ministry, Acts 1.2.

10. In His bestowment of the Holy Spirit, John 15.26; Acts 2.33; Eph. 4.8. See Psa. 68.18.

11. In His representation by the Holy Spirit, John 14.16.

12. In His intercessory ministry, Rom. 8.26, 27, 34.

13. In His return, Rev. 22.17.

14. In His millennial reign, Isa. 32.15.

TOPIC THREE: THE HOLY SPIRIT IN THE SCRIPTURES.

In the Holy Scriptures, the Spirit of God has performed one of His greatest works: II Tim. 3.16; II Pet. 1.20, 21. This subject has been fully developed under Bibliology. Here we briefly notice a threefold work in giving the Scriptures:

1. Revelation, Gen. 3.16; Ex. 20.1-12; Rev. 1.1-12.

NOTE: Revelation in this connection means the giving new

truth which the unaided human mind could not discover.

2. Inspiration, II Sam. 23.1, 2; John 14.26; 15.26;

NOTE: Inspiration concerns the transmission of truth, both old and new.

3. Illumination, I Cor. 2.10-12; Eph. 1.17, 18.

NOTE 1. Illumination concerns the apprehension of revealed truth.

NOTE 2. The Holy Spirit also seals, interprets, and applies the Scriptures to our hearts.

TOPIC FOUR: THE HOLY SPIRIT IN THE OLD AND NEW DISPENSATIONS.

By the Old Dispensation is meant the period from Adam to Pentecost; by the New Dispensation is meant the period from Pentecost to the Second Coming of Christ.

A. Distinction between Dispensations.

The distinction between the work of the Spirit in the old dispensation and in the new is a difficult subject. After all is said that can be said, much more light is needed for clearness of apprehension and accuracy of statement. To begin with, it is quite commonly said that the difference is expressed by two Greek prepositions: *Upon* (*epi*), and *in* (*en*), i. e., that the Holy Spirit in the old dispensation came *upon* men, while in the new dispensation he *indwells* them. But this distinction will not hold, because in the Old Testament the Holy Spirit indwelt men, while in the New Testament He came upon men, that is, baptized them: Gen. 41.38; Ex. 31.3; Num. 27.18; Dan. 5.11; Luke 24.49; Acts 1.8 .   Perhaps the best point of approach to the subject is the Christian Church. In the Old Testament, except in type and symbol, there is no church, the body of Christ, of which He is the Head and which is the temple of the Holy Ghost. Have we not here the essential distinction in the office work of the Spirit of God in the two dispensations?   May we not say, then, that in the Old Testament age, *chosen individuals* were the objects of the Spirit's grace for life and gifts for service; while in the New Testament and the present age He works in and upon the *body of Christ* and individuals as *members* of that body? Individual persons—the body of Christ; these expressions give the key to the difference between the two dispensations: I Cor. 12.13.

B. The Work of the Spirit in the Old Dispensation.

Generally speaking, in the Old Testament age, we trace a threefold work of the Spirit:

1. His action upon the hearts of individuals, in saving grace; for example, Abel, Enoch, Noah, Abraham, Moses, Samuel, David, etc.: Gen. 5.22, 24 (Enoch); Heb. 11.5. (grace for life); Jude 14, 15 (gifts for service).

2. His action upon prophets, priests, and kings—a

wholly external operation to qualify them for office: Lev. 8.10; I Sam. 10.1.

3. His action upon divinely appointed workmen, in conferring gifts and talents for the service of the people: Ex. 31.2, 3, 6 (Aholiab and Bezaleel); Isa. 45.1; Zech. 4.6.

NOTE I. In his book on the Holy Spirit, Dr. G. Campbell Morgan mentions a fourfold work of the Holy Spirit in the Old Testament:

1. Coming upon men, literally, clothing Himself with them. For example, Judges 6.34.

2. Coming upon men mightily, literally, forcing them into something. For example, Samson, Judges 15.14.

3. Indwelling men; for example, Joseph and Joshua, Gen. 41.38; Num. 27.18.

4. Fitting and filling men for special service, Ex. 31.1, 2 (Aholiab and Bezaleel).

NOTE 2. In his little book, "Plain Papers on the Doctrine of the Holy Spirit," Dr. Scofield says, "In the Old Testament the Spirit of God is revealed as a divine person. As such He is associated in the work of Creation; strives with sinful man (Gen. 6.3); enlightens the spirit of man (Job 32.8; Prov. 20.27), gives skill to the hand (Ex. 31.2-5); bestows physical strength (Judges 14.6); and qualifies the servants of God for a varied ministry (Ex. 28.3; 35.21, 31; Num. 11.25-29; I Sam. chaps. 16, 17; II Sam. 23.2). To this should be added that operation of the Spirit by which the men of faith in the Old Testament ages were regenerated. While this doctrine is not explicitly taught in the Old Testament (except prophetically) our Lord's words in John 3.5 and Luke 13.28 leave no doubt as to the fact itself. Since the new birth is essential to seeing and entering the Kingdom of God, and since the Old Testament saints are in that

Kingdom, it follows necessarily that they were born of the Spirit. But, since that was the period of nonage as Paul explains (Gal. chaps. 3 and 4) they had not the indwelling Spirit of sonship. They were minors (under tutors and governors). It should be remembered also that to the Old Testament saint no way was revealed by which he might receive the Holy Spirit. All the offices of the Spirit were reserved within the sovereign will of God. He sent His Spirit upon whomsoever He would. That the Spirit came upon an individual did not by any means prove him to be in salvation. Even a sincere believer had no assurance that the Holy Spirit might not forsake him (Psa. 51.11), whereas, the believer of this dispensation has an express promise of the abiding of the Spirit."

C. The Work of the Spirit in the New Dispensation.

In the new dispensation, we may distinguish a three-fold work of the Holy Spirit.

1. Giving birth to the Christian Church on the day of Pentecost, as a body of living members of which Christ is the risen Head: I Cor. 12.12-27; Eph. 1.22, 23.

2. Informing and infilling the Church with His presence and power: Eph. 2.19-22.

3. Conferring gifts and graces upon the Church: Rom. 12.6-8; I Cor. 12.4-11, 28-31; Gal. 5.22, 23.

TOPIC FIVE: THE HOLY SPIRIT IN THE CHURCH.

This subject has been anticipated in the work of the

Holy Spirit in the Old and New Dispensations. Moreover, the work of the Spirit of God in the Church and in the believer is much the same, for whatever is true of the Church as the body of Christ is also true of the believers as members of that body. But in a general way we may trace a sevenfold work ot the Holy Spirit in and through the Church:

1. Organizing it at Pentecost, as the body of Christ, Acts 2.1-4; Eph. 1.22, 23.

2. Possessing it, as the temple of God, I Cor. 6.19, 20; II Cor. 6.16; Eph. 2.21, 22.

3. Equipping it with gifts and graces for service (see last topic).

4. Giving it the body of inspired truth (see Topic III).

5. Giving it the Spirit of illumination and guidance into all truth, John 16.13; I John 2.20, 27.

6. Presiding over and guiding the Church into all the will of God, Acts 15.28.

7. Completing the body of the Church by calling out a people for the name of Christ, Acts 15.14-18.

TOPIC SIX: THE HOLY SPIRIT IN THE WORLD.

There are some who hold that the Holy Spirit has no office work in relation to the world. It is clear, however, that He has a threefold ministry:

1. He restrains the development of evil until God's purpose is fulfilled, II Thess. 2.7.

2. He convicts of sin, righteousness, and judgment, John 16.8-11.

3. He bears witness to the truth of God in preaching and testimony, John 15.26, 27; Acts 5.30-32.

TOPIC SEVEN: THE HOLY SPIRIT IN THE BELIEVER.

The work of the Holy Spirit in the believer is a vast subject. It covers, indeed, the whole field of the Christian life, which in every phase and development is the result of His gracious and glorious activity. It will be well, then, to study the subject from more than one point of view.

A. UNION WITH CHRIST.

One of the most striking and beautiful ways in which to study the work of the Spirit of God in the children of God is to look at it in relation to our own union with Christ.

I. MEANING.

Union with Christ means such a connection of the believer with the Lord Jesus Christ as constitutes a just and reasonable ground for his inheritance by faith of all the benefits of the atonement. This just and reasonable ground is our being made partakers of the divine nature: II Pet. 1.4.

In our study of the atonement, we sought for a just and reasonable ground for Christ's assuming our guilt and bearing our penalty; and we found it in His partaking of our nature: Heb. 2.14. So, likewise, for our inheriting Christ's righteousness and bearing the weight of His glory, both here and hereafter, we find a just and reasonable ground in our being made one with Him by spiritual birth: I Cor. 6.17. There is an exact parallel here; by incarnation Christ rightly takes our place in penalty, and by regeneration we rightly take His place in holiness.

II. SYMBOLISM.

There are five New Testament symbols of the believer's union with Christ. (See "The Crisis of the Deeper Life," pp. 10-17.)

B. GENERAL SCRIPTURE ASPECTS.

We group here a number of passages in which the work of the Holy Spirit in the believer is set forth:

1. Regeneration, John 3.5; Titus 3.5.
2. Sanctification, II Thess. 2.13; I Pet. 1.2.
3. Freedom from sin and death, Rom. 8.2.
4. Strengthened with power, Eph. 3.16.
5. Sonship, Rom. 8.14.

6. Witness to sonship, Rom. 8.16.

7. Produces fruit, Gal 5.22, 23.

8. Guides into all truth, John 16.13.

9. Divine Remembrancer, John 14.26.

10. Reveals the deep things of God and interprets and applies them, I Cor. 2.9-14.

11. Confers power to communicate revealed truth to others, Acts 1.8; I Cor. 2.1-4; I Thess. 1.5.

12. Guides in prayer, Rom. 8.26; Eph. 6.18; Jude 20.

13. Inspires thanksgiving, Eph. 5.18-20.

14. Inspires worship, Phil. 3.3. R. V.

15. Separates for definite service, Acts 13.2-4.

16. Guides in the minutiæ of life, Acts 8.27-29; 16. 6, 7.

17. Quickens the mortal body, Rom. 8.11.

C. SPECIAL DOCTRINAL ASPECTS.

As to the work of the Holy Spirit in and upon the believer, two views are held:

1. He begins His work at the time of conversion. This view is held by those who believe strongly in the freedom of the human will.

2. He begins His work before the time of conversion—perhaps as early as birth or even before birth. This view is held by those who believe strongly in the sovereignty of God.

There is truth in both views. In those who are to become children of God by faith in Jesus Christ, we must believe that the Holy Spirit works before conversion—providentially guiding, preserving, and controlling their lives: Psa. 139.13-18; Jer. 1.5; Gal. 1.15, 16.

Of the many words and expressions used in Scripture to set forth the special work of the Holy Spirit in the believer we choose six New Testament terms as comprehending and representing the extent and intent of Christian experience, namely: Election, Calling, Conversion, Justification, Regeneration, and Sanctification: Act 3.19; Rom. 4.25; 8.29, 30; II Thess. 2.13; II Pet. 1.10; Titus 3.5.

I. ELECTION.

1. Kinds.

There are three distinct elections mentioned in the Scriptures: First, National, as in the case of Israel: Rom. 9.11; 11.5-28; Second, Official, as in the case of Aholiab and Bezaleel: Ex. 31.1-6; and Third, Redemptive, as in the case of the Church and the believer: I Thess. 1.4; II Pet. 1.10.

2. Redemptive Election.

Redemptive Election may be defined as God's determination from eternity to save certain individuals, apart from any merit of their own, on the ground of their foreseen faith. This is predestination.

NOTE: In Romans 8.29, two verbs occur, namely, "foreknow" and "predestinate." The Greek word translated "foreknow" occurs in Acts 26.5; Rom. 8.29 and 11.2; I Pet. 1.20; II Pet. 3.17. The Greek word translated "predestinate" occurs in Acts 4.28; Rom. 8.29, 30; I Cor. 2.7; Eph. 1.5, 11. The Greek word rendered "foreknow" implies prescience of character; the Greek word translated "predestinate" implies determination founded on such prescience of character.

II. CALLING.

There are two distinct callings mentioned in the Scriptures: First, **General**, through the public proclamation of the Gospel: Isa. 45.22; 55.6; 65.12; Ezek. 33.11; Matt. 11.28; 22.3; Mark 16.15; John 12.32; Rev. 3.20; and Second, **Special**, through the personal call of the Holy Spirit: Luke 14.22; 14.23; Rom. 1.7; 8.30; 11.29; I Cor. 1.23, 24, 26; Phil. 3.14; Eph. 1.18; I Thess. 2.12; II Thess. 2.14; II Tim. 1.9; Heb. 3.1; II Pet. 1.10.

NOTE: The general call of the Spirit may be called *ordinary;* the special call of the Spirit, *extraordinary.* The former is external, the latter is internal. While the latter can be resisted unto destruction, it is generally efficacious unto salvation.

III. CONVERSION.

1. Definition.

Conversion may be defined as that voluntary change in the mind of the sinner in which he turns, on the one hand, from sin, and on the other hand, to God. This turning away from sin is a negative element and is repentance; the turning to God is a positive element and is faith.

NOTE: Conversion is the human side of salvation. The word "conversion," from the Latin, means a turning again—a right-about-face movement. While God is said to convert men and they to convert their fellow-men, yet the Scriptures uniformly call upon men to convert themselves; that is, to turn away from sin to God: Psa. 85.4; S. of S. 1.4; Prov. 1.23; Isa. 31.6; 59.20; Jer. 31.18; Ezek. 14.6; 18.32; 33.9, 11; Joel 2.12, 14; James 5.19, 20.

2. Repentance.

Repentance may be defined as the voluntary change in the mind of the sinner whereby he turns from sin. It involves a change of view, a change of feeling, and a change of purpose.

NOTE: The Greek word translated "repentance" means a change of mind.

3. Elements of Repentance.

These are three:

a. Intellectual. This is a recognition of sin as personal guilt and defilement: Psa. 51; Rom. 1.32; Rom. 3.19, 20.

b. Emotional. This is heart sorrow for sin as committed against God: II Cor. 7.9, 10.

c. Volitional. This is a renunciation of all sin: Jer. 25.5; Acts 2.38, Rom. 2.4.

NOTE: Repentance that stops short of the volitional element is not true Scriptural repentance. Along with repentance must go reparation and restitution. (See "The Crisis of the Deeper Life," page 33.)

4. Faith.

Faith may be defined as that voluntary change in the mind of the sinner whereby he turns to God. Like repentance, it involves a change of view, a change of feeling, and a change of purpose.

5. Elements of Faith.

These are three:

a. Intellectual. This is belief in the existence of God and in the teaching of the Scriptures: John 2.22, 23; James 2.19.

b. Emotional. This is personal faith that Christ is the only Saviour from sin: Matt. 13.21; John 5.35; 8.30, 31.

c. Volitional. This is the actual surrender to Christ and present trust in Him as Saviour and Lord: Acts 16.31; Rev. 3.20.

NOTE: Faith that stops short of the volitional element is not "saving faith." All three elements are found in Heb. 11.6.

IV. JUSTIFICATION.

1. Definition.

Justification may be defined as that judicial act of God by which, on account of Christ, to whom the sinner is united by faith, He declares that sinner to be no longer exposed to the penalty of the law but restored to divine favor.

NOTE: In the New Testament, the word "justify" means not to make righteous, but to declare righteous. And justification is the state of one who is thus declared righteous: Rom. 8.10; I Cor. 1.30.

2. Elements of Justification.

These are two, namely: the remission of punishment and the restoration to favor.

A. The remission of punishment. The penalty of sin is remitted to the sinner on the ground of what Christ has done on the Cross.

1. As the act of a Judge, there is *pardon*, Mic. 7.18.

2. As the act of a Father, there is *forgiveness*, Psa. 130.4.

B. Restoration to favor. The sinner is restored to God's favor on the ground of Christ's perfect obedience to the law of God.

1. As an act of restored friendship, this is called *reconciliation*, II Cor. 5.18.

2. As an act of created sonship, this is *adoption*, John 1.12; Rom. 8.15; Gal. 4.5; Eph. 1.5; I John 3.2.

3. Ground of Justification.

This is not the works of the Law, nor human desert, Acts 13.39; Rom. 3.20; Gal. 2.16; but it is the blood of Christ, Rom. 3.24, 25; Rom. 5.1, 9; Gal. 3.13; I Pet. 2.24.

4. Condition of Justification.

This is faith, Acts 13.39; Rom. 3.26; 4.5; 5.1.

NOTE: The ground and the condition of justification must not be confused. What Christ has done is the ground of justification; our faith in Christ is simply the means whereby we receive the blessings of this atoning work.

These are peace, Rom. 5.1; freedom from condemnation, Rom. 8.1; heirs of God, Titus 3.7; saved from wrath, Rom. 5.9; glorification, Rom. 8.30.

V. REGENERATION.

1. Scripture Definitions.

There are a number of Scriptural representations of regeneration which are not so much exact definitions as vivid descriptions of the truth.

a. A new heart and a new spirit, Ezek. 36.26.

b. Born again, or born from above, John 3.3.

c. A passing from death unto life, John 5.24; Eph. 2.1, 5; I John 3.14.

d. A new creation, II Cor. 5.17; Gal. 6.15.

e. A partaking of the divine nature, II Pet. 1.4.

f. A making anew of the mind, Rom. 12.2.

NOTE: Regeneration is not a Scripture term, but it means a rebirth. The word does occur in the English translation, but in the sense of a spiritual generation or birth: Titus 3.5.

2. Theological Definitions.

Following are a few theological definitions of regeneration which more or less approximate the truth.

a. Regeneration is a spiritual work wrought by the Spirit of God in the spirit of man.

NOTE: This definition does not define regeneration. It could be applied to any work of the Spirit in the Christian life.

b. Regeneration is the giving of a new bent or direction to the affections and will.

NOTE: This is an inadequate description of regeneration; it covers a part but not the whole.

c. Regeneration is the communication of the divine nature to man by the operation of the Holy Spirit through the Word.

NOTE: This is from Dr. A. J. Gordon of Boston, and is perhaps the best available.

3. Necessity.

The necessity of regeneration is expressed in the divine "must" of Jesus in John 3.7. One can pass from natural life, or the flesh, into supernatural life, or the Spirit, only by new birth: John 3.6.

4. The Agent, or Instrument.

This is the Holy Spirit applying and working through the Word of God: John 15.3; 17.17; I Cor. 4.15; Eph. 5.25, 26; I Pet. 1.23-25.

NOTE: For a brief statement of the doctrines of Justification and Regeneration, see "The Crisis of the Deeper Life," pp. 35-42.

VI. SANCTIFICATION.

1. Scriptural Definitions.

The holiness of the Christian flows from vital contact with God. This contact has both a divine and human side.

2. The Divine Side.

On the divine side there are two points of contact, namely, the Cross of Christ and the Gift of the Spirit.

a. The Cross of Christ.

The first point of divine contact, whereby holiness is received, is the Cross of Christ, and the first step in the path of victory is the vision of the Cross. In Christian experience the apprehension of divine truth comes before its appropriation and realization. Vision precedes victory. The child of God must see his spiritual inheritance before he can enter upon its actual possession. In sanctification the highlands of deliverance loom up while the believer is struggling along on the lowlands of defeat.

Let us try to see clearly just what the vision of victory is. It is all wrapped up in the simple phrase: "through Jesus Christ our Lord." This expression means three things: First, our identification with Christ in His crucifixion; second, our identification with Christ in His resurrection; and third, Christ's identification with us through His personal indwelling.

1. Our identification with Christ in His crucifixion.

There are two aspects in which the believer stands related to the cross of Christ, viz.: **substitution** and **identification.**

Of these truths, perhaps substitution is the more familiar. Christ died for us. He bore our sins on the cross. He took our place under wrath and endured the penalty which we deserved. This is the vision of the cross which comes to the helpless sinner; and when he appropriates it by faith it brings salvation from the guilt of sin. This is the meaning of "Christ our Saviour": Isa. 53:6; Heb. 13:12.

The second aspect of our relation to the cross—identification—needs special emphasis, because it is not well understood by all Christians. Christ died for us—that is true; but it is only half the truth. We died in Christ—that is the other half of the truth. The statement is only partially true that Christ died for us that we might escape punishment. It requires also to be said that God regards us as having been punished in Christ. To make the truth individual, in the person of my Substitute I bore the penalty of sin. In Him the law exhausted its power of death upon me. When Christ died, I died too. With reference to the claim of the law and the power of sin, I am, in the sight of God, counted as a dead man. This is what Paul meant, when he declared, "I am crucified with Christ," Gal. 2.20. This also is the clear teaching of such passages as the following:

Rom. 6.4, 5, 8, 11; 7.4; II Cor. 5.14; Col. 3.3; Col. 2.12.

2. Our identification with Christ in His resurrection.

This is the second part of the vision of victory. In the same two aspects in which the believer stands related to the crucifixion of Christ he also stands related to His resurrection—substitution and identification. Christ was our Substitute both in His crucifixion and in His resurrection; not only did He die for us on the cross, for us also He arose from the grave.

Now, in His resurrection, as well as in His crucifixion, the believer is identified with Christ. This is what Paul meant when he said, "I am crucified with Christ; *nevertheless I live*," Gal. 2.20. To make the truth personal, I died with Christ; but I also rose with Him. I was in Him when He hung on the cross and when He lay in the grave; but I was also in Him when He burst the bands of death on the morning of the resurrection. Indeed, the Apostle Paul carries the identification still farther: "Crucified with Christ"—this expresses the death-side of our union with the Lord. "Risen with Christ"—this expresses the life-side of our union with Him. Let us take a few verses which bring out this life-side of our union with Christ—our identification with Him in His resurrection: Rom. 4.25; I Cor. 15.14, 17, 20; Rom. 6.4, 11; II Cor. 5.14, 15; Col. 2.12; 3.1, 3.

Of this twofold identification of the believer with Christ in His death and resurrection, baptism is an impressive symbolical representation.

Baptism has a twofold significance. In the first place, it is the outward sign and visible seal of the inner work of grace wrought by the Spirit of God in regeneration.

But, in the second place, baptism in its deeper spiritual meaning is a symbol of death. It is not a rite of cleansing, but a type of crucifixion and resurrection: Rom. 6.3, 4; Col. 2.12.

3. Christ's identification with us through His personal indwelling.

This is the last part of the vision of victory and the most glorious of all. Christ Himself, by the Holy Ghost, will come and dwell in our hearts and live out His own life within us: Gal. 2.20; John 14.20, 21; Col. 1.27; Rom. 15.29.

It cannot be too strongly emphasized that the Christian life is a Christ-life. It is not an imitation, but an incarnation. We do not copy Christ, we reproduce Him; or, rather, He reproduces His own life within us by the indwelling of the Holy Ghost.

> Once there lived another man within me,
>   Child of earth and slave of Satan he;
> But I nailed him to the cross of Jesus,
>   And that man is nothing now to me.
>
> Now Another Man is living in me,
>   And I count His blessed life as mine;
> I have died with Him to all my own life;
>   I have ris'n to all His life divine.
>   —Rev. A. B. Simpson.

b. **The Gift of the Holy Spirit.**

The identification of the believer with Christ in His death and resurrection is the historical and incomplete side of holiness; the transformation of the believer in character and conduct through the reception of the gift of the Holy Ghost is the experimental and complete side of holiness.

1. The Experience of the Apostolic Church.

In the experience of the Apostolic Church, as recorded in the book of Acts, there were three things that were closely connected, namely: Conversion, Baptism, and the Reception of the Holy Ghost: Acts 2.38, 39.

Three facts would seem to be clear: First, conversion, baptism, and the reception of the gift of the Holy Ghost are three separate and distinct things; second, these three things, while separate and distinct, are yet closely related both as doctrines and as experiences; and third, these three things are here stated in their normal order and Scriptural relationship. A careful examination of the book of Acts leads to two conclusions, namely: First, in some instances the Holy Ghost was received *at the time of* conversion; and second, in other instances the Holy Ghost was received *subsequent to* conversion.

In the following instances the Holy Ghost was received at the time of conversion: Acts 2.38-41; 10. 44-48.

In other instances the Holy Ghost was received subsequent to conversion: Acts 8.12-17; 19.1-6; 9.17, 18.

2. The Teaching of the Apostolic Writings.

We have studied the experience of the Apostolic Church, with reference to the definite reception of the Holy Ghost, as recorded in the book of Acts. Now, let us turn to the teaching of the Epistles.

Let us cite a few passages which refer to the possession of the Holy Spirit or to the indwelling of the risen Christ. These two classes of passages may be grouped together, for it is the baptism of the Holy Ghost which brings to our hearts the revelation of the indwelling Christ: I Cor. 3.16, 17; Rom. 8.9, 10; I Cor. 12.13; II Cor. 13.5; Gal. 3.2; 4.19; Eph. 3.14-19; Col. 1.27.

A careful examination of the above and similar passages discloses two striking facts, namely: First, in some instances the baptism or possession of the Holy Spirit is closely identified with regeneration or conversion; and Second, in other instances these experiences are separated in point of time. But this is just the conclusion which we reached from our study of the book of Acts. Thus the experience of the Apostolic Church and the teaching of the Apostolic writings agree: and, indeed, this must be so, for the Holy Spirit was the Inworker of the one as He was the Inspirer of the other.

3. The Spiritual Crisis in the Life of our Lord.

At thirty years of age a marked crisis came in the life of our Lord. It was then, at the river Jordan, that Christ was not only baptized in water by John the Baptist, but also baptized with the Holy Ghost by His Heavenly Father.

What was the significance of this crisis in the life of Christ? From His birth till His baptism the Holy Spirit was *with* Christ; but from His baptism till His passion the Holy Spirit was *within* Him. After the crisis at the river Jordan two Divine Personalities were inseparably united—Jesus of Nazareth and the Spirit of God.

Now, the Apostle John tells us that "as He is, so are we in this world" (I John 4.17). In this experience, therefore, as in all other things, Christ is our Divine Pattern. So, after we have been born of the Spirit—and it should not be long afterwards—we must be baptized with the Spirit. It is then, in connection with taking Christ as our sanctification, that we receive the Person of the Holy Ghost as our indwelling and abiding Comforter. When once He comes into our hearts, He never leaves us.

3. The Human Side.

Contact with God, whereby the Christian becomes partaker of the Holiness of Christ, has a human as well as a divine side.

On the human side, contact is formed by a step of entire surrender and an act of appropriating faith.

a. A Step of Entire Surrender.

Another name for surrender is consecration. But as consecration is really a divine work, surrender is a better term. The Christian can yield his heart and life, but he cannot consecrate them; only God can do that. Thus, the Old Testament priests did not consecrate themselves; Moses, acting for Jehovah, consecrated them; the priests could only yield themselves to be consecrated.

Surrender is giving up—a yielding to God. The believer must lay his whole life on the altar, relinquish all right to its control, and count himself henceforth and forever the Lord's. Surrender is a painful act. It means separation; it means sacrifice; it means self-denial; it means death: Lev. 8.1-13; Rom. 6.13; 12.1; Matt. 16.24.

Self-denial, which is the essence of surrender, does not mean giving up *things;* it means giving up *self.*

Surrender to God must be voluntary, complete, and final.

1. It must be voluntary.

Unless the step of surrender be taken voluntarily, the surrender will be made only in name, and will have no spiritual value. God calls men, but does not coerce them. In making choices and in deciding destiny, the will is free. It is true that God will supply motives to right action, but He will not arbitrarily determine the decision of the will. Accordingly, if the will does not yield, there is no surrender; and if the will is not free in its action, the surrender is not voluntary. Compulsory surrender is the result of force; voluntary surrender is the result of love: Gen. 22.16, 17; Phil. 3.7-11; Psa. 40.6-8; Heb. 10.5-9; Phil. 2.5-8; Rom. 12.1, 2.

2. It must be complete.

Unless surrender be complete, it is not surrender at all. A partial consecration is not sufficient; God will not accept a divided heart. We must not keep back part of the price. If we expect God to give Himself wholly to us, we must give ourselves wholly to Him. In the hour of surrender it is a good thing to make a mental inventory of our lives—spirit, soul, body, strength, time, talents, character, reputation, possessions, etc.—and then lay everything absolutely and unreservedly upon the altar: Mal. 3.10.

3. It must be final.

Unless surrender be final, it cannot be called true surrender. When rightly understood, surrender to God can neither be repeated nor recalled; it is unalterable and irrevocable. There are Christians who have a habit of making a reconsecration of their lives on every favorable occasion. Indeed, some believers give themselves anew to God with each recurring day. The motive which prompts to this act is of course entirely right, but the practice itself is clearly unscriptural. Thus Paul declared, "that He is able to keep that which I have committed unto Him against that day": II Tim. 1.12. See also John 10.27-29; Psa. 118.27.

b. An Act of Appropriating Faith.

The gift of the Holy Ghost is received not only by a

step of entire surrender but also by an act of appropriating faith. These two conditions must go together and in this order. Surrender is yielding to God; faith is taking from God. Again, surrender is negative and passive, while faith is positive and aggressive. Moreover, just as the step of surrender must be voluntary, complete, and final, so the act of faith must be definite, vital, and appropriating.

QUESTIONS FOR STUDY.

1. Prove from Scripture that the Holy Spirit is a Person.
2. Prove from Scripture that the Holy Spirit is God.
3. Mention ten names of the Holy Spirit with references.
4. What are the symbols of the Holy Spirit? Discuss briefly any one of them.
5. What is the erroneous classification of Sabellius concerning the work of the Trinity?
6. What is the true Scriptural view?
7. In every work of God, what is the particular function of the Father? Of the Son? Of the Spirit?
8. What are meant by the indwelling and outgoing works of God?
9. What would be an example of the indwelling work?
10. What is the work of the Trinity in Creation?
11. What is the special work of the Holy Spirit in Creation? Mention five particulars.

12. Trace the various stages of the work of the Holy Spirit in the Person and career of Christ.

13. What is the special work of the Holy Spirit in the Scriptures?

14. What marked distinction can be made between the work of the Holy Spirit in the old dispensation and in the new dispensation?

15. What was the special work of the Holy Spirit in the old dispensation?

16. What is the special work of the Holy Spirit in the new dispensation?

17. What is the special work of the Holy Spirit in the world?

18. What is the special work of the Holy Spirit in the Church?

19. Discuss briefly the subject of the believer's union with Christ.

20. Mention ten general Scriptural aspects of the work of the Holy Spirit in the believer.

21. What two views are held with respect to the time when the Holy Spirit begins His work in and upon the one who is to become a Christian?

22. What six fundamental doctrines may be taken as comprising the Christian life?

23. How is the term "election" used in the Scriptures?

24. Define redemptive election.

25. How is the term "calling" used in the Scriptures?

26. Distinguish between the general and special call of the Holy Spirit.
27. Write a brief but comprehensive paper on the Doctrine of Conversion.
28. Write a brief but comprehensive paper on the Doctrine of Justification.
29. Write a brief but comprehensive paper on the Doctrine of Regeneration.
30. Write a brief but comprehensive paper on the Doctrine of Sanctification.
31. Show the relation of the Holy Spirit to the healing of our bodies.

DOCTRINE EIGHT: ECCLESIOLOGY.

Topics.

I. The Idea of the Church.

II. The Twofold Meaning of the Church.

III. The Local Church.

IV. The Organization of the Church.

V. The Government of the Church.

VI. The Worship of the Early Church.

VII. The Discipline of the Church.

VIII. The Ordinances of the Church.

IX. The Ministry of the Church.

X. The Destiny of the Church.

CHAPTER VIII.

ECCLESIOLOGY.

TOPIC ONE: THE IDEA OF THE CHURCH.

The fundamental New Testament idea of the Church is brought out in the Greek verb *kalein*, signifying *to call*, with its derivatives and compounds.

1. *Kalein*: This Greek word, which means "to call" denotes the first act of Christ in point of time in connection with the Church: Rom. 8.30; I Cor. 1.9; II Thess. 2.14; I Pet. 2.9.

2. *Kleetoi*: This word, which means "the called," designates the members of the Church: Rom. 1.6, 7; 8.28; I Cor. 1.1, 2; Jude 1.

3. *Kleesis*: This word, which means "calling," denotes the peculiar vocation of the Church: Rom. 11.29; I Cor. 1.26; Eph. 4.1, 4.

4. *Parakleetos*: This word, which is commonly translated "comforter," designates the indwelling and informing Spirit in the *Kleetoi* (the called): John 14.16, 17; Rom. 8.9, 11; I Cor. 3.16; Eph. 2.22.

5. *Epikalein*: This word points out the distinct and distinguishing act of the *Kleetoi*—to call on Christ, i. e., to invoke Him in prayer: I Cor. 1.1, 2; Rom. 10.9, 13; Acts 22.16; Acts 9.14, 21; 7.58, 59.

6. *Parakalein*: This word points out the distinct and distinguishing act of *Kleetoi* towards one another—to call to, exhort, or strengthen in the faith: Heb. 3.13; 10.25; I Thess. 3.2.

7. *Ekkleesia*: This word designates the company, body, or organism of the *Kleetoi*, i. e., the Church: Matt. 16.18; 18.17.

NOTE: Gathering up the combined meanings of all these Greek words, we may say that the root idea of the Church is that of a company of believers called out from the world and indwelt by the Spirit of God, whose special and peculiar ministry toward God is prayer, and toward one another is exhortation and consolation.

TOPIC TWO: THE TWO-FOLD MEANING OF THE CHURCH.

There are two usages of the Greek noun *Ekkleesia* or Church in the New Testament:

I. The **Church Universal**, a Spiritual Body, composed of believers of all ages and times who are united to God by faith in Jesus Christ: Eph. 1.2; 3.21; Heb. 12.23.

II. The **Church Local**, a Visible Body of believers united to God by faith in Jesus Christ. Of this usage of the word there are three special applications:

1. A small company in a house: Rom. 16.5; Philemon 2.

2. The Christian congregation of a town or city: I Cor. 1.2; I Thess. 1.1.

3. The group of churches in a country or nation: Gal. 1.2.

NOTE 1. To the above New Testament usages of the word Church we may add two later and modern meanings: namely, the branches of Christendom, as the Greek Church, the Roman Church, the Protestant Church, the Protestant Episcopal Church, the Methodist Church, etc.; and the material building in which the members of a church worship, as the First Reformed Church of Nyack, New York.

NOTE 2. The word Church occurs twice in the gospels, both instances being in Matthew, and both in the future. In chap. 16.18 Christ refers to the spiritual and invisible church universal; and in chap. 18.17, He refers to the church local and visible. As a spiritual organism, the church may be viewed in two aspects, namely: in *time*, Matt. 16.18, and in *eternity*, Eph. 3.9-11. When the Christian Church of a city or town is mentioned, the word *Ekkleesia* is in the singular number; when a country or nation is spoken of, the plural number is found, Acts 13.1; Gal. 1.2.

TOPIC THREE: THE LOCAL CHURCH.

From this point onward we shall confine our attention to the Local, or Visible Church; and it will be desirable to get a clear working definition of a New Testament church. Of these we give three.

I. The **Local Church** is "a body of professed believers in Christ, baptized on a credible confession of faith in Him, and associated for worship, work, and discipline" (H. G. Weston).

II. "The **Local,** or **Individual, Church** is a company of believers voluntarily united together in accordance with Christ's laws, for the purpose of maintaining worship and observing the ordinances" (F. W. Farr).

III. A **Church** is a company of believers called out from the world, voluntarily joined together and meeting at stated times, among whom the Word of God is preached, discipline is administered, and the ordinances observed.

NOTE: There are those who would add to this definition the two ideas of regeneration and baptism; and we feel that this would be in full accord with the New Testament teaching on this subject.

TOPIC FOUR: THE ORGANIZATION OF THE CHURCH.

The Church Universal and Invisible is an organism, but the Church Local and Visible is an organization. This is shown by three facts:

1. **Stated meetings.** The Apostolic Christians met regularly for worship from house to house—at first every day in the week, but later, on the first day of the week, or Sunday, which was called the Lord's Day because it celebrated His resurrection from the grave: Acts 2.46, 47; 20.7; I Cor. 16.2; Rev. 1.10.

2. **Election or appointment of officers:** Acts 1.15-26; Acts 14.23; Titus 1.5.

3. **Officers.** There were two officers of the local church in New Testament times, namely: the Deacon, and the Elder, or Bishop.

In post-apostolic times and in later church history, the elder and the bishop represented two distinct offices, the latter being the higher. But in the New Testament, the terms elder and bishop represent one office: Acts 20.17, 28; Phil. 1.1; I Tim. 3.1 8; Titus 1.5, 7; I Pet. 5.1. The word **bishop** in Greek means an overseer, and the word **elder** in Greek means one of adult years, possessing experience and counsel. The word **deacon** means "minister," or "helper." The elder, or bishop, had oversight of the spiritual interests of the church, while the deacon was in charge of the temporalities. While both "bishop" and "elder" come from the Greek, the word "bishop" is taken from the municipal usage of Greek cities, while the word "elder" is taken from the Jewish usage of local synagogues. The date of the appointment of deacons was about 33 A. D.: Acts 6.1-6. The date of the appointment of elders was about 45 A. D.: Acts 11.30.

Two other officers of the early church may be mentioned, namely: the deaconess, Phil. 4.3; Rom. 16.1; and the evangelist, Eph. 4.11. The evangelists were itinerating preachers, not restricted to any one local church.

NOTE: Pastors and prophets are also mentioned among the officers of the early church: I Cor. 12.28; Eph. 4.11. While

22

Agabus and the daughters of Philip predicted the future, yet the New Testament gift of prophecy corresponded to our present conception of the ministry of the true preacher of the Word: I Cor. 14.3.

TOPIC FIVE: THE GOVERNMENT OF THE CHURCH.

There are three forms of church government, namely:

1. The Episcopal, or government by bishops.

2. The Presbyterial, or government by elders.

3. The Congregational, or government by members themselves.

There is no rigid system of church government prescribed in the New Testament. While there are suggestions of Episcopal and Presbyterial government (Acts 20.17, 28; 14.23; Titus 1.5), yet there are indications that the Congregational form of government prevailed over the other two. Three points may be mentioned.

1. Every church had the power of disciplining and excluding its members: Matt. 18.17; I Cor. 5.1-5; II Thess. 3.6.

2. Each church elected its own officers: Acts 1.26; 6.1-6.

3. Each church had the power of determining all matters not already determined by the Scriptures: I Cor. 11.34.

TOPIC SIX: THE WORSHIP OF THE EARLY CHURCH.

There were seven features in the public worship of the early church, namely:

1. Praise (Singing).
2. Prayer.
3. Prophecy, I Cor. 14.3.
4. Scripture reading with comment.
5. Reading of apostolic letters.
6. Collections for the poor.
7. Celebration of the Lord's Supper (weekly at first).

NOTE: The spirit of worship was characterized by four things.

1. It was humble.
2. It was reverent.
3. It was grateful.
4. It was joyful.

(Luke 24.52, 53; Acts 2.46.)

TOPIC SEVEN: THE DISCIPLINE OF THE CHURCH.

I. **Definition.** Discipline may be defined as the correction or expulsion by the church of one or more of its members for immorality of life, or heresy of doctrine.

II. Kinds of offenses. There are two kinds of offenses of which a church member may be guilty, namely, public and private. And there are two kinds of discipline corresponding to these offenses, namely, public and private.

III. Forms of Discipline. Church discipline, whether private or public, may take one of three forms.

1. Private reproof.
2. Public reproof.
3. Excommunication.

The law of private discipline is found in Matt. 5.23, 24; 18.15-17. And the law of public discipline is found in such passages as I Cor. 5.3-5; 5.13; II Cor. 2.6-8; II Thess. 3.6.

NOTE: There are only three ways for a member to get out of a local church, namely: by death, dismissal by letter, and exclusion by trial or withdrawal under charges. After a church member has been excommunicated, he should be dealt with tenderly as a brother, and his restoration sought through repentance and faith.

TOPIC EIGHT: THE ORDINANCES OF THE CHURCH.

I. DEFINITION.

The **ordinances** are those outward rites which

Christ has appointed to be administered in each church as visible signs and seals of the saving truth of the Gospel.

II. NUMBER.

The ordinances are two in number and only two, namely, Baptism and the Lord's Supper.

NOTE: The Church of Rome makes seven ordinances or sacraments, namely, Ordination, Confirmation, Matrimony, Extreme Unction, Penance, Baptism, and the Lord's Supper.

A. BAPTISM.

I. Definition. Baptism is the initiatory rite of admission into the Christian Church. It is the symbol of union with Christ: Matt. 28.19; Mark 16.15, 16.

II. Significance. This is twofold, namely:

1. It is the badge of discipleship, the public confession of Christ as Saviour and Lord.

2. It is the sign and seal of participation by faith in the death and resurrection of Christ.

NOTE: Baptism is not the New Testament equivalent of the Old Testament rite of circumcision; for circumcision was a symbol of cleansing, while baptism is a symbol of death. The conditions of baptism and the mode of baptism, as well as the subjects of baptism, are controversial topics among Christians. The writer feels free simply to express his personal view and conviction as to the teaching of the New Testament. In his judgment, adults and only adults are the proper subjects of baptism; repentance and faith in Christ are the essential conditions of baptism, and immersion seems to be clearly indicated by the symbolism of the ordinance: Acts 2.38-41; 8.12; Rom. 6.1-4; I Cor. 10.1, 2; Col. 2.12.

B. THE LORD'S SUPPER.

I. Definition. The **Lord's Supper** is an ordinance instituted by Christ for observance by His followers, and consisting in the consecration of bread and wine with the words of institution and the subsequent eating and drinking of the consecrated elements. The Lord's Supper is a symbol of the believer's communion with Christ: Matt. 26.26-30; Luke 22.19, 20; I Cor. 11.23-34.

NOTE: Baptism may be called the sacrament of regeneration; the Lord's Supper, the sacrament of sanctification. There are various names in use for this latter ordinance, namely: The Lord's Supper, the Communion, the Eucharist, the Sacrament of the Lord's Supper, the Memorial Supper, and the Ordinance of the Lord's Supper.

II. Views. There are four principal views of the Lord's Supper that are current among Christians:

1. **Transubstantiation.** This is the Roman Catholic view. It holds that through the consecration by the priest the elements of bread and wine are converted into the real body and blood of Christ. Thus the communicant partakes of Christ, physically, through the mouth, entirely apart from spiritual apprehension by faith.

2. Consubstantiation. This is the Lutheran view. It holds that while the bread and wine are unchanged, there is yet a real, though mystical, partaking of Christ through the mouth. This, however, is not apart from faith, but is the mystery of the sacrament and is not explainable.

3. The Zwinglian view. This holds that the Lord's Supper is simply a commemoration of His person and sacrifice. It is merely a memorial feast. The Lord is not present to devout feeling and spiritual apprehension, except as our departed loved ones are present, when we call them to mind and dwell upon their virtues and good deeds.

4. The Calvinistic view. This is the generally accepted evangelical view of the Protestant Church. Contrary to the Romanist view, it holds that there is no conversion of the elements into the real presence of Christ. Again, contrary to the Lutheran view, it holds that there is no physical partaking of Christ through the mouth. Still again, contrary to the Zwinglian view, it holds that the Lord's Supper is more than a memorial feast. The Calvinistic view holds that after consecration the elements remain unchanged, and that apart from devout feeling and spiritual apprehension the Supper has no value. But it does maintain that through the elements, in a way that can be realized by no other means of grace, the believer is brought into vital touch with Christ, and

by faith may eat His flesh and drink His blood, and thus abide in Him. The truth symbolized by the Supper is unfolded in John 6.51-58. Augustine, in the fourth century, expressed the very heart of the spiritual significance of the communion when he said, "Believe, and thou hast eaten."

TOPIC NINE: THE MINISTRY OF THE CHURCH.

The Ministry, or Mission of the Christian Church is twofold: Evangelization and Edification.

I. EVANGELIZATION.

Evangelization may be defined as the efforts put forth by the Church for the salvation of men from sin and error. It is the primary mission of the Church. Contrary to the post-millennial view, we are not to bring the world to Christ, but to bring Christ to the world. There is a vast difference. To preach the Gospel as a witness to all nations and to take out of them a people for Christ's name is the fundamental mission of the Church in the present dispensation: Matt. 28.19, 20; Mark 16.15; Acts 1.8; 15.14-18.

Note: There are two beautiful symbols of the ministration of the Church to the world; these are salt and light. Salt is a preservative, giving both savor and flavor to society. Light is a symbol of testimony, the witness which the Church bears to the world, both by the purity of its doctrine and the piety of its members.

II. EDIFICATION.

Edification may be defined as the building up of the Church in truth and grace. After sinners have been saved, they must be indoctrinated in the truth of the Scriptures and possessed and filled by the Holy Spirit. There are five agencies which contribute to the edification of the Church:

1. The Christian Ministry, Eph. 4.11, 12.
2. The Word of God, Col. 3.16; I Pet. 2.2; Heb. 5.14.
3. The Holy Spirit, Gal. 5.25; Eph. 5.18.
4. The Gifts of the Spirit, I Cor. 12.4-12.
5. The Sacraments.

TOPIC TEN: THE DESTINY OF THE CHURCH.

The Destiny of the Christian Church is threefold:

I.   To be married as a chaste virgin to Christ, Rev. 21.9; II Cor. 11.2; Eph. 5.27.

II. To reign with Christ as a Royal Consort, Rev. 1.6; 3.21; I Pet. 2.9; Rev. 20.6.

III. To show forth throughout all the coming ages the praise, the grace, and the glory of God, Eph. 1.6, 12; 3.10.

NOTE: There are three words that bring out these three relationships of the Church to Christ: Bride, Queen, Jewel.

QUESTIONS FOR STUDY.

1. What is the fundamental New Testament idea of the Church?
2. State as clearly as you can what the Church is, as derived from a careful study of the seven Greek words which were mentioned.
3. What are the two New Testament meanings of the Church?
4. Define a Local Church.
5. How may it be shown that the local church is an organization?
6. What are the New Testament offices of the Church?
7. According to the New Testament usage, do the words Bishop and Elder designate the same office or different offices?
8. What are the three forms of Church government?
9. Do you find Scriptural ground for any one form of government more than the others?
10. Describe the features of early Church worship.

11. What is Church discipline?
12. How many forms of Church discipline are recognized and what is the order of procedure in each?
13. What are the ordinances of the Church?
14. Define baptism.
15. What is the twofold significance of baptism?
16. Define the Lord's Supper.
17. What are some of the names used for this ordinance besides "the Lord's Supper"?
18. What is the error known as Transubstantiation?
19. What is the error known as Consubstantiation?
20. What is the Zwinglian view?
21. What is the Calvinistic view?
22. What is the twofold mission of the Church?
23. What is its threefold destiny?

DOCTRINE NINE: ESCHATOLOGY.

Topics.

CHAPTER IX.

ESCHATOLOGY.

TOPIC ONE: THE DISPENSATIONS.

Seven different dispensations are generally recognized by all prophetic teachers.

1. **The Age of Innocence**—from man's Creation to his Fall.

2. **The Age of Conscience**—from the Fall to the Flood.

3. **The Age of Government**—from Noah to Lot.

4. **The Patriarchal Age**—from Abraham to Moses.

5. **The Age of Law**—from Moses to Christ.

6. **The Age of the Church** —from Pentecost to the Rapture.

7. **The Millennium Age**—from the Revelation to the loosing of Satan.

NOTE: The brief periods between the Crucifixion and Pentecost and between the Rapture and the Revelation are of the nature of parentheses.

TOPIC TWO: THE SECOND COMING OF CHRIST.

1. **Its Place in Scripture.**

a. The Second Coming is mentioned eight times as often as the first.

b. It is the theme of several whole books, e. g., Thessalonians, and of certain chapters, Matthew 24; Luke 21.

c. The Old Testament prophets bear witness to it: Isa. 45:23; Ezek. 21:25-27; Zech. 14:16.

d. The angels know of it: Acts 1:11.

e. The apostles preached it: Acts 3:19; I Thess. 4:16; I John 2:28; Jude 14.

f. Jesus Himself frequently mentions it.

2. **What It Is Not.**

a. It is not death.

The dead rise when Christ comes: I Thess. 4:16, 17. At death we go to Him.

At the rapture He comes for us: John 14:3. Certain verses have no meaning unless we distinguish death from His coming: John 21:23; Phil. 3:20.

Death is an enemy. At the Second Coming we overcome death: I Cor. 15:50-57. We are nowhere commanded to watch for death, but we are repeatedly enjoined to look for His coming.

b. It is not the descent of the Holy Spirit.

The Holy Spirit is a distinct person and His coming is not the Coming of Christ. Again many of the passages referring to the coming of Christ were given after Pentecost: Phil. 3:21; II Tim. 4:8; I Thess. 4:16, etc.

c. It is not Universal Christianity apart from the person of Christ: I Thess. 4.16.

d. It is not the destruction of Jerusalem. John 21:21; Rev. 22:20, were written after the destruction of Jerusalem.

The Coming of Christ is a comfort; the destruction of Jerusalem is a judgment.

3. The Signs of the Lord's Coming.

(1) The last days will be full of peril: II Tim. 3:1.

a. Physically—from pestilence, earthquake, famine, etc.: Matt. 24.

b. Socially—anarchy and socialism, lawlessness.

c. Nationally—wars and rumors of wars.

d. Religiously—seducing spirits and doctrines of devils: I Tim. 4:1.

(2) There will be apostasy of the Church: II Thess. 2:3.

(3) Satan's counterfeits will be circulated: Spiritualism, Christian Science, etc.: I Tim. 4:1.

(4) The Gospel will be preached in all the world: Matt. 24:14.

23

(5) Knowledge will be increased, and facilities for travel will be enlarged: Dan. 12:4.

(6) Riches will be multiplied: James 5:1, 8.

(7) Israel will be revived as a nation: Ezek. 36:37; Acts 15:16; Mark 11:13, 14, 28.

All these signs are general and have been sufficiently fulfilled to warrant our expecting the Lord to return at any time.

NOTE: While Jesus warns us that we are not in darkness that that day should overtake us as a thief, yet we are to be on our guard about naming days and hours.

Many prophecies refer to the Revelation of Christ, which is the second event in the future. If we see indications of their being fulfilled in our day, it is evidence that the first event is being crowded that much nearer.

4. The Two Aspects of the Coming of the Lord.

a. The Rapture.

Just as the First Coming of the Lord extended over a period of thirty years, so the Second Coming includes different events. At the First Coming He was revealed as a babe in Bethlehem, later as the Lamb of God at His Baptism, and as the Redeemer at Calvary. At the Second Coming He will first appear to His own secretly and suddenly to catch them away to the Marriage Supper of the Lamb: Matt. 24:40, 41.

This appearance is called the Rapture or the Parousia.

NOTE: Immediately after the Rapture there comes a period of terrible tribulation known as the day of Jacob's trouble: Jer. 30:4-7; Zech. 13:9.

b.   The Revelation.

Following the tribulation there is another sudden but open manifestation of the Lord in Heaven with His accompanying saints and holy angels, for the purpose of establishing the long-promised Messianic Kingdom in the earth. At this time He overthrows Satan, binds him for a thousand years, and brings in the Millennial Age.

TOPIC THREE: THE MILLENNIUM.

1.   The Restoration of Israel.

Israel is to return to the Promised Land and become a nation again: Gen. 12:1-3; Deut. 4:30, 31; Deut. 30: 1-6; II Sam. 7:10; Amos 9:11-15; Isa. 27:12, 13; Isa. 60:1-22; Jer. 16:14-16; Ezek. 20:36-44; Rom. 11:11-27; Acts 15:13-16.

2.   The Cleansing of Israel: Ezek. 36:24-28.

God promises to cleanse Israel finally from all filthiness and idols, to renew them inwardly and cause them to keep His statutes and judgments.

At the revelation of Christ when He shall stand upon Mount Olivet, Israel, as a nation, will believe upon Him and will accept Jesus, the crucified Saviour, as their Messiah and Lord: Zech. 12:10-14; Jer. 31:9; Jer. 23:3-6.

3. The Reorganization of Nations.

The governments of the earth will be overthrown and all peoples will be subservient to the King of kings: Dan. 2:44; Micah 4:1, 2; Isa. 49:22, 23; Jer. 23:5; Luke 1:32; Zech. 14:9; Isa. 24:23; Psa. 90:11; Psa. 22:8; Rev. 11:15.

4. The Reestablishing of the Kingdom of David.

All the Old Testament prophecies that remain unfulfilled of the future glory of Israel find their consummation in the Millennium: Jer. 22:4; Ezek. 37:22-28; Zech. 12:8; Acts 15:16. Jerusalem shall become a world center and David's Greater Son shall rule not only over His own patrimony, but shall be Suzerain over the whole earth.

5. The Lifting of the Curse.

The curse which sin brought upon the whole creation of God will be finally lifted. The effects of the great catastrophe of man's fall will be eliminated from the earth. The whole earth will be filled with beauty, peace, and plenty: Isa. 32:15, 35; 51:3; Ezek. 36:33-36; Isa. 11:6-9.

"No more let sin and sorrow grow
  Nor thorns infest the ground,
He comes to make His blessings flow
  Far as the curse is found."

TOPIC FOUR: THE RESURRECTION.

1. The Certainty of the Resurrection.

(1) Witnesses from the Old Testament.

Abraham: Gen. 22:5; Heb. 11:19.

Job: Job 19:25-27.

Isaiah: Isa. 26:19.

Daniel: Dan. 12:2, 13.

Hosea: Hos. 13:14.

(2) Instances of the dead being revived.

NOTE: This is different from the resurrection; but is corroborative evidence.

a. Elisha raised the son of the Shunammite: II Kings 4:18-37.

b. The man who was raised by touching Elisha's bones: I Kings 13:21.

c. The raising of Jairus' daughter: Matt. 9:25.

d. The raising of the widow's son: Luke 7:15.

e. Lazarus: John 11:43, 44.

f. Dorcas: Acts 9:41.

(3) Our strongest ground for believing in the resurrection is found in the rising of Christ from the

dead. No fact in history is better attested than this. Jesus Himself told of His death and resurrection during His life: John 10:18; Luke 24:1-8.

2. The Nature of the Resurrection. The believer's new body is related to his present one: I Cor. 15. It is also like unto Christ's glorious body. It is spiritual not natural, incorruptible not corruptible, literal not figurative. This is the redemption of the body: Rom. 8:23.

3. The Time of the Resurrection.

(1) The Resurrection of the righteous, or the Resurrection of life, will occur when Christ comes again, at the end of this age: I Cor. 15:22, 23; I Thess. 4:14-17; John 5:28; Rev. 20:4.

(2) The Resurrection of the wicked will occur at the end of the Millennium: Rev. 20:13.

TOPIC FIVE: JUDGMENTS.

1. The Judgment of believers for their sins at Calvary: John 5:24; Rom. 6:8; 7:4, showing His estimation of its character by the terrible penalty inflicted on His Son. God judged all sin at Calvary.

We are identified with Christ in His crucifixion. We take our place under condemnation as worthy of death before ever we can claim forgiveness and the privilege of rising in Him to newness of life.

2. **The Judgment of Rewards for Believers:** II Tim. 4:8; Rev. 11:18. Believers do not earn their salvation, for it is a free gift of God, but after they are saved they earn their crowns and rewards by faithful service through the Spirit.

There are at least five crowns spoken of in the New Testament that are bestowed upon the believer.

a. The incorruptible crown: I Cor. 9:25.

b. The crown of righteousness: II Tim. 4:8.

c. The crown of life: James 1:12; Rev. 2:10.

d. The crown of glory: I Pet. 5:4.

e. The crown of gold: Rev. 4:4.

Rewards are according to the works that are built upon the foundation of Christ. It is possible to be "saved yet so as by fire" (I Cor. 3:15) and be ashamed before Christ at His appearing.

On the other hand, one may build gold, silver and precious stones which will abide the testing day and bring additional reward.

3. **The Judgment of the living nations.**

Since nations have their existence in this world only, it is necessary that they be judged here. In a sense God is always judging the nations by ordaining great calamities or blessings in accordance with their national deserts. But there is to be a final judgment

of the nations before the judgment seat of Christ:
Matt. 25.

4. The Judgment of the wicked dead.

This is the great day of judgment that is spoken of
most frequently in Scripture and that occurs after the
Millennium. It is called the day of wrath and revelation of the righteous judgment of God: Rom. 2:5; the
day of destruction, etc.

The saints will sit with Christ, who will administer
this judgment: John 5:22. All men will be gathered
together, both small and great, the quick and the
dead: Rev. 20:12; II Tim. 4:1. God's books will
be opened: Dan. 7:10, and He will judge in righteousness the actions, words, and thoughts of men: Eccle.
12:14; Matt. 12:36, 37; Jude 15; I Cor. 4:5.

NOTE: To the above are often added the judgment upon
the race in Adam, the judgment of self by believers, the judgment of angels by the saints, and the judgment of Satan by God.

TOPIC SIX: THE CLOSING SCENES OF TIME.

1. Satan is loosed for a little season.

After the Millennium, there is a final uprising of the
forces of evil against God and His Christ.

Satan is overthrown and cast into the lake of fire.
Then follows the last resurrection, that of the wicked

dead; the judgment of the great white throne; and the casting of death and hell into the lake of fire: Rev. 20:11-15.

2. The New Heaven and the New Earth.

The old order of creation has been destroyed by fire, and God fulfils His promise of making all things new: II Pet. 3.12, 13.

The New Jerusalem comes down from God out of Heaven and becomes the tabernacle of God with men: Rev. 21:2, 3.

3. God's revelation to men of His plan for the ages is nearing its close.

We know that in ages to come He will shew the exceeding riches of His grace in His kindness toward us through Christ Jesus: Eph. 2:7. In I Cor. 15:24 we see the ringing down of the curtain upon the great drama of the world's history and then cometh the end, when He shall have delivered up the Kingdom to God, even the Father, when He shall have put down all rule and all authority and power, and the Son also Himself shall be subject unto Him that put all things under Him, that God may be all and in all: I Cor. 15:24-28.

Thus our Bibles begin with "In the beginning God," and the verse that looks farthest into the dim future closes with "God all and in all."

"Wherefore, beloved, seeing that ye look for such

things, be diligent that ye may be found of him in peace, without spot, and blameless": II Pet. 3:14.

QUESTIONS FOR STUDY.

1. Name the different dispensations.
2. Show the position of the Second Coming of Christ in Scripture.
3. Give the erroneous explanations of the Second Coming of Christ.
4. Enumerate the signs of the Lord's Coming.
5. Differentiate between the Rapture and the Revelation.
6. Give the prominent characteristics of the Millennium.
7. Describe the two resurrections.
8. Name and describe the four principal judgments.
9. Mention the events that follow the Millennium.

INDEX.

[The numbers refer to the pages. For general subjects see Table of Contents, page 3.]